Broken
Harts

Broken Harts

The Life and Death of Owen Hart

Martha Hart

with Eric Francis

M. EVANS
Lanham • New York • Boulder • Toronto • Oxford

Published by M. Evans
An imprint of The Rowman & Littlefield Publishing Group, Inc.
4501 Forbes Boulevard, Suite 200, Lanham, Maryland 20706

Distributed by NATIONAL BOOK NETWORK

First published in Canada by Key Porter Books Limited,
70 The Esplanade, Toronto, Ontario, Canada M5E 1R2

First United States Edition published in 2004 by M. Evans and Company, Inc.

Library of Congress Cataloging-in-Publication Data

Hart, Martha (Martha Joan)
    Broken Harts : the life and death of Owen Hart / Martha Hart with Eric Francis. —
1st U.S. ed.
        p.   cm.
Includes Index.
    ISBN 1-59077-036-6 (pbk.)
    1. Hart, Owen, 1965–1999. 2. Wrestlers — United States — Biography. I. Title: Life
and death of Owen Hart. II. Francis, Eric (Eric Michael) III. Title.
    GV1196.H34H37 2004
    796.812'092—dc22   2003020139

Text design: Peter Maher
Electronic formatting: Heidy Lawrance Associates

Printed in the United States of America

This book was written for my precious children,
Oje and Athena,
so they would know the truth
about their father's life and the
events surrounding his death.

*"My strength is as the strength of ten,
because my heart is pure."*

—LORD ALFRED TENNYSON

Contents

FOREWORD

Writing is a wonderful tool to help the healing of the soul.

Putting down on paper the journey I traveled before and after Owen's death has been both intensely emotional and extremely liberating. Expressing my pain has helped me leave it behind, making *Broken Harts* crucial in my recovery.

In writing this book, the words and tears flowed openly as I relived the most painful moments of my life. Having suppressed the bulk of my emotions while I spent almost two years fighting for justice for Owen, I finally allowed myself to let go of the feelings that tortured me.

While piecing the book together I struggled a lot with the emptiness I felt. I found myself writing many poems to express my feelings of imprisonment—how the demons constantly haunted me, how I was trapped in a life I didn't want and didn't choose, and how my pain pierced me to the core of my being. I felt lost for a long time.

For the better part of a year, on an almost daily basis I worked on documenting my life with and without the only true love of my life. While most of the book was written in an office set up in my Calgary home, I found myself chronicling various aspects of this book at the base of ski hills, at the Science Centre, on picnics, at the lake or anywhere else I brought my two energetic young children.

Some of the most emotional parts of this book were written while traveling through Africa with my children and my good friends Karim, Shemin and Hussein Bhojani. Due to the time difference I had difficulty adjusting my sleeping schedule, so I wrote great amounts of the book in a dimly lit bathroom in the middle of the night while Oje and Athena slept.

Another trip that proved quite productive was to O.K. Falls, British Columbia, with my dear friend Karen Dudelzak, her husband Richard and their family. Karen was an incredible friend who took the kids on a number of outings in order to give me quiet time to work. She listened endlessly as I tried to sort out my feelings on our many lovely walks through the area's vineyards. I thank her for her support.

Following Owen's death I relied heavily on support from various people who were there to help me carry on without him. In the early days and throughout the lawsuit Bret Hart, Owen's brother, was key to my survival. He helped me more than he will ever know. He was the only person who could truly comfort me, as he was the closest thing, physically, to what I had lost. He gave of himself freely to do anything to help. His support came at a cost to him and his family as his assistance often interfered with his own life and responsibilities. I am so glad I had him as a friend at the most critical time and that he stood by me until the very end of the lawsuit.

We have since gone our separate ways and our lives have taken us down very different paths, but I will always wish the best for him and keep a special place in my heart for all he did for me.

Of all the lawyers who walked me through seventeen months of hell, no one deserves more thanks than my lead counsel and good friend Pamela Fischer. There were so many times we cried together as we slugged through all the proceedings, which forced me to relive the same nightmare over and over. Although I thank Kansas City's Gary and Anita Robb and their staff as well as Calgary's Ed Pipella, I give Pam full credit for arranging and concluding the settlement in the case—she was truly amazing throughout.

Colleen Gray, a longtime acquaintance of mine, became an extremely significant person in my life after Owen's death. She too had been hit by tragedy when her brother, his wife and two children were killed in a terrible plane crash just eleven months before Owen died. Our similar pain bonded us—I could talk to Colleen about grief issues others couldn't understand. She was also instrumental in helping me start up the Owen Hart Foundation for which she still donates her time as public relations manager.

Choosing Eric Francis as my co-writer turned out to be the smartest decision I made in writing this book. We spent endless emotional hours together discussing every aspect of my life with Owen and without. The task of compiling the information in this book was more than daunting, but together we managed to pull it off. Eric was a better friend to me than he needed to be. I will be forever grateful for all his help, guidance, patience and hard work. Eric is a true gentleman.

Outside of my family, my best and truest friend is Lisa Hartzell, who was always there to put a smile on my face. She is a constant supporter and a very bright spot in my life.

Other great friends that were a pillar of support were Dr. Paul Wellings, John and Charlotte Esser, Jeff and Jill Jarrett, Wade Hartzell, Charles Ruff, Pino Mancuso, Stan and Shirley Schwartz, Peter Steinmetz, Brian Olsen, Ron Kincaid and family, Stan and Ester Oh, Mia and Vernon Schlinger, Frank Sisson, Bev Kolis, Wolfgang Stach, Peter Ginakes, Jeff McWhinney and the Osler family.

Special thanks also to Sharon Falk, Magdi Wellings and Tammi Christopher, who taught me true friends are the ones who are there not only when the bombs hit, but also when the dust settles.

Keith Hart, another of Owen's brothers, was also good to me, Oje and Athena. He was so deeply affected by Owen's loss that every time I see him (to this day) he cries. He knew what Owen and I shared, and he will forever grieve his brother and the love between Owen and me that was lost.

Thanks also to Owen's sister Alison, his brother Wayne, the Rockyview Grief Group and the staff and parents at both Christopher Robin and Strathcona Tweedsmuir schools.

I'm so grateful to Anna Porter and Susan Renouf of Key Porter Books for giving me the opportunity to tell my story and for believing I had something worthwhile to share with the world.

Finally, I want to thank my family.

My mother Joan has always been my hero and someone I've leaned on heavily throughout my life, especially after Owen died. Her wisdom and experiences have helped me successfully face many challenges in my life.

My sister Virginia and her husband George Xavier have been important people who also supplied endless support. Virginia was a major source of encouragement as I started the foundation as well as this book. As my older sister she has always taken the role of protector over me, a position she still proudly maintains. I love my sister dearly as we have always been able to count on one another throughout our lives. She is one of the best people I know.

The two whom I owe the most thanks to are Oje and Athena. Without them my life with Owen would have been all for nothing. They are the reason I get out of bed every day and the reason life is worth living. Without them I would have slipped away. They will grow up and thank me for being strong and raising them, but what they might not realize is that if it wasn't for their dependency on me I might not have survived. They deserve my highest order of thanks as they were the source of my strength.

My final thanks go to God and to Owen, who now walk together as one, for it was faith in them both that gave me the courage to walk on.

OUR LAST NIGHT TOGETHER

"When death to either shall come—I pray it be first to me."
—ROBERT BRIDGES

Whether Owen was home or not, Friday night was always pizza night. After a swim at the Killarney Pool our two kids, Oje and Athena, always looked forward to dropping by Spiros Pizza to pick up a Hawaiian Special on the way home. Friday, May 21, 1999, was no different in this respect, but what made the evening so special was Owen's rare presence.

As was usually the case when Owen was home, it had been a busy day. I worked all morning at the post office, where I had been walking a route for seven years. As a part-time psychology student at the University of Calgary, as well as a full-time mother, I still felt it important to keep what I saw as a terrific, stress-relieving job.

After I finished my route at 11 A.M., Owen joined me as we went to Christopher Robin Junior School to pick up Athena for an afternoon at the Science Centre. Our first and only house of ten years was up for sale and we were asked to vacate it for the day so the realtor could show it.

Acting goofy as always, Owen flipped up his collar to look like some sort of nerdy Dracula and thoroughly enjoyed watching our precious, pony-tailed daughter, then three years old, discover the wonders of science.

A big kid himself at 229 pounds, with a neck practically as big as my waist, Owen seemed equally as enthralled with the various hands-on exhibits and challenges aimed at children twenty years his junior. He and Athena were adorable to watch together.

Soon thereafter we made a quick trip south of the city to the house we had been building for the better part of the last two years. Situated half an hour from downtown Calgary in the Elbow Valley community, our home was mere days away from completion. It featured a two-acre lot with a brilliant panoramic view—the Canadian Rockies to the west, city lights to the east, foothills to the north and a forest-covered coulee behind the house. The 5,000 square foot house was designed entirely by the two of us as a larger scale derivative of our current home, using red brick as part of a unique combination meshing Victorian, country and executive styles.

Inside there were five bedrooms, four bathrooms, three fireplaces, vaulted ceilings, a spiral staircase, an office, a large den, a Victorian snuggery with mountain views and a spacious country kitchen. Downstairs was a fully finished basement with a family room, games room, playroom and workout facility.

It was all tied together with our favorite cherry wood finishing. No detail was left to chance. We had worked so hard for this and wanted everything to be just right.

As part of his final touches to the place, Owen had just painted a bench swing for our wraparound porch. Here we planned on spending evenings snuggling up together with mugs of hot tea while the kids would play in the big backyard.

I was puttering around the kitchen, contemplating the hanging of a cast-iron pot rack and bubbling with excitement over our long-awaited moving day, when Owen called me outside to get my approval on a few more things. He wanted to make sure everything was perfect in my eyes. After all, this was our dream home.

Owen was scheduled to fly out the next day for a typical ten-day stretch of wrestling shows and a pay-per-view event as part of the World Wrestling Federation's traveling soap opera/freak show. The next time he was scheduled to be back in town the new house would be our home.

Although I was in charge of the entire move, he wanted to help as much as he could before he left, to ensure it would be a smooth transition without him.

As one of the WWF's highly touted international stars, Owen was on the road up to 250 nights a year. I had long become accustomed to "running the show" in Calgary while he put on shows all over the world.

We were a great team. With his grueling schedule and the taxing nature of his job on his body, I tried to make Owen's trips home as stress-free and relaxing as possible. I didn't expect him to do much menial labor and he appreciated that immensely. I took out the garbage, cut the lawn, weeded the garden, shoveled the driveway—in our neighborhood I was like one of the boys, minus the beer.

We both fit comfortably into our roles in the marriage. He was the bread-winner and devoted husband, offering plenty of love and support to me and the kids; I also worked, oversaw our finances, ran the household, took care of our beautiful children and yearned for the precious days my soulmate and best friend would return for moments like these. Everything seemed so perfect.

Later that night at the pool, I watched as Owen ran into one of his favorite people, Bill Breen. He was our next-door neighbor who always seemed to enjoy a laugh with Owen. With imminent plans on moving his family as well, Bill found plenty to talk about with Owen as I watched the kids.

Owen was a baby-faced giant whose twenty-one-inch neck and ability to bench over 350 pounds were a strange fit for his boyish grin and playful personality. Everyone seemed to like him—not just because he was recognized around the city and the world as a high-profile wrestler, but because he loved to laugh. He was a good listener with a heart of gold and an infectious grin. He made me proud everywhere we went. Yes, there were times he'd frustrate me to no end with his incessant pranks and pratfalls, but that was also part of his charm.

Wrapping up his conversation with Bill, Owen told him he was "just like a brother to him."

The words meant plenty considering Owen was the youngest of twelve children born into Canada's undisputed first family of wrestling.

Growing up in a red-brick Victorian mansion perched on Calgary's west side overlooking the city's ever-growing skyline, Owen was taught early on about the importance of family. You look after your family members and you stick together.

Yet his home was managed more like a decrepit, broken-down hotel for freeloading wrestlers, sideshow freaks and animals used in his father's *Stampede Wrestling* circuit.

Owen's lifelong goal was to simply be normal. While his life on the road or in the WWF was anything but, I like to think our little family of four gave him the love, attention and nurturing he missed out on in a childhood house that had its share of misfits.

Coincidentally, I too grew up the youngest in a large family that had a number of drifters roving in and out of the house. With my father abandoning us at an early age and my mother left to raise her kids in our modest, two-story home in southeast Calgary's Inglewood, she still had a huge heart that welcomed outsiders in for food and shelter. For several years she allowed an acquaintance named Frenchie Joe to park his tiny caravan in our backyard. When not working on the oil rigs across central Alberta, this sweet old man from Moncton, New Brunswick, would return to our backyard, where he lived for years. Although he'd walk in the back door whenever he needed to use the bathroom or get some water, he generally kept to himself. Between him and various guests of my brothers and sisters, we always seemed to have someone who wasn't family lodging in or around the house.

The Hart house was even more crowded with outsiders, including various mechanics who worked on any number of the broken down Cadillacs Owen's father, Stu, kept strewn across his acreage.

In both our houses, the intrusion of strangers did well to disrupt what little family unity we had, as nameless, faceless strangers would routinely sit down at the dinner table with us. They were generally harmless folk who were down on their luck and needed help getting back on their feet. However, as children, Owen and I similarly resented their presence. Although we appreciated our respective parents' kind intentions, we could think of plenty of other ways to help those in need without disrupting family life.

Although his good looks and brilliant smile were what initially attracted me to Owen, I think it was our similar backgrounds that truly brought us together. We both wanted the same things in life. We wanted a normal existence with a nuclear family and good, strong values. We did neighborly things, got involved in our children's schooling and were active in our children's lives. Neither one of us had that while growing up, but we had it now, and our Friday night ritual drove that point home.

Returning to our southwest Calgary home with pizza and two starving children in tow, we settled down for a quiet evening in the family room. Owen stoked the fire and put a Disney movie on for the kids. There were plenty of laughs and plenty of smiles.

Just over an hour later, we put the children to bed and reconvened on the sofa to watch one of our favorite movies, *Father of the Bride*. We spoke briefly about how proud we were of our two kids and the direction we had them going.

Wanting to give them everything we never had as children, we had enrolled our son Oje—which was Owen's nickname—in piano lessons and art classes. He also played hockey and soccer. A polite little seven-year-old with brown hair, his father's deep blue eyes and good looks, he was one of the top students in his Grade One class. He had all the talent in the world, just like his father.

Our daughter Athena was enjoying figure skating, ballet, soccer and music classes. She was daddy's little girl. Despite Owen's schedule, he took such an active role in parenting our daughter. He delighted in taking her for ice cream or to gymboree or ballet class. Sometimes he'd even take her along to the gym when he worked out, allowing his little blonde-haired beauty to crawl around with a big smile on her face. As was always the case, he'd be thrilled to show her off to even the newest of acquaintances.

Blessed with such an easy disposition, Athena was always so giving. If her brother dropped a piece of cake or a sandwich, she'd be the first to cut hers in half and offer it up to him. Owen was particularly moved by her kind-heartedness when he brought her along to the home of a terminally ill Calgary boy who had made a dying wish to meet his wrestling hero.

Upon seeing the balding boy in his sickly condition, Athena showed no fear and approached the boy to hold his hand.

Owen and I were especially pleased the children were not interested in following wrestling in any way.

Both kids loved swimming and, despite a WWF schedule that almost always included Friday night cards, Owen tried as hard as he could to be there for our week-ending routine. If at all possible, he'd reschedule Friday night flights to the midnight milk run so he could enjoy the evening, kiss the kids goodnight and travel overnight to his next match.

One Friday night he made sure never to miss was the annual family camp-out at Butterfield Acres. It involved setting up camp, singing songs and sleeping in a tent together with other families setting up nearby. Every year he would book off that night so he could camp by flashlight with us. One year it got rained out and was switched to the following week. He was so upset. Despite the rain, we went camping that night anyway. We were soaked to the bone, shivering and uncomfortable. I felt like a cavewoman. He loved it, though, because we were together, doing something normal families did. (That said, I'm not sure how many "normal" people would have chosen to brave the elements if given the choice.)

One year he flew home from California just so he could watch Oje perform in his school's Christmas concert. All the kids thought it was so cool Oje's dad flew two-and-a-half hours to see the show before racing back to the airport for a return flight an hour later.

While some days I felt like a single parent, having to raise the two all by myself, Owen's time at home was a powerful reminder the kids and I were not alone. The two children had given us so much joy through every stage of their young lives that we had planned to have a third child within the next year. It was with that in mind we decided we'd need the bigger house. We were so excited about the idea of having another child, we painted a bedroom in the new house yellow, so it could be a nursery. Sadly, it remains empty.

Before we delved into what would be the most memorable conversation of my life, Owen said something out of the blue.

"This is your life, isn't it—just you and the kids?" He smiled, tilting his head and wearing a look that made it clear that he too would love to be a bigger part of that life.

Although I love my children dearly and have always treasured the ability to spend plenty of time watching and helping them grow up, I longed for the day when Owen's traveling would end and we'd get to be a true family unit. Yes, this was my life but it could've been so much better with Owen by my side more often.

We both knew that wasn't going to happen anytime soon. Despite the fact Owen grew up wanting to be a school teacher and later tried to join the fire department, we both realized a few years earlier that he would likely wrestle for a while longer. He figured his body could stand up to the rigors of pro wrestling until at least age forty, if not longer, and he was only thirty-four. As disenchanting as the WWF had become, the money was good and we had a new house to pay for.

We had accepted wrestling as his career—that was our life.

As the movie progressed that evening, so did a heart-to-heart discussion that eventually turned to his job—something we rarely talked about.

He had been informed just a few days earlier that he'd be required to descend eight stories, from the rafters to the ring, for an upcoming pay-per-view show. He admitted to me he was scared about it. It wasn't that Owen was afraid of heights, but having done two previous stunts in which he first rappelled into the ring along a guide wire and later descended from high atop a building, he was uncomfortable with the idea. What was heightening his fear was that, for the very first time, he would descend straight down into the ring hooked up to a harness from behind—there would be no guide wires. It was a long way to go with nothing to hold onto.

Scheduled just two days later, for the "Over the Edge" pay-per-view show in Kansas City, Missouri, there was little time for him to protest the decision. Owen was assured he would be in the hands of top stunt experts so he figured there was little point in ruffling feathers among show writers. He had already spent a lot of time over the last several years arguing with WWF brass who wanted him to take part in a variety of lurid storylines.

Whereas wrestlers had once been a collection of comic-book super-heroes battling evil challengers, the WWF had degenerated into a sleazy soap opera that suddenly revolved around immorality, sex and vulgarity—a world in which good is bad, and bad is better. Owen figured there were only so many times he could charge into the production room and beg off from yet another sick or ridiculous gag aimed at bolstering all-important TV ratings.

Years earlier, when he began souring on the business and its rigors, he wouldn't have cared if he had lost his job. However, things had changed. We now had a new home to pay for as well as costly designs on private schooling for Oje and Athena. In addition, we'd hopefully have a third child on the way soon, which would mean even more bills.

Promising himself and me he'd never sell out for the money, he decided he wouldn't be part of any storylines or antics his children couldn't watch on TV. That was his barometer and it was forever being tested. Truth is, we never let the kids watch wrestling anyway.

Still, there were certain aspects of the job he knew he would have to endure, despite his displeasure. This stunt planned for Kansas City was obviously one of them.

As we sat chatting in our cozy living room surrounded by framed family photos, I knew Owen was having a hard time saying goodbye to our modest digs. He would have been content to stay in our original home the rest of our lives. The house had a sentimental value he figured could never be replaced no matter what price we sold it at. It was the house we brought our first bundled-up newborn to on March 5, 1992. Three-and-a-half-years later, on September 23, 1995, we did the same with Athena.

The first night we ever spent in the house was our wedding night, July 1, 1989. For a year leading up to that warm summer evening, we had the house built to our specs without telling anyone in either family. It was our little secret. Using the money we had diligently saved for years, we fully furnished the place two months before we officially moved in. We were so proud.

We loved our neighbors, Bill and Gail Breen, as well and Dave and Jacquie Wilson. Our kids got along well with theirs. In the backyard, Owen had built a swing set for the kids and loved to watch them play on it. In the winter Owen would brave the cold to make a tiny ice rink so Oje could learn to skate. Although Owen was never given the chance to play hockey or taught to skate—his parents hadn't the time or money for either—he would strap on the blades and try gliding alongside his son. Although both used their hockey sticks for balance much more than for puck handling, the two beginners seemed to have a great time out there.

We set up floodlights, allowing Owen and Oje use of the rink at night, and we often piped Christmas music through the patio speakers. As a homebody who loves to bake pies and spoil everyone with culinary delights, I always had hot chocolate ready to pour when my two beloved boys shuffled into the house half-frozen.

The bulk of our most cherished moments were in that old house of ours.

With this being our last night together at 2028 Sirocco Drive S.W., I didn't want his final memories of the place tarnished by seeing it full of boxes, ready for the movers. I had delayed packing until after he left the next day and he was glad not to have to see that.

Soaking up his final night in our home, he reiterated just how lucky we both were. Yet, with all wrestling had provided, I pointed out to Owen a stunt like the one scheduled for Kansas City was way above and beyond his job description. He was a wrestler, not a stuntman. I told him he should get the WWF to sign a waiver in case something happened and he was unable to work for a while. He agreed.

It was then he rattled me with words that will stay with me forever.

"You know, if anything ever happened to me I'd want you to find someone else."

"Especially for Athena," he added. "Oje will be fine because he's really close to you. It would be Athena that would need someone."

I grew extremely upset. Getting up off the sofa and standing to face him, my voice began rising. I told him not to talk that way. He too grew more and more serious and reiterated his stance.

My worst fear for years had been the prospect of losing Owen. I worried he'd die in a plane crash or car accident, or that he'd be crippled by something gone terribly awry in a wrestling match.

I suppose most happy couples worry that way. Given that Owen was my high school sweetheart and the only man I've ever loved, I needed him in every way. We needed one another. We were soul mates and nothing could be allowed to ruin all we had hoped and dreamed of together. How would either one of us be able to go on alone?

Shuddering at the thought, I returned to the sofa, cuddled up to him and buried my head in his broad chest. I told him if something ever happened to him I would be so terribly alone. He disagreed, reminding me people like my dear mother Joan and my sister Virginia would do anything to help. As for his family, which we had purposely distanced ourselves from for years, he told me Bret could be counted on for anything. He also pointed out that my closest girlfriends, Lisa Hartzell, Sharon Falk and Tammi Christopher, were really good people.

With all that was said, it was nevertheless a strange and foreboding moment.

Owen came from a family of seven brothers and four sisters, in which Bret was the eighth-oldest sibling and the one Owen knew best. As two of the WWF's most popular attractions, they had traveled all over the world together, occasionally dabbling as both partners and opponents.

Wrestling was Bret's passion, which accounts for why he was so successful professionally. Owen's passion was his family—wrestling was just a job. As a wrestler, Owen always took solace in the fact he could count on dependable advice from his big brother, "The Hitman," who is a multi-millionaire and was widely considered the most famous Albertan, if not one of the most famous Canadians, alive. Despite being radically different individuals, they were close at times.

Getting up to pour a cup of tea, I confided to Owen my belief that if something ever happened to me I would feel as though I hadn't truly lived yet. As happy as I'd been through the years, and as excited as I was about our future, I just felt there was more for me to experience out there.

He felt completely differently about himself. "I feel I've done everything in life," he said, his face lighting up. "I've reached all my goals, I've traveled all over the world, ridden a camel in the desert, I've been to Africa, India, Japan, Mexico, all over Europe. I'm married to the woman I love, we have two great kids … I feel I've lived the most incredible life and all I want to do is keep living it."

At first I was somehow angry at his words, although I quickly realized I was envious more than anything else. Only now do I see his words as so terribly sad. He just wanted to keep living.

With a busy day ahead of us, we decided to skip the rest of the movie. Instead, Owen suggested we pop in a home video. We selected our recording of the day Oje was born. It was a great choice as it's one of the only videos we have in which neither one of us is behind the camera filming. We're both sitting together with Oje, talking to the camera.

With a deep sigh Owen sank back into the sofa, put his hands behind his head and said, "This is so nice. You can just never have enough of this stuff. We have to watch more of this, it's so precious." I agreed.

Capping off a wonderful day with a kiss from the man I so dearly loved, we went to bed. It would be the last night we'd ever spend together.

The next morning, Owen woke up early and went downstairs to grab the Saturday paper and make coffee. Returning to the bedroom after rousing the kids and getting their day started, he climbed back into bed with a steaming cup of coffee for me. I flipped on the TV and we cuddled. A brilliant sunshine blanketed the room when he opened the curtains.

I treasured mornings like these—there were too few of them. I felt like life was too good to be true, that I had everything I could ever want. It was one of those rare moments I actually thought about my happiness. Owen crawled back into bed and we spooned, holding each other tight. It was wonderful.

Knowing how much I loved a particular gardening show that was on TV, he instructed me to stay in bed while he got up to make his famous French toast. A half-hour later we assembled as a family at the kitchen table for breakfast, something the kids loved as much as I did.

Forever wanting to spend every possible minute at home, Owen had rescheduled his 8 A.M. flight to noon. Yet, as always seemed to be the case, he suddenly found himself rushing to get out the door. Quickly packing his two small carry-on bags—a task he had down to a science—he ran down the stairs and clamored to throw on his boots. Since I had to drive

Athena to soccer, he decided to spend a little extra time with Oje by driving with him to the airport. The plan was he'd pick my mother up on the way so she could drive Oje and the minivan back.

As we gathered in the garage to see him off, Owen was in such a scramble to get going I was reluctant to even hug him for fear of slowing him down. I elected for a brief embrace and a quick peck on the cheek as he tied his boots. It was then he stopped, pulled me into his arms and kissed me on the lips. I remember thinking how incredibly thoughtful it was of him to do that. As much of a hurry as he was in, he wanted me to know he was never too busy for his wife. It was our last kiss—a moment I'll forever cherish.

Having made his way to Chicago for a show that night, he called for our nightly chat shortly after midnight. Typically spending at least an hour on the phone with one another every evening, it wasn't uncommon for us to rack up monthly long distance bills in excess of $400. Because we couldn't share our days together, we spent countless hours rehashing them over the phone.

We were always very connected, taking one another on a chronological review of our respective days. Even though we had spent the morning together, much was discussed. I was particularly intrigued by the conversation he told me he had with Oje en route to the airport.

Before picking up my mom, Owen said Oje was kind of quiet and listened closely to his father's words. Owen told Oje, "When I'm not home you're the little man in the house and it's your job to be good to your mom and sister." Owen gave him this little pep talk about what it's like to be a good person.

Little Oje, all of seven years old, then asked his dad how one goes about picking a wife. Owen said you have to pick someone who's going to be your best friend and help you.

When I think of how everything unfolded, I think it's just so incredible Owen had this talk with him and that Oje has this final memory of his dad giving him such great advice.

Given how perfect our last couple of days had been together, I didn't want to let him hang up. After ninety minutes of chatter into the wee hours of the morning, it became apparent to both of us I was simply stalling him—I even asked what he ate for dinner. It was silly but I just wanted to hear his voice. Our conversation the night before had stuck with me and I didn't want to hang up.

Finally he said, "Martha, you know I love you. I'm so tired, I just want to go to sleep." A minute later we exchanged goodbyes and he told me once more how much he loved me.

We'd never speak again.

A STAR IS BORN

"The child had every toy his father wanted."
—Robert E. Whitten

From as early in his childhood as he could remember, he told me there were screams: the wails of breathless victims shrieking for mercy, begging for any sort of assistance in escaping a pain so excruciating it drove grown men to the verge of tears. Often they were the horrid howls of strangers crying out for a respite or rescue they knew would never come. The only thing young Owen knew of the desperate shouts was that his father was the man responsible for the invisible horrors conducted in the bowels of his childhood home.

It haunted him for years.

Born May 7, 1965, Owen James Hart was the last of Stu and Helen Hart's twelve children. Raised in the family's twenty-one-room, red brick mansion on a Broadcast Hill spread overlooking Calgary, Owen was exposed to wrestling every day of his rather unusual childhood.

As headquarters for Stu's beloved *Stampede Wrestling* circuit, which entertained wrestling fans throughout western Canada for more than forty years, the house played host to a steady stream of wrestlers ever since the newlyweds bought it in 1951.

Built in 1905, the stately home had previously been occupied by two wealthy families and had also been used by the Red Cross to help orphans and sick children. In many ways, the Hart mansion would continue to be a house of pain for years to come. Using the world-famous "Dungeon" in his basement to implement a lifetime of wrestling maneuvers on his students as well as his sons, Stu ensured the house was often filled with the wails that terrified Owen.

A cramped enclave, bordered by knotty pine paneling and filled with custom-made free weights, it was in the Dungeon, on a thin wrestling mat soiled with sweat, dirt and the odd spot of cat urine, that Stu gave life to a wrestling show that was eventually syndicated worldwide.

Over the years, Owen had heard his seven brothers and four sisters talk about the Dungeon and the torment manufactured within its confines. Too young to understand why his father would do such horrible things to his brothers or visitors, Owen quickly developed a tremendous fear of his father that lingered through adolescence. Stu's gruff, raspy voice, thick forearms and massive hands only served to heighten Owen's concern.

To keep control of twelve kids Stu figured you had to flex your muscles a bit. Although nothing ever needed to be said, it was understood among the children that if they stepped out of line Stu would take them downstairs to "stretch" them—a similar practice to the ancient ordeal of putting someone on the rack. Victims were subjected to any number of threadthroughs or submission holds to test their pain threshold and, more importantly, their character.

Stu thought of it as toughening them up. Others saw it as cruel and unusual punishment. Once in his grasp, there was no escaping any of Stu's moves—the more you tried, the more searing the pain.

"I was intimidated by my dad and respected him," said Owen in a 1997 interview for Bret's documentary, *Wrestling with Shadows*. "That fear of ever doing something wrong kept me from doing something wrong."

Stu didn't confine his deeds of discipline to the Dungeon either. He wasn't averse to swooping up a wrongdoer at any time to be placed in one of his myriad moves. Immersing his family in a world dominated by the sport he so dearly loved, no one was safe from Stu's playful or not-so-playful pretzel holds. Even his daughters got a taste of his power from time to time.

The first time I formally met Stu was at his son Keith's wedding in December 1982. I was completely intimidated, as he had a reputation and persona that had people in awe. Stu could tell I was at a loss for words so he said little and just kept winking at me throughout the night. It was his way of telling me he liked me and that he approved of Owen having a girl-friend. Thank God, I was safe. Or so I thought. In time Stu managed to start putting some of his holds on me as a playful gesture. Several times I thought I'd black out.

Even at his eighty-second birthday party, on May 3, 1997, he delighted in showcasing his past greatness by folding up grandchildren and guests alike into quivering balls of hurt on the living room floor—this despite the fact his once perfectly sculpted body had deteriorated from a lifetime of body slams and hard labor, not to mention parenthood. Yet, his passion for wrestling endures, and he takes every chance he gets to talk about his days in the Navy or wrestling at Madison Square Garden.

Armed with a limited education, Stu certainly made quite a success of his life. He grew up on a humble Saskatchewan homestead where he learned to milk cows and work the farm. Stu's father eventually lost the house, and the family was forced to live in a tent for two harsh prairie winters. Eventually, ten-year-old Stu, his two sisters and his mother were taken by the Mounties to become wards of the Salvation Army. They were reunited as a family several months later in Edmonton, where Stu took up wrestling as a teenager at the YMCA. He was manhandled there regularly —a hardship that only served to toughen him up.

A brilliant athlete who played virtually every sport available, Stu had a short stint with the Canadian Football League's Edmonton Eskimos. Although he was nearly killed in a bicycle accident at age twenty-six (when he was launched more than fifteen feet into the air by a speeding fire truck), Stu soon returned to the YMCA to continue wrestling despite serious disk damage in his back. He became one of Canada's top amateur wrestlers through the late '30s and early '40s.

Stu met his bride in New York after a stint in the Navy, then moved back to Calgary to buy their house—now a provincial historic site—and start his legendary wrestling promotion. So highly regarded for his tireless contribu-tions to the community, Stu was recognized in 2001 with the Order of Canada.

In the early days, Stu's custom-made Dungeon was reserved for his workouts and for prepping talent for his upcoming shows. Anyone with designs on wrestling in one of Stu's shows had to first prove himself against the Hart patriarch. Even the strongest of challengers often bowed to Stu's grappling talents, which he honed in the Navy. There was always something about the fear in their whimpers and pleas that made him stretch them a little further, a little longer, a little harder. Yet, somehow, many saw it as a sort of badge of honor to be manhandled by such a wrestling genius. Besides, Stu was always careful not to apply too much pressure. He seemed to know the other person's limits of tolerance even if they didn't. His stretches may have scared some but I think it's fair to say he never seriously hurt anyone physically. Mentally, maybe.

Known in wrestling circles around the world, the Dungeon not only produced hundreds of combatants to stock Stu's storied wrestling loop, it's also credited with helping many of the best modern-day wrestlers hone their craft. World-renowned talents like the Dynamite Kid, Davey Boy Smith, Chris Benoit, Angelo Mosca, Archie "The Stomper" Gouldie, Junkyard Dog and Chris Jericho all have vivid memories of the extremely cramped, ill-designed chamber.

Limited by a low ceiling decorated with massive holes (courtesy of wrestlers' flailing feet, arms and heads), maneuvers were further restricted by low-lying water pipes. Some of the athletes who trained in the room recall having to constantly duck or squat to avoid cranial collisions with the ceiling. The thin floor mat provided very little in the way of cushioning—the paneling bordering the room was equally inefficient.

One step down from the small matted area was a tiled floor littered with custom free weights bearing the Hart name. As time wore on these became increasingly scarce as hopefuls and even family members would steal them as souvenirs.

A bench press, weight rack, speed bag and a pulley system were also crammed into this room, where the air was constantly filled with the thick stench of sweat and dust.

Other musty rooms downstairs housed the furnace, water heaters, a treadmill, shower, office, laundry area and sink as well as an industrial meat slicer Stu used to help prepare meals.

As part of Stu's kind and trusting Prairie mentality, the door was literally always open to wrestlers or other acquaintances to stay in the basement quarters. The house was also open to any number of cats and dogs, which would occasionally have their kittens or puppies in the dark recesses of the basement's makeshift bedrooms.

Living in a place in which wrestling midgets, seven-foot monsters like Andre the Giant or a Bengal tiger could be spotted in or around the house as part of Stu's wrestling stable (yes, Stu once wrestled a tiger in the ring) nothing ever shocked Owen. There were always plenty of sibling squabbles to be broken up or settled with might, while Stu acted as the iron-fisted mediator.

Yet, while boxing legends like Jack Dempsey, Rocky Marciano, Jersey Joe Walcott, Joe Louis and Olympic runner Jesse Owens made pilgrimages to Stu's wood-paneled fear factory, young Owen generally steered clear of the area. While he never let on his fears to his brothers or sisters, for years he avoided climbing down the cold, metal-grated industrial stairs to the basement of horrors.

So upsetting were the screams, Owen decided one day to secretly record them using his brother's beat-up tape recorder. He kept the cassette as a strange reminder of the shrieks and wails he grew up fearing.

As junior member of the world's first family of wrestling, Owen learned at a young age to fend for himself. It was a skill he counted on heavily throughout his life.

Whether it was a fight among siblings, schoolyard bullies, amateur wrestlers or WWF behemoths, Owen went in well prepared with a master's from the School of Hard Knocks and a minor in diplomacy. Not to be mistaken for someone who set out looking for conflict, he often stumbled upon it by virtue of the fact he was a member of one of Calgary's most notorious families.

With eleven brothers and sisters to learn from, he quickly discovered the importance of sticking up for siblings who were often targets in schoolyards, bars or wherever the well-known family would venture in and around Calgary or western Canada.

Several of the older Hart boys had gained quite a reputation around town, becoming local celebrities by virtue of *Stampede Wrestling* broadcasts, which aired every Saturday in Calgary with local sportscasting icon Ed Whalen anchoring the antics.

It was there, at Calgary's Victoria Pavilion, that wrestlers from around the world would grapple amidst thick cigarette smoke that, at times, mixed with the stench of farm animals occasionally housed in stalls behind the stands.

Far from the glamor that appears to be the WWE these days (a recent lawsuit forced the WWF to rename itself), Stu and his wrestlers drove as many as 3,000 kilometers (1,900 miles) a week through prairie blizzards to make regular stops in cities like Edmonton, Saskatoon, Regina and Red Deer. There were also plenty of shows put on in smaller towns like Banff and dots on the map like Oyen, Alberta, a town so small you could send someone from one end to the other with a simple drop kick.

Dedicated to his show as he was, Stu often filled in on the card when a scheduled wrestler didn't show up.

Whether his wrestling promotion was packing them in with headliners in Edmonton or drawing flies in small towns around British Columbia, Stu was always a fiercely proud man who kept up the image of having lots of money.

Be it the massive foyer chandeliers that could be seen through his front windows from miles away or the two custom-made driveway pillars that welcomed guests to the Hart house, Stu took great pride being able to successfully grow his western Canadian promotions while building a massive family.

But despite the high profile of *Stampede Wrestling* and the mansion from which it was run, the Hart children grew up relatively poor. With a long line of broken down Cadillacs strewn around his majestic, thirty-acre yard propped high atop the city, Stu insisted on driving the children around town in an aging limousine, which was both practical and somewhat flashy. However, when it pulled up to a local gas station, the kids would sometimes jump out of the vehicle in the dead of winter without socks or shoes.

"We thought we were rich, but sometimes there wasn't even enough money for gas," Owen often told reporters.

At Christmas, Stu and Helen filled stockings for all the kids, who received little outside of the necessities. Sure, they grew up in a harsh environment, but that was part of being a Hart. You fought for whatever you could get and you also learned to make do without.

The Harts were unable to afford the cost of suiting up any of the boys for hockey. However, Owen was always one of the best schoolyard athletes at Wildwood Elementary or Vincent Massey Junior High, where all his siblings had gone before him. In high school, he was a four-star letterman at Ernest Manning where he played rugby, football, wrestled and enjoyed track and field.

Although there were plenty of kids who used to tease the Harts about their father's fake wrestling business, there was no shame in being a Hart. All were very proud children who would back one another up if push came to shove around the bike racks after school.

"I don't know if it was a false sense of security … [but] there was no fear," Owen said in *Wrestling with Shadows.* "We had this image like, 'We're the Harts and we're invincible.'" It was an attitude that translated well into the ring as all the boys dabbled in wrestling to varying degrees. "We had our own house league," joked Owen.

Whether they blossomed into stars in the ring or were simply referees, matchmakers or program sellers, each of the boys had an understanding of and appreciation for wrestling. They all played a role that assisted their dad in elevating *Stampede Wrestling* to cult status.

From age five, Owen spent every Friday night at the smoke-filled Pavilion on Calgary's Stampede grounds selling programs or doing whatever else he could to help ensure the show ran smoothly. His early fear of the sport, brought on by the Dungeon screams, was heightened further once he set eyes on Abdullah the Butcher, a popular character who entered the ring wielding a butcher's knife. Owen had nightmares of this cleaver-wielding assailant for years.

Armed with enormous respect for his father, Owen saw how Stu got up every morning to make the children oatmeal while Helen slept. This, despite the fact Stu typically arrived home from his shows in the wee hours of the night. Stu also made their lunches, though they were never pretty. While many other children had peanut butter and jam on soft white bread with the crusts cut off, Stu slapped together thick corned beef sandwiches on hard crusty bread. Instead of a nice crunchy apple, Owen would often find a tomato in his little brown bag. Owen made a habit of eating everything for fear of upsetting his father. Besides, he was made well aware his father used to have to shoot rabbits with a slingshot for his dinners. With that in mind, messy sandwiches didn't sound all that bad.

Vowing his children wouldn't go hungry as he once did, Stu always ensured the kids were well fed. Stu did all the grocery shopping and cooking, which always included a feast on Sundays when the family would gather for a traditional sit-down dinner. It's a tradition carried on to this day, with any number of sons, daughters and grandchildren popping by.

As baby of the bunch, when Owen was born he shared a room with two of the girls, Ellie and Georgia, the two oldest sisters. He was affectionately known as "the girls' project."

The other two girls, Alison and Diana, shared another room, which Owen often avoided. He rarely got along with Diana, who made for an obvious rival by virtue of being closest to him in age.

To three of the girls he was better than a doll—he was the real thing. They'd brush his hair, dress him up and play house with him. They babied him so much he was "kind of like the fifth girl," joked Bret.

Meanwhile, the other Hart boys were split into three rooms. Oldest brothers Smith and Bruce shared a room upstairs in the attic, as did third- and fourth-born Keith and Wayne. On the second floor Bret and Ross shared a room with Dean (who died in 1990 due to kidney failure).

One morning at the kitchen table, Helen informed everyone Owen was old enough to make the switch to the boys' room, a prospect which had several of the boys looking forward to exacting a little revenge on the little boy from across the hall.

"In a family like ours there were lots of tattle tales and he was on the girls' side, ratting on everybody for everything," recalls Bret of the day of reckoning. "We were waiting for him."

That afternoon, hours after Owen had moved in to his new digs, a typical brawl broke out upstairs, punctuated by a lot of yelling and finger pointing.

"My dad came in and asked who started it and looked at Owen," said Bret. "Owen pointed to Ellie and said, 'She did it.'" He immediately became one of the boys. He was no dummy.

Because of Stu's responsibilities as an entrepreneur and head of this massive family, it wasn't easy to gain his attention without doing something wrong. And everyone knew the quickest way to Stu's heart was through wrestling.

Even though Stu was fifty when Owen was born, Owen would wrestle with him because his dad enjoyed it. Owen disliked the sport as a youngster but wanted to make his father happy. It was a great way to connect. As father and son wrestled or talked about wrestling, emotions were displayed that built a strong bond between them.

It was easy to see his dad was not proud of some of his kids. It was equally as obvious Owen and Stu shared a special relationship. Although Stu never said it to Owen while he was growing up, it was evident he was very proud of his youngest son. Owen knew it and worked hard to ensure that would never change. It helped that Owen wasn't a troublemaker and needed little guidance or punishment from his parents.

As Owen got older, Stu could see his youngest son was a lot like him. Owen was practical, hard-working, strong and decent—a man's man. Stu wasn't a drinker or womanizer and was very dedicated to his family. He admired the same qualities in Owen and the respect was mutual.

However, as an adult Owen often grew frustrated with Stu as every conversation eventually deteriorated into the business Owen so despised. The final time the two saw one another ended with Owen stomping out of the house, telling his father he didn't want to talk about "that garbage"—wrestling.

Owen had a different type of respect for his mother. A kind, gentle soul who married Stu on the premise he'd abandon the wrestling business within a few years, Helen always hated the sport. She disliked everything about it, especially the participation of her young boys, who she long feared would be injured in the ring.

Yet all her children got involved in wrestling to various degrees. Bret, Bruce, Keith and Owen became professional wrestlers, Wayne became a wrestling referee and Ross got involved in *Stampede Wrestling*'s TV productions. Dean and Smith also dabbled in it. Adding to her horror, all four of her daughters—Ellie, Alison, Diana and Georgia—married wrestlers.

Helen met Stu in her native New York City in 1947 following his naval career. After two years of trying, Stu finally convinced this beautiful young woman—a daughter of Olympic runner Harry Smith—to marry him and move to Alberta, a place she had never heard of. "We were married in a blizzard," she liked to joke, "and I've been snowed in ever since."

In 1951, Helen asked Stu how long he'd remain in this silly wrestling business. "Just a few years," was his response.

Because Helen was born prematurely, doctors told her she'd likely never be able to bear children. This, of course, was not the case.

"Every time Stu hung his pants up I was pregnant," she used to laugh. "But that's okay. It's cold in the winter and we love children."

Owen loved both his parents a great deal. Although he enjoyed talking to his mother more than his father, he felt closer to his dad. Helen was a strong communicator and was much more grounded than Stu. She provided the kids with someone to talk to about anything other than the wrestling they had all been force-fed for years.

However, Owen would often comment that his mother's hands were so soft because she never had to lift a finger. Helen was not a conventional mother as she never really cooked or cleaned. For the most part it was Stu who took on the responsibility of raising the children.

Helen's role revolved around the family business, for which she was the bookkeeper. Working feverishly to ensure every performer was paid, regardless of fluctuations in gate receipts, Helen grew frustrated over the years at a business that failed to provide the financial comfort she long desired.

Always a lady, Helen welcomed even the strangest of guests into her home with a "Hello, dahling," issued in her unmistakable New York accent. Because she was charming to everyone, first impressions of Helen would have you believe you were meeting a happy woman. Although there were many good things in her life, there was a side of Helen that was very sad. She was often a woman in turmoil, who fought with Stu over the stresses of running a business together and raising a large family.

While their arguments were contained in their own home and were nothing out of the ordinary, Owen was embarrassed to bring friends to the house for fear of stumbling across such confrontations.

At times unhappy with the path she chose in life, I think Helen envied all of her sisters to some degree because she thought their lives resembled the life she wanted—normal, balanced and topped off with a white picket fence. Marrying Stu and becoming a wrestling promoter's wife was not what she had in mind. But while Helen may have compromised some things in her life to marry Stu, he really was a good match for her. She needed someone strong like him to take care of her. And he did.

Stu was an ambitious, hard worker who pampered his wife for their entire lives together. He took care of her and the children without demanding a lot in return. He was the chef, disciplinarian, caregiver, businessman, housekeeper and shopper. He even set Helen's hair on a daily basis, cooked her meals and hand-delivered them to her room where she would often eat in private. He never complained about the seemingly endless workload. He did it gladly because he loved her deeply. No husband could have been better.

I had long admired and respected Stu for his devotion. There was no doubt he was a good man. Despite Helen's occasional complaints, it was clear she loved Stu immensely and would be lost without him. Still, Helen had difficulties coping with the stresses in her life and often needed an escape from the unorthodox world around her. For years she suffered in relative silence, drinking behind closed doors to cope with her chosen path.

She was a recluse, preferring to stay in her well-equipped bedroom as it was her safe haven. It was the only part of the house that was really hers. Her affection for wine and vodka was no secret to the children. They did what they could to temper her drinking by secretly hiding her bottles, watering them down or pouring them out. To her credit, she drank far from the sight of her children.

However, it upset several of her kids. Owen didn't like alcohol at all and would rarely drink. He didn't like the taste or the smell and I believe it was largely due to seeing the negative things it brought out in others when they indulged.

While the rest of the house was open to the world, the kids knew their mom's room was off limits. Adding to Helen's isolation was the fact she couldn't drive. In many ways she was stuck in the house. Shortly after marrying Stu, Helen was in a near-fatal car accident while pregnant with Bruce, their second child. Following major reconstructive surgery to her shattered face, she never drove again.

I liked Helen a great deal and found her to be an extremely interesting woman to chat with. She always had the unique ability to light up a room.

As Owen got older it became clear that he was Stu's favorite. It was no coincidence Owen was one of the only boys who called him Dad. The rest would usually call him Stu. Owen brought out a gentler side of his father that few saw with any regularity.

A large part of the bond that drew Stu and Owen together was Owen's wrestling abilities. Learning quickly from his father and brothers in the Dungeon, Owen was a natural athlete who seemed destined to fill the shoes of talented Hart wrestlers before him, like Dean, Keith and especially Bret.

It wasn't hard to see Stu wanted all of the boys to be wrestlers, as wrestling was his life. He certainly never discouraged it.

Once Owen got to high school he started to develop physically and became a real wrestling force. Owen knew his dad had tremendous respect for amateur wrestling, even more so than for the professional ranks. With that in mind, Owen wanted to be a good amateur wrestler for his dad. Having missed his own chance at Olympic wrestling glory due to World War II, Stu had Olympic aspirations for several of his boys. As great an amateur wrestler as Bret was, Owen later compiled an even better record.

Gradually, Owen grew out of his childhood fear of the Dungeon and began using it frequently to work out. While down there, he couldn't help but pick up the odd wrestling tip from dad or a brother, whom he'd never allow to watch him wrestle in high school. He hated the extra pressure it added. At one high school meet his brother Keith showed up with Stu unannounced, infuriating Owen and prompting him to be flipped on his back seconds into the match.

It wasn't easy being a young Hart wrestler. "I was living my dad's dream, being an amateur wrestler and going for the Olympics," Owen told High Road Productions in his biography. "But I hated it. I didn't like dieting. I didn't like being Owen Hart, the famous Hart boy—Stu Hart's son. But I always had this feeling: 'When I come home I want to please my dad.'"

By his mid-teens, Owen would regularly come home with gold ribbons and medals won at local high school wrestling meets. Proud to inform his father of his accomplishments, Owen frowned upon his father's insistence on announcing such results at the Friday night *Stampede Wrestling* shows. Such accolades made Stu proud. He wanted to tell the world he had yet another young wrestling star waiting in the wings. Despite his son's objections, if Owen won gold Stu would announce it anyway.

As good a young wrestler as Owen was, he insisted at every turn he wanted nothing to do with it career-wise. He wanted to be a teacher.

Owen had seen the putrid underbelly of the wrestling game first-hand—how wrestlers behaved, how they were treated—and he knew it wasn't for him. At least he hoped it wasn't.

HIGH SCHOOL CONFIDENTIAL: 1982

"True love is like ghosts, which everyone talks about and few have seen."
—François, Duc de La Rochefoucauld

It had been a long day at school, topped off with a grueling gymnastics practice. One of the two gyms at Western Canada High School was being renovated and the basketball team won the remaining gym for their practice, so we gymnasts got stuck in the grungy basement.

I was in Grade Ten, my first year of high school, and I found it more difficult than I thought to juggle homework with sports. By the time I rode the city bus home it was typically well after six o'clock, leaving me just enough time to do my homework before going to bed.

With a bag full of gear slung over my shoulder, I sluggishly walked up the steps and into the main corridor. The school was like a ghost town. At the end of the long hall I could see what was left of the sunlight shining through the exit doors. The gymnastics season was just about over and I was glad I'd soon be able to get home a little earlier for a change.

As I made my way towards the door I noticed this striking, blond teenage boy loitering outside the wrestling room. The wrestlers were another athletic team that got ripped off when they closed the gym, but their fate was even worse than the gymnasts—they got stuck in a classroom. It was pathetic. They had to remove all the desks and then throw down a bunch of wrestling mats.

There was no missing the wrestling room—it stank of sweat. Nearing the point in the dreary hallway where I'd normally take my last breath before plugging my nose, I approached this boy who I figured must be a wrestler. I knew most of the wrestlers, if not by name then by face, and clearly he wasn't from my school. This mystery boy was cute and very well built. As I passed, he smiled at me.

"Too bad he doesn't go to this school," I thought.

Four weeks later, I could finally hang up my gymnastics tights, leaving me with more time to dedicate to my homework. I was hardly a straight-A student and I had to work hard for my marks. My friends thought I was a boring stick-in-the-mud because I would actually stay in on weekends to do homework while they went out to have fun.

My longtime friend Odette Beaudette had been bugging me for some time to go with her on Friday nights to the local *Stampede Wrestling* show. I didn't know much about it but from what I had heard and seen on TV I was not interested in the least.

She religiously attended every Friday's show and bought me tickets to accompany her on many occasions, but I always managed to decline at the last minute. Finally, a weekend arrived when I had no homework on my plate for a change, so I decided to appease her and go for the very first time. She was thrilled.

Sitting ringside in Calgary's age-old Pavilion, I couldn't believe I had come to such a dingy, rundown place. A thick smoke wafted throughout the poorly lit building and a few bright lights cascaded into the wrestling ring from high atop the stands. It was like something out of the movie *Rocky*.

The announcer made his entrance into the ring, prompting the throaty crowd to throw out its first roar of the night. Everyone was staring at a set of blue curtains that the wrestlers would soon burst through.

The first to come out was a young guy dressed in jeans and a T-shirt. He walked to a ringside table and I instantly recognized him as the boy I had seen in the hallway at my school.

I tugged on Odette's sleeve, asking who he was.

"That's Owen Hart," she explained. "His dad, Stu Hart, owns *Stampede Wrestling*."

I didn't know much about wrestling but I had heard of Stu. He was an icon in Calgary.

The show began with a parade of all the wrestlers, good and bad, which walked around the ring. They were a motley collection of old and young, muscular and just plain fat. Shortly after the introductions the matches began.

I was a little nervous because it wasn't long before these big brutes were hurling each other all over the mat, through the ropes and onto the floor next to my feet. Shocked by a kind of graphic violence I had never before been exposed to, I buried my head into my friend's shoulder on several occasions. She got a kick out of seeing me so shaken.

The predominant thought running through my mind was, "What am I doing here?" I looked at Odette—a smart, athletic girl—and was a little surprised at how mesmerized she was by it all. I couldn't understand the attraction.

Between matches, I watched to see exactly what this boy, Owen Hart, did. He intrigued me. He appeared to be operating the sound system that welcomed each wrestler into the ring with a theme song. When the noise in the place wasn't too loud, I asked Odette if she knew anything about him.

"A bit," she said. "He goes to Ernest Manning High School." That explained his presence at my school—we competed in the same sports division.

Filled with schoolgirl nerves, I wanted to introduce myself but didn't know how to approach him. I deliberated for a short period before something came to my mind.

"Remember our old phys-ed teacher, Mr. Margetts?" I asked Odette. "Didn't he transfer to Ernest Manning?"

She confirmed indeed he had.

"Owen must be a pretty good athlete, I bet he'd know him," I said. "Maybe I'll ask him if he does."

Odette told me the show would soon break for an intermission, so I built up my nerve to approach him then. I was glad I had an opening line, even if it wasn't a very good one. When the break came, I waved him over.

"Did you want something?" were his first words.

I proceeded to ask him about his school and if he knew my old gym teacher. He said he didn't.

What was I to do now? With my big opening line smashed to pieces, I searched frantically for something else to say before the situation became as uncomfortable as I had been all night.

I told him I thought I saw him at my school a few weeks ago, standing by the wrestling room. He confirmed it was probably him. What little conversation I had initiated was waning and neither one of us had much else to say.

He asked if I liked the show so far. I admitted I didn't know much about professional wrestling and that my friend had talked me into going. As he was pressed for time, our conversation was cut mercifully short. Still, I was glad I talked to him. In addition to being good-looking he had been polite and friendly.

Suddenly the evening didn't seem like such a bust after all. I actually kind of enjoyed the second half—well, more than the first anyway. In the same breath, I was glad when the show was over.

By the end of the night the crowd's aggressiveness had reached dizzying heights. Those shoehorned into the small arena grew increasingly drunk and unruly, spurred on by the highs and lows of each match. There was a restless, rowdy attitude pulsating throughout the capacity crowd of 2,500 and I was worried some of the audience members might start fighting among themselves. It wasn't my scene at all. Yet, Odette seemed right at home with the chaos that somehow bonded the intense mob.

I was more than a little worried about leaving the building amidst these charged-up wrestling fans. Thankfully we were able to leave the Stampede grounds without incident and we walked towards my Inglewood home chatting about our night.

We were hungry so we decided to stop at the neighborhood pizzeria for a bite. Although it was only a few blocks from my house, I had never been there before. To my surprise I walked in to see Owen sitting with some of his friends. He recognized me from our short conversation and walked over to say hello.

"Are you guys stopping in for a quick drink?" he joked, knowing we were well under Alberta's legal drinking age of eighteen.

"No, we don't drink," I replied in a stern, matter-of-fact tone.

He chuckled at my seriousness.

Chatting briefly, I told him I found the show unusual but added it was kind of fun.

"Maybe you should come down again sometime," he said.

"Maybe I will," I smiled.

I thought briefly about how nice it would be to get to know him better but doubted I could put up with the crazy fans and the filthy surroundings.

He went back to sit with his friends and we ordered our food. By midnight Odette and I realized we had to get going, said goodbye to Owen and headed home. I went to bed thinking about the interesting night I'd had.

Several weeks passed and I hadn't returned to *Stampede Wrestling*. Still, I thought a lot about Owen and went to watch whenever we hosted his high school for various sporting events.

At one of his rugby games, he spotted me on the sideline and gave me a little wave. I definitely had a crush on him and thought maybe he liked me too. I wanted to talk to him but it was awkward. There were too many people around, and after the game was over his team quickly boarded their bus and went back to their school.

I couldn't stop thinking about my memorable meeting with Owen. I probably overanalyzed what he said but I thought maybe he really meant it when he suggested I should go to the wrestling matches again sometime. I decided to put some effort into getting to know him, so against my better judgment I went to the wrestling show again with Odette.

Owen appeared happy I had taken him up on his suggestion to return to the show and came over to talk to me right away. With the end of the school year approaching and the athletics seasons finishing, I knew that the best place to see Owen and get to know him better was at the wrestling show. He kept encouraging me to attend, so I did.

We chatted every Friday night at the matches then met for further discussions at the pizza place. I knew I really liked him because every time I saw him my heart raced and my mind would nearly go blank. There was a real chemistry between us—one that left me feeling warm and happy inside. I was utterly smitten, and I was pretty confident he felt the same way about me.

The situation wasn't perfect, though. Although I really looked forward to seeing Owen, I hated going to the wrestling shows to do it. My mother was also becoming concerned. She began questioning my sudden interest in going out every Friday night. I confessed I liked this nice boy that worked at the wrestling matches and she exploded.

"Those wrestlers have the worst reputations," she ranted. "I don't want you going down there anymore."

My mother was petite and I towered over her, but her word was law. I was very respectful of her opinion and never wanted to disappoint her. I carefully explained that Owen wasn't a wrestler. He was a decent boy. His dad ran the shows and Owen was simply helping him out as the music operator.

She didn't like it one bit, but after endless discussions, she eventually agreed to let me go on one condition: that my older sister Virginia accompany me. I was fifteen and she was nineteen. It was humiliating to have my big sister chaperoning me, but I wasn't about to rock the boat. I told Virginia how much I liked Owen and that I didn't want her wrecking it. I begged her not to say anything derogatory about Owen or the wrestling exhibition to our mother.

"I won't if there's nothing bad to tell," she said.

Virginia knew I didn't care much for the wrestling itself and that Owen was the only draw for me. I found the whole wrestling environment disgusting. What made matters worse was that after attending for over a month, some of the regulars took notice that Owen had a fondness for me. Even though Owen wasn't one of the wrestlers, he was still a member of the Hart family, and some of the girls in the crowd became jealous. I started to worry about these groupies and told Owen a few times I wasn't comfortable going to the shows anymore.

Some of these girls were rough, harsh people, and initially I wasn't sure what they were capable of. I soon found out at one show when I narrowly avoided being hit by a thrown bottle. On another occasion one of them saw me coming and told security my sister had drugs in her purse. He frisked us and made poor Virginia dump her purse, sending her running into the bathroom in tears, humiliated by the process.

My dislike of the wrestling environment was reinforced even further during a subsequent show when Owen got involved in an audience fight. Several fans started a shoving match and when Owen and his brother Ross tried to quell the situation, things got out of hand. Owen had a reputation as a great amateur wrestler, which probably deterred some people from fighting him, but when push came to shove, he'd leg-dive people to get them out of the arena. Although he wasn't a fighter, and certainly wasn't a bully, I remember being turned off by it.

"Oh, you're kind of violent. Do you hit girls too?" I half-joked with Owen, who I nicknamed "Scrapper."

As the summer wound down, I attended the last Friday night show before school started up again. As had become our ritual, Owen and I met at the show before reconvening at the pizzeria. One of Owen's buddies had a hip new Trans Am, and as we were leaving the restaurant Owen asked my friend and me if we'd like a ride home with him and his two buddies. I trusted Owen and accepted without hesitation.

There were five of us stuffed into this little car so I had to sit on Owen's lap—the old high school trick. The guys thought we'd like a tour of the city so we found ourselves cruising downtown.

Owen was apparently getting fairly comfortable with me sitting on his lap and thought it would be funny if he snapped my bra strap. It was a loud snap and everyone in the car heard it. Big mistake.

I thought it was completely disrespectful of him and was utterly insulted. "I don't know what kind of girl you think I am but you can't do that to me," I yelled, turning a car of giggles into silence the rest of the drive home.

I felt he had taken an uninvited liberty with me and I was furious. Plus, I was sick of going to the wrestling shows to see him and I was starting to wonder if he really was a nice guy or not. Even worse, I was worried he saw me as just another one of those "ring rats" that hung around the shows, dying to hook up with a wrestler.

When we pulled up to my house I jumped out without saying good-bye. Owen clamored after me and ordered his friends to stay while he walked me to the door. Despite this, as soon as Owen closed the car door his friends abruptly drove off.

I didn't want to leave him alone on the street so I sat on the porch steps, knowing his pals would return momentarily. Our old, Victorian-style house in southeast Calgary was surrounded by a tall hedge and enormous poplar trees so I didn't know if he could see I had waited for him. He stood on the sidewalk for a minute before walking up the path to my house and sitting down. At first, neither one of us said anything.

I broke the ice by telling him I was a nice girl and expected to be treated that way. He apologized and told me he was only kidding around.

"I didn't think you would react so strongly," he said.

It dawned on me that this was the first time the two of us were able to talk without our friends being within earshot. I could tell he was sorry, not because he thought what he did was so wrong but because he could see it bothered me. At once I reconsidered the negative thoughts I started to have about him and resolved he really was a nice guy after all.

It wasn't long before we heard the sound of his friend's car returning. Our brief time alone was most satisfying and I wished his friends could have given us more of it.

As he got up to leave, I took out a pen and quickly wrote my phone number on a piece of paper. "I know you already have my number but I'm going to give it to you again," I said.

I had something else to say but I didn't know if I should, as I worried it would offend Owen. I knew the wrestling business was his father's livelihood but at the last minute I dared to say my piece.

"Owen, I like you a lot but from now on you'll have to call me if you want to see me," I said. "I don't like wrestling and I'm never going back to that wrestling show."

He had no response. He took the paper out of my hand, leaving me with no indication of his future intentions, and jumped in his friend's car.

Three weeks went by and not a word from Owen. School was well under way and my fun-filled summer memories were fading. Despite my feelings for Owen, I meant it when I said I wasn't going back to the wrestling show.

Meanwhile, football season was kicking off and our school had already played a few games. I liked going out to support the school team so I decided to go to the next game. The cold bite of the oncoming winter was already in the air. Sitting on the outdoor bleachers was brutal—I was freezing and the game hadn't even started yet. The teams ran onto the field for pre-game warm-up and I noticed we were playing Manning, Owen's high school. I wondered if he was there. I searched until I spotted him—number 41. He was easy to find as he was the only one wearing a gold helmet.

As I watched Owen play, warm thoughts of our Friday nights together flowed through my mind. I was sad he hadn't called as I missed talking to him. Walking out of the stadium after the game I saw Owen's dad and his sister Diana, who had come to watch him play. I doubted they knew who I was but I wanted to leave a good impression just in case, so I said hello.

On the way home all I could think of was soaking in a hot bath. I was absolutely chilled to the bone. I climbed into the tub soon after I walked in the door. Soaking contently, I could feel the warm water slowly extracting the coldness out of me when my sister Virginia called me.

"I'm in the bath. What do you want?" I snapped at her.

"You're wanted on the phone," she replied.

It was almost 10:30 P.M. Who would be calling me this late?

"It's Owen Hart."

I jumped out of the bath as fast as I could, grabbed the nearest towel and ran upstairs to the extension phone.

"Did you go to the game? I didn't see you," were his first words.

After weeks of silence I had all but given up hope on him. I was so thrilled to hear his voice that we talked blissfully for two hours and arranged our first official date.

It had been over six months since I met Owen, and on October 9, 1982—I'll never forget what day it was—he came over to my house to help me babysit. It wasn't the most glamorous date but I was excited.

I prepared all day by cleaning the house from top to bottom. Owen arrived and everything was going so well until he took his shoes off. He wasn't wearing any socks and I had to do my best to pick my eyes up off the floor. He had the world's ugliest feet! He had big flat toes and, worst of all, the baby toe on each foot rested on top of the toe next to it. I tried not to stare but they were so hideously strange I couldn't help myself.

It was so silly but I honestly thought I might have to forget about this guy because his feet were so weird. Then, I'd look at his face and realize I liked him too much. I figured if he kept his socks on the relationship would work.

When my mom came home from work and suggested it was "time for my friend to leave," I walked Owen to the door. I wasn't sure if he would try to kiss me but I hoped he would. We stood awkwardly at the door shifting our eyes until he finally put his hands on my shoulders, pulled me closer to him and kissed me.

It was great! The kiss itself wasn't his best, but the moment was priceless. I closed the door behind him and floated up to bed.

Our second date was more eventful, as Owen's car ran out of gas. I would soon accept this as a common occurrence in our relationship as he was forever borrowing any number of his family's cars and praying two dollars of gas contributions would get us from A to B.

As time went on we began to see a lot of each other. Owen was such a nice guy. It sounds silly, but ever since the "bra strap" incident, he knew I demanded complete respect from him, and he gave it to me 100 percent. In some ways I always felt that little episode set the tone for our relationship. It was like a small statement of what I would put up with and what I wouldn't.

I adored him. He was so sweet and sensitive—not just to me, but to everyone.

The more time Owen and I spent together, the more we realized just how much we had in common. Both of us were the youngest in large families, growing up in extremely unconventional households.

My mother had been divorced after having nine kids. She later had two more children—Virginia and me—with our father in a subsequent relationship. My dad was a wealthy, self-centered man who broke up with my mother when I was three and refused to contribute to our upbringing, financially or otherwise. Even though I would see my father on occasion, our meetings were hollow. We never bonded. I despised him and thought my mother should have taken him to court for child support payments. However, she was afraid of him and chose to raise us herself.

After her relationship with my father, my mother, who was a very attractive lady all her life, sadly remained alone and never remarried. Watching her raise a large family on her own, I admired her work ethic and ability to cope with all the stresses life and parenting brought. Her responsibilities were so great I tried to make her life easier when I could. We have always been very close.

On top of her parenting duties, my mother also had health problems, battling breast cancer before I was born. Following a complete mastectomy on her right side, she came away with an incredibly positive outlook on life that she passed on to me. She always felt she was living on borrowed time so she made the most of each day and never seemed to worry what tomorrow would bring. Her life experiences made her a very wise woman and I respected her opinions a lot.

She kept a close eye on me and had problems warming up to the idea of me having a steady boyfriend, let alone one affiliated with professional wrestling. She was polite but short with Owen.

He worked overtime on her, getting her coffee or washing her car. He was good at picking appropriate times to do his good deeds, avoiding being a brown-noser. It didn't take long to win her affection. In fact, I think she grew to like him more than she liked me! In short order, she couldn't resist him. Nobody could.

Like Owen's parents, my mother was a firm believer in helping the down-and-out get back on their feet. Through word of mouth, individuals like the dishwasher from the restaurant she worked at or one of my brothers' friends would hear of my mother's kindness and request temporary lodging.

Accustomed to such an open-door policy, Owen was most gracious and helped our visitors as much as she did, if not more. Listening to their stories softened him. He sympathized with their plight and I was pleasantly surprised at Owen's acceptance.

As much as I hated to admit it, sometimes I could be less than kind to some of my mother's visitors. I tried to treat these people with humanity but I also viewed some of them as intruders. I thought some of them should work harder to make a better life for themselves, rather than rely on others to do it for them. They were all harmless but I didn't have the tolerance Owen had. I couldn't accept everyone at face value as easily as he could. I distinguished the ones I thought worked hard and deserved a break from those I felt were loafers. Owen didn't seem to have an opinion either way. He treated everyone with dignity regardless of the way they lived their lives.

I vowed never to fall into the same traps these freeloaders did. It helped me build ambition and a work ethic I've long prided myself on.

In addition to his compassion, smarts and athletic ability, Owen had an incredible sense of humor. He was always well-stocked with comeback lines, and his pranks were legendary and unbelievably original.

His mind was invariably scanning the scene, waiting for the right opportunity. I couldn't believe it when he tied a piece of bacon around my one cat's neck and watched with amusement while my other cat chased it around. While his tricks were always harmless, playful fun, his desire to toy with people was sometimes overdone and annoying. His jokes never ended.

We would often jog by the river, and one day as I lagged behind he started screaming just as a group or runners passed by.

"Would you quit chasing me! I told you I don't want to go out with you," he wailed.

All I could do was hang my head until they passed.

Christmas was also an interesting affair, as one year he gave me a diamond ring, which he stuck in a smelly old size twelve sneaker.

Owen was quite clever with the production of his pranks, as many times he wasn't even in the vicinity when the height of the joke unfolded. One night he came over to my house, knowing I had to go to bed early for a big exam the next day. At my insistence, he left early and I went upstairs to go to sleep. To my horror, someone was sleeping in my bed. For quite some time I stood in my doorway, trying to figure out how to wake this stranger. With no movement or response to my prodding, I finally got the nerve to whip off the covers only to discover Owen had put a wig on a big stuffed toy my brother had won at Stampede.

He was naturally funny and made me laugh all the time, even when I didn't want to. Of course, I wasn't the sole victim of his follies. No one escaped the wrath.

One day I told him very seriously that his jokes had to stop—they were driving me crazy. Wearing a somewhat mischevious grin, he said he'd really, really try.

Alas, the hijinx continued.

For quite some time, Owen shielded me as best he could from his family. He knew what his various siblings were all about and he didn't want me to meet them. We dated for more than three months before I was introduced to any of his siblings or parents and I was starting to wonder if there was something wrong with me. I hadn't met anyone in his family and he was a fixture in mine.

He had become quite comfortable with my mom and my sister Virginia and cultivated a friendship with both. When I questioned why we never visited his house he told me he was embarrassed by some members of his family. He didn't want any of his siblings to do anything to scare me away like they had done to his other brothers' girlfriends. He said some of his sisters were so critical.

I told him he didn't have to worry about that. It wasn't as if I was exempt from oddballs in the family—I had my fair share too.

They weren't going to change my feelings about Owen and, as it turned out, nothing ever would.

I finally met the family at his brother Keith's wedding, New Years Eve, 1982. He figured the house would be clean for a change and everyone would be on their best behavior.

I was a little surprised to see broken down jalopies everywhere as well as several animals wandering in and out of the house. Owen told me there were a number of mechanic types living with them who forever seemed to be working on the vehicles.

I quickly realized why it didn't faze Owen to have a stranger at my house for dinner—he had ten of them at his house. My mom and his dad were from the same era—they lived on farms and that's how they did things. Everybody helped one another and trust was inherent.

For all of Owen's great characteristics, he seemed to be lacking somewhat in moral guidance. He knew what was right and wrong to a degree, but he had witnessed several siblings doing the wrong things in life without being corrected or punished. He watched one of his brothers steal cars and bikes, among other things, which he stored at his parents' house. Stu and Helen either turned a blind eye or were too busy to notice.

Another brother dated a girl less than half his age, resulting in a pregnancy, without reprimand from his parents. Owen listened to vicious rumors spread by a sister he knew were out and out lies, yet he never tried to set the record straight.

Owen's parents didn't necessarily condone their children's behavior, but they were not actively correcting it either. They would complain about the unfavorable conduct of their children but not directly to the children themselves. There didn't appear to be any control or ground rules laid down for the Hart kids to follow. They were all taught to get an education, but there was no consistency on how to live an honest, decent life. Their lifestyles were similar to the wrestling business itself—as long as it looked good on the surface it would suffice.

Throughout his childhood, Owen longed for stability and clear expectations. I think he found comfort and clarity in my values and they began to rub off on him.

I found what I needed too—a strong but tender male figure that I had been lacking all my life. We brought out the best in one another and, as we would discover throughout the next seventeen years, we fit together like two puzzle pieces.

There was good balance between our personalities. Owen was a laid-back type of person and I was intense, with strict morals. He knew what I wanted in life—a solid family structure, kids, a good job—and that I was willing to put the effort in to get it.

I had seen people from every walk of life sail through my house and I really did know the type of person I wanted to be. My belief was that everyone should be responsible for the choices they make and be brave enough to own their decisions, good or bad. I just figured that even if you can fool the whole world you can't fool yourself. You know who you are and what you've done, and you have to look in the mirror every day and live with the person you see. I always wanted to be proud of that reflection and didn't want to disappoint myself.

Six months into our relationship, our feelings for one another had become so strong he turned to me at the end of a date and made my heart skip a beat.

He told me he loved me.

"I think I love you too," I said.

But as our relationship progressed my earlier concerns about Owen's involvement in wrestling intensified. I couldn't imagine spending any time, let alone the rest of my life, with someone who toiled in such a seedy, unsavory environment—a place where violence ruled and decency disappeared. Although he chose to look at the scene as more of a joke than anything else, he agreed it wasn't the sort of environment he wanted to spend any prolonged periods of time in.

I vividly remember one night we were at his brother Bret's house, mere blocks from the Stampede grounds. The lights were off and we were watching some sci-fi movie, the type Bret was crazy about in those days. I remember Bret asking Owen matter-of-factly, "You want to wrestle, right Owen?"

I jumped right in. "Oh no, he's going to be a teacher," I said. Owen and I were both taking summer school in preparation for university. Wrestling was out of the question.

Still, Bret was taken aback by the comment and remembers the conversation to this day. To him, any notion that a talented young brother like his would pass up the opportunity to wrestle was unheard of.

THE ROAD TO FAME

"Happy is the man who hath never known what it is to taste of fame—to have it is purgatory, to want it is a hell!"
—EDWARD BULWER-LYTTON

As promised, I didn't go back to *Stampede Wrestling* for close to four years. I was never a fan of wrestling, and never will be. It wasn't a part of our relationship, although Owen dutifully continued his role as his father's ringside deejay until he finished high school.

Despite repeated inquiries into his wrestling future beyond high school, Owen had no interest in doing anything to interfere with his plans to one day be a teacher—despite the fact he was good enough to win the city and provincial wrestling championships in 1983 before finishing tenth at nationals in Toronto. By then he already had the looks, the build, the genes, the athleticism and the personality to be every bit as popular on the pro scene as his brothers before him. And that's exactly what his father and brothers had in mind all along.

He was always the entertainer of the bunch, the kind who lit up in front of any sized gathering, be it in the schoolyard, gym, pizza parlor or living room. Owen was a natural to continue climbing the ladder that would one day lead to the ring.

However, from early on he always made it clear to me he didn't want any part of it. Owen wasn't interested in the travel and circus-type atmosphere that enveloped his father's *Stampede Wrestling* as it toured across western Canada. He wanted to live a normal life.

That said, he continually impressed family and friends with an incredible repertoire of high-flying maneuvers and counter-moves while fooling around in the dungeon or the family's outdoor ring. It was there Stu and several of the other brothers still ran regular wrestling camps, known by many as the School of *Hart* Knocks.

Owen was a natural, and this kept his brother Bruce, who ran their dad's shows, salivating at his potential in the family business.

Owen graduated high school in 1983 and decided that summer he would travel through Europe for a few months with his brother Ross, who was four years his senior. However, just prior to their departure, Owen went on the road one night to fill in for an injured Stampede wrestler. Donning a mask to conceal his identity and preserve his amateur eligibility, Owen teamed up with one of the best wrestlers in the business, Dynamite Kid, to take on Ross and a wrestler named Gary Eichenhauser.

Owen was the talk of the match. Still, he wasn't going to tell me about his in-ring experience until I questioned one of the battle wounds he tried hiding. I was concerned, but he convinced me it was a one-shot deal.

Weeks later the two brothers toured through Germany, France and England, staying with his father's wrestling promoter friends. Well aware of his physical talents and potential drawing power, their European hosts quickly convinced Owen to wrestle for their various shows so he could earn pocket money. He was a big hit, which was hardly surprising given he was a great athlete who had long amazed his brothers by picking up wrestling moves with ease.

The trip was longer than either of us could manage. Owen sent postcards and letters every few days and we spoke on the phone on Sundays. I was still in Grade Twelve and was working at a laundromat, providing change and doing people's laundry. Every cent of my paycheck went to our inflated telephone bill.

When Owen returned to Calgary, his only association with the sport was through university. Although content to hang up his wrestling strip for good, his high school wrestling heroics had earned him the Jimmie Condon Athletic Scholarship. He contemplated the option of attending the University of Alberta in Edmonton three hours north, where his dad once coached the school's wrestling team. Instead, he decided to continue living at home while attending the University of Calgary. It was there, starting in January 1984, he wrestled for the U of C Dinos varsity team while simultaneously pursuing a degree in physical education. He didn't like the long hours the team demanded of him because it interfered with his studies, but he knew he had to do it to satisfy his scholarship.

"It sounded kind of neat to come home and say, 'Dad I got a wrestling scholarship,'" Owen recalled in a 1997 documentary by High Road Productions. "I should have said, 'I don't want this.' It took precedent over the whole purpose why I was going to university—to get a degree. It's like I'm back in this wrestling ...the curse of wrestling."

That same year, 1984, Stu shut down *Stampede Wrestling* after selling the territorial rights to an upstart wrestling promoter's son named Vince McMahon Jr. As part of the ill-fated deal that saw Stu receive a paltry sum up front for his life's work, a handful of his dad's top wrestlers were also welcomed into the big time of McMahon's upstart World Wrestling Federation. Those wrestlers included Bret, the Dynamite Kid and Davey Boy Smith, who was married to Owen's sister Diana. Jim "The Anvil" Neidhart, who was married to another of Owen's sisters, Ellie, also made the jump to the WWF.

With *Stampede Wrestling* gone, there seemed to be a better chance that Owen would never end up wrestling as a pro. There were no more regular local shows and the WWF was strictly for super heavyweights.

I had joined Owen at university in January 1985 but left when I was offered a good full-time job with benefits at the Canadian Imperial Bank of Commerce. I had worked so hard to gain entry into university I wasn't thrilled about giving it up, so I dabbled in night classes before the workload and scheduling conflicts forced me to put school on hold once again.

While I worked and saved money by living at home, Owen spent the next two-and-a-half years wrestling for the university. All the while, he kept his eyes firmly fixed on the teaching career his brothers Bruce and Keith had told him so much about. In fact, they had both been substitute teachers of Owen's while moonlighting as *Stampede* wrestlers.

Even when Stu and several of the brothers decided to re-open *Stampede Wrestling* in 1985, it mattered little to Owen or me. We never went and we never talked about it—it was as if it didn't exist.

Owen worked menial jobs each summer. He was a rigger in Alberta's oilfields one year and the next he was laying gas pipes throughout rural Alberta for seven dollars an hour. In the spring of '86, his father's Stampede circuit was struggling following the highly publicized departure of Bret and his biggest stars two years earlier. Besides, local wrestling fans were now preoccupied with the spectacle McMahon had turned the WWF into.

Bruce approached Owen with a proposal. They needed new blood and no one had been as popular over the years as the Harts had. In desperate need to rekindle interest, he pleaded with Owen to be their savior of sorts. Thinking it would strictly be a summer gig that would allow us to be together more often, Owen figured it made sense to stay in town making decent money doing something he was extremely good at. Besides, it would also help his father out. He decided to give it a whirl.

Following in the footsteps of several of the Hart brothers before him, he became an instant crowd favorite, rejuvenating the territory mere weeks after making his ring debut in May 1986. Attendance improved dramatically as he became their new star. Not only was Owen an entertaining, high-flying wrestler to watch, he was blond, blue eyed, well-built, tanned and expressive in interviews. Best of all, he was a Hart—the same kid many patrons had purchased programs from years earlier.

Already intimately familiar with what made for a good wrestling match, Owen poured his heart into his craft. He bulked up in the gym and watched countless hours of video of a brilliant, high-flying Japanese wrestler named Tiger Mask. Owen wasted little time setting himself apart from anyone else in the business by incorporating a combination of styles and techniques he picked up from wrestlers who had paraded through Calgary over the years.

Thrilled with the fact he was making reasonably good money for the first time in his life, he was proud to be able to take me out for a change. Throughout our young relationship, I always had a job at the bank, supermarket, Spa Lady gym, 7-11 or laundromat while in high school. He said he felt like such a loser without money and hated the fact I was always the one paying for our dates. Now he was making $500 a week and felt like the world was his oyster.

The money, combined with his overwhelming success in the ring, prompted him to skip university enrolment that fall. He enjoyed entertaining the crowds, and liked the idea of helping to make money for his dad.

Still, we didn't talk too much about it because it was only temporary. Everyone told him university would always be there but wrestling wouldn't. I wish that were the case.

By this time Owen and I were starting to make serious plans about our future together and he decided he would take an entire year off of school, fully intending to return to university down the road to finish his degree. I supported his decision but urged him not to get too caught up in wrestling as it might derail his original plans to teach. As it turned out, wrestling ended up carrying him far from his original plans. Despite repeated attempts to escape the jaws of wrestling years later, Owen never returned to school—a choice he often regretted.

As he traveled in beat-up old vans across the Canadian prairies to cities like Regina, Medicine Hat, Moose Jaw and Edmonton to entertain thousands alongside his brothers who now ran the promotion, it quickly became apparent Owen was every bit as talented and popular as anyone his father's storied company had ever seen.

A star had not only been born, but was flourishing.

With Owen doing shows in various cities almost every night of the week, our plan to spend more time together wasn't working out very well. I worked all day at the bank and, for a time, attended the University of Calgary at night. It left us precious little time to meet late in the afternoon before he jumped in a van with a handful of others for the next city and the next show. He was always gone.

After talking about marriage for a few years, in 1987 we decided to get engaged. By then we had been dating for five years. I was twenty, he was twenty-one.

We both saved money aggressively so we could do things right by springing for a nice wedding and buying a house we could move into on our wedding night. We picked out the ring together and were waiting for a good chance to start telling people. However, we had learned over the years that success and happiness were not things you could always share with the Harts. There was too much jealousy, too much competitiveness.

One night we decided to drive up to his parent's house at 10 P.M. to tell Stu and Helen of our wedding plans. There was little response—they reacted with no enthusiasm whatsoever.

It wasn't long before other promoters in the wrestling industry took notice of Owen as a real up-and-comer. In particular, an outfit named New Japan Pro Wrestling was very interested in Owen's repertoire of new style, high-flying moves. Their agent in Calgary, Tokyo Joe, kept a close eye on Owen's progress. In those days, going to Japan to wrestle was considered a major boost to your career. Japan wouldn't take just anyone. They only wanted the best, and they paid very well for it.

Owen stayed with *Stampede Wrestling* in 1986 and '87 before being offered a stint in Japan. They loved him there and called him Owen Hart-o.

Partly because he was raised watching wrestling, Owen always had a certain psychology that was needed to put together a great match. He could carry any match by walking his opponents through it. Often times he had taken an overweight wrestler, like Mahkan Singh (Mike Shaw) at the Stampede shows, and created a great rivalry. He had the ability to make all his opponents look better, a rare and crucial tool in the wrestling game.

I hate to admit it, but the first handful of years I dated Owen I thought wrestling was real. I had my suspicions it was fixed but, to be honest, because we tried to minimize the impact of wrestling on our lives I never cared enough to ask. I'd seen his uncomfortable reaction when asked by fans if it was fake, and I didn't want to put him on the defensive.

When Owen started wrestling professionally I decided to return to the Pavilion to support him, with the provision I'd only stay to watch his matches. I remember being genuinely horrified to watch him. I really thought he was getting hurt. There was one point where I thought about taking off my shoe to throw it at a hulking wrestler named Bad News Allen, who had Owen in excruciating pain week after week. He seemed so irrational, throwing chairs into the crowd and scaring people. He would lunge at me and even started yelling one night because I think he suspected I thought it was real. I was terrified but I remember yelling back at him once, saying something stupid about my shoe threat.

Owen saw how upset I got, especially after the matches when I'd see the bruises and welts. Thankfully, he soon felt the need to set me straight. "You have to stop getting upset," he said, probably trying hard not to laugh at my naivete. "I'm not getting hurt—it's not real."

It made me think back to a day Bret asked Owen in front of me, "Is Martha *smart?*"

Pausing before answering Bret's question, Owen responded hesitantly. "Not really," he chuckled.

Wrestling had a language of its own, which Owen kept scrambled until that time. So, not knowing what he meant, I was furious. I started yelling at him, pointing out I was going to university and wasn't just some bimbo.

He said he was just kidding but couldn't tell me just then what it meant.

A couple days later he let me know *smart* meant you were smart to the business and you knew wrestling was fixed. While most of the world knew by then that pro wrestling was indeed scripted, it was still considered a bit of a trade secret among the Harts.

I knew there was a technique involved but I had no idea it was completely fake. The finishing moves, the outcome, the injuries, the blood—it was all rehearsed to some degree.

Feeling like a complete idiot, I remember being comforted by the knowledge Helen thought the same thing when she first met Stu. When she found out wrestling was fixed she had no respect for it.

It was a relief to know Owen was okay in the ring, but afterwards I felt kind of the same as Helen, thinking, "Oh brother, this is a joke—it's not really even a sport." However, it was a breakthrough in our relationship, as he finally trusted me with something like a family secret. It was like revealing a magician's tricks.

The next secret he told me all about was "getting juiced." He explained how the Stampede wrestlers would conceal a razor blade in the tape around their wrists. When they'd get knocked out of the ring they'd roll under the skirt of the canvas, take their blade out, do their "gig" and throw the blade under the ring. They'd then re-emerge bleeding profusely. It sounded like an awful sacrifice for a few minutes of entertainment but Owen reassured me it was harmless. He explained that although it looked horrific, the cuts generally amounted to little more than a scratch.

Owen tried it a few times to help his father's business but didn't like it so he stopped. While some wrestlers took it too far, Owen didn't think it was necessary to have to cut yourself to get a reaction.

As I expected, there were plenty of times the injuries weren't self-inflicted or scripted. While most moves in the ring were loosely choreographed and the ultimate goal was to both protect one another from injury while entertaining the crowd, Owen routinely came home with stitches or staples in his head, face, neck or upper body.

As fake as it is, every wrestler knows one mistake in the ring by either man could wind up causing a major injury. Opponents loved wrestling Owen because he was known for being so technically sound and would never hurt anyone. Yet, some wrestlers were clumsy and capable of inflicting real pain and injuries with one miscalculation.

There was a right way to do everything, by minimizing pain while maximizing effect. Owen said even the classic chair smash over an opponent's head would hurt, but not much if it was executed and absorbed properly. The key was ensuring the flat part of the seat connected with the opponent's head.

To "potato" someone was to punch, drop a knee or kick someone particularly hard, making it hurt more than it was supposed to. It was usually countered with a "receipt," or payback potato. Owen told me some guys did have genuine issues with their opponents and would really hit a guy. But most often, a potato prompted a quiet apology in the ring.

While the finish of each bout is always discussed long before the evening begins, wrestlers often talk to one another through matches. While engaged in headlocks or any other position in which a wrestler's mouth can't be seen, instructions or key words will be said to trigger the next series of events.

It was the job of promoters or those "carrying the book" to give wrestlers storylines and guidelines surrounding the match. It was up to the wrestlers to pull it all off with an artistic flair that set the stars apart from the jobbers.

Owen explained the key to success as a wrestler was to "get over" with the crowd, which meant drawing a reaction. One way to do that was when the "heel" (bad guy) would be cued mid-match to "get the heat," prompting him to do something underhanded to anger the fans. It was followed by the "comeback" which typically saw the "baby face" (crowd favorite) turn jeers into cheers with a successful counterattack.

"High spots" were also crucial as matches reached a crescendo due to some sort of spectacular exchange or turnabout. It could come in the form of any number of difficult wrestling moves. The finish usually came when either the referee or one of the wrestlers said "Let's go home." It meant the match was to wrap up. The finish, which was discussed before-hand, generally ended with the baby face executing his trademark finishing move.

A win by the heels routinely came courtesy of some sort of outside interference or chicanery, which further riled the crowd.

Outside the ring, Owen's colleagues would often utter the words "kay fabe," signaling them to stay in character while in front of fans. Owen knew all the tricks of the trade early on and did well to pull them off in a fashion so convincing that I still cringed with regularity while he was in the ring. That said, my disgust with wrestling was such that I would only watch Owen's match before scurrying out of the arena. A few years down the road I wouldn't watch him at all. He, too, lost interest in reviewing his matches on TV, flipping past wrestling whenever it was on.

Owen's first tour to Japan in August 1987 was a huge success. By that time everyone in wrestling had heard about the blond kid from Canada and his unique style. He took several four-to six-week tours to Japan only to return to Calgary for *Stampede Wrestling* mentally and physically exhausted.

Japan was one of the toughest places to wrestle because the promoters expected a lot out of their performers nightly. It was also hard because there were few Western comforts of home. It was difficult to order food or get it when you wanted it. There was no English TV, it was a chore to find a gym to work out in and the language barrier proved to be a daily challenge.

Many of the other American wrestlers would take prescription pills or drink to cope with the long stays in Japan. Owen rarely took part in such libations, so he found little or no companionship among the crew. It was there he started writing long, heartfelt letters to me about the loneliness and isolation he felt on the road.

Owen was a relatively big man by Japanese standards. At five-foot-ten and 210 pounds at that time, he was one of the only Western wrestlers who could fight with the same stamina as the junior heavyweights, who had incredible cardio strength. His matches were legendary and his name on the card always helped to pull in the crowds. Owen was even crowned with the IWGP Championship belt, which, even though it was fake, was an incredible honor since he was one of the first foreigners to be so adorned.

Japanese wrestling is the closest to real wrestling in the professional field and is taken seriously as a mainstream spectator sport. Match results are even published in the daily sports pages. The only thing predetermined is the finish.

Every time I picked Owen up from the airport after one of these grueling trips he was so happy to be home he would practically kiss the ground. I was always thrilled to see him. His trips abroad were really hard on me emotionally. The days would just drag on as I battled loneliness and considered the sacrifices I made to have a boyfriend who was never around. On weekends all of my friends were out on dates while I stayed home waiting for my guy to call from God knows where.

During those calls Owen would constantly encourage me to remember that with every trip he brought us one step closer to a brighter future for us.

"All our hard work will pay off," he'd say.

He would ask me repeatedly not to give up, "because one day you will have so much time with me you won't know what to do with it all."

When Owen returned from one particular six-week trip he seemed more smitten with me than usual. We had been engaged for just over a year but had not yet set a wedding date.

"You are the most important person in my life," he said. "You are the reason I rush home after every trip. I want to marry you."

I looked at him and said, "I know."

"No, you don't understand," he said. "I want to marry you *now*."

I was so thrilled I jumped into his arms with a grin that stuck for weeks.

As exciting as it was, the practical side of me kicked in. I had always wanted to get married in July and it was already June. There was no way we'd have time to set up a proper wedding. Besides, why would we want to rush such a grand occasion?

Waiting an extra year would also allow us to save more money to buy a house. We talked it over and decided to get married the following year, on July 1, 1989. Scheduled for the same day as Canada's birthday, we joked that no matter what, Owen and I would always have fireworks on our anniversary.

We decided we would announce our plans at Christmas, giving us six months to prepare. It was one of the happiest days of my life.

In the ring Owen had become hugely popular in such a short time, prompting the World Wrestling Federation to take notice. In the spring of '88 he went for a weekend tryout, wrestling as Owen James. The WWF decided they wanted him in some capacity or another but he turned them down so he could spend more time at home.

Stampede Wrestling was barely hanging on at that point and Owen felt like he was onboard a sinking ship. He was now getting paid close to $1,000 a week as their headliner but he hated to see his dad losing money. He frequently told Stu he should shut it down if it wasn't producing anymore.

A few months after turning down the WWF, Owen was re-approached by WWF officials who told him they had a good idea how they were going to use him. He then decided to give it a try.

By that time Bret, known worldwide as the "Hitman," was well on his way to becoming one of the biggest superstars in wrestling history. Bret had teamed up with brother-in-law Jim "The Anvil" Neidhart to form the Hart Foundation, which was crowned World Tag Team champs several times through the late '80s and early '90s. It was no coincidence their greatest matches came against the British Bulldogs, featuring former *Stampede Wrestling* pals Davey Boy Smith and the Dynamite Kid (Tom Billington). Davey was still married to Bret's sister Diana, and Billington married the sister of Bret's wife, Julie.

Like Owen, Bret never intended to be a pro wrestler. He, too, wrestled as an amateur to impress his father, eventually becoming a two-time provincial amateur champ. However, his childhood dreams revolved around being a film director. Bret had enrolled at Calgary's Mount Royal College to study film before dropping out a year later to work as a part-time referee for his dad. The next thing he knew he was touring western Canada, Japan, Germany and England as a headliner before landing in the WWF.

His success and reputation as one of wrestling's best technical wrestlers, the "Excellence of Execution," as he was known, helped open the door for Owen, who was getting his big wrestling break at age twenty-three.

Owen was scheduled to start working for the WWF in July 1988, just months after Calgary had played host to the Winter Olympics. It was a very exciting time for Owen and a great opportunity to make some good money. It appeared all his hard work had finally paid off as he was hitting the big time.

Outfitted with a blue mask and a fur-lined blue cape, Owen essentially debuted as a ridiculous character named Blue Blazer. His colleagues referred to him and his do-gooder comic book character as the Blue Sports Coat.

Owen went from being the star of the show everywhere he went to being one step above being a "jobber." In the early days, jobbers were generally overweight, sloppy, nameless guys who got squashed by the stars every night. Owen felt he deserved better.

The money was good but that wasn't what mattered most to Owen. He was disgusted at having to predominantly wrestle in the early matches where he was given little respect and no major "push" or storylines. He resented the fact WWF bigwigs made it seem like the wrestlers should be so grateful to be working there. Although most wrestlers felt that way, Owen didn't.

Disenchanted with what he expected to be a step up from his family's loop, his visions of grandeur quickly washed away. Despite making close to $100,000 US in his first year, his increasing unhappiness at living out of a suitcase reinforced his desire to escape the business. There were more important things in life than money, especially when you could see your employer blatantly exploiting you and your talents.

Then came his first major injury. Attempting to leapfrog opponent Greg Valentine as part of a choreographed move, Owen was hit in the groin. He was unable to walk or wrestle for more than a month, and the doctors considered surgically removing one of his testicles, which had ballooned to the size of an orange. Hospitalized for a week and bedridden for much longer, he couldn't even get up to go to the washroom.

I helped Owen through it all any way I could and the setback strengthened our bond, making us realize the most important thing we had was each other. With plans to start a family in the next few years, the injury really prompted him to question whether risking his health every night was worth it.

Returning to the road, where he roomed with Jim Hellwig, a.k.a. the "Ultimate Warrior," Owen openly discussed returning to Japan where he could spend less time on the road and still have the same amount of take-home pay.

In June of 1989, mere weeks before our wedding date, he shocked his family and everyone in the wrestling industry by quitting the WWF less than a year after starting.

Some figured he was crazy to walk away from the Coca-Cola of wrestling but his refusal to accept the McMahon mentality ultimately gained him a lot of respect in the business. The experience also helped Owen see the other side of how people can be. He was young and it changed the way he looked at his career. He didn't care as much about the money as he did his happiness.

With a wedding to plan, I was looking forward to getting some help and support from Owen's family. I had always helped out the Harts when I could. Whether it was buying Christmas gifts for each and every family member, baking pies for Stu or helping clean their house for gatherings, I did what I could to fit in. I enjoyed contributing to their family functions.

I had booked the historic Palliser Hotel in downtown Calgary for our wedding before Owen told me Stu and Helen really wanted to host the wedding at their home. They had already hosted weddings for others, like Diana and Davey Boy, Keith and his wife Leslie, Ellie and Jim Neidhart, Bruce and Andrea, and Alison and her wrestling husband Ben Bassarab.

I hesitantly canceled the hotel because we didn't want to upset anyone in the family. However, as the wedding approached I could see such respect wasn't going to be reciprocated. I started seeing a real ugly side of the siblings I suspected had always been there. I knew there were personality conflicts and obviously not everyone could possibly like everyone, but weeks before our wedding it all came to the surface. Suddenly everyone was fighting.

Diana had a falling out with a seamstress friend over a business venture of theirs. As part of their little war, the seamstress started calling family members a month before the wedding to tell them of nasty comments Diana had made about them. Owen and I had nothing to do with their squabble but suddenly everybody was mad at everybody.

It wasn't that the news was much of a surprise to anyone, it was just that it had never before been so blatantly exposed. People starting canceling, saying they wouldn't come if so and so was coming. It was childish and got out of control so I went to talk to Helen.

She immediately started to cry, wondering why there was all this anger and bitterness from a daughter like Diana who should have had so much to be happy about. Diana had two healthy children, she was young and pretty, and she was married to Davey Boy, who was a successful wrestler with a good income. There was no reason for all the ugliness.

Owen asked his brother Bruce to be his best man as the two had been close when Owen was young. However, weeks before the wedding Bruce got into a fist fight involving Davey Boy and Dynamite Kid. Bruce was left with a broken jaw that had to be wired shut before the wedding.

Bret's wife Julie was mad because Diana made derogatory comments about her, including a scathing ethnic slur among other things. Julie decided she wasn't going to attend my wedding.

Owen's sister Georgia said she wanted to make the wedding cake but then decided at the last minute she didn't want to. Georgia also cried on my shoulder because she had eloped with husband B.J. and hadn't had a proper wedding. I liked Georgia and felt bad about the fact she had been denied an elegant wedding, but that was not my fault.

We wondered if Davey Boy would attend the wedding after his altercation with Bruce. Sister Ellie then chimed in, saying, "If Davey Boy isn't coming, I'm not coming."

"Who cares if you don't come," I thought. Owen's brother Dean was dating a young girl and had a baby with her, prompting Ellie to stomp in one day to warn me to be nice to the mother of Dean's child at our wedding. It was way out of line. I had no issues with whomever Dean dated and I didn't care for Ellie's tone or suggestion I'd be anything but nice to her.

Diana fueled the fire by making harsh comments about Bruce's wife, Andrea, and then topping it off by criticizing Andrea's mother. Now Andrea declared she wasn't coming to the wedding either.

Owen's sisters then started calling their brother Owen Patterson (my maiden name) because they were angry he was more like my family than his. It was so petty. If Jerry Springer was doing his show ten years earlier they could have all been stars.

It was disappointing to see that the support I gave over the years was not going to be reciprocated by most of the Hart siblings. It turned out to be a harsh awakening for me.

I had hoped at a time like this there could be some sort of brief harmony. Not so. However, I didn't care if any of them came. At that point I would've been happy if some family members were excluded altogether.

One day, in disagreement over the wedding dinner menu, Georgia, who had obviously been stirred up by someone as she was usually quite docile, took a verbal jab at me. "Oh, go have your Victoria Park wedding," she said. (Victoria Park is one of the only truly run down, inner-city districts in Calgary.)

Owen was outraged by Georgia's comment, because, as he pointed out, the Hart house was run like a barn, where animals were allowed to eat off the dinner table. There was no organization or cleanliness, as a rule. He slammed his hand down on the table and ordered her not to speak to me that way. This was his wedding and he wanted things done the way we liked.

It was clear these people weren't accepting me into the family, which was fine. With the welcoming I had been receiving so far it wasn't a place I wanted to be anyway. From the snide comments they had made to me over the years I gathered they disliked that I worked, had my own money and could take care of myself—unlike many of them. They knew I'd never put up with the disrespect their spouses had shown them through physical abuse, adultery, failure to come home some nights, spending their money on drugs, excessive alcohol use or simply denying access to any money.

Owen was clean cut, he respected me and it drove them crazy.

The wedding seemed to bring out the worst in everybody. Although we appreciated all Stu and Helen did to try hosting a nice wedding, the home-made food ran out, just as Owen worried it would. We didn't even get a chance to eat. Several of the Harts left early, including Bret who still had a bad taste in his mouth over the mudslinging incidents that preceded the whole debacle. Many family members didn't even buy us a gift.

However, none of it ruined our day. It is no big surprise for siblings to have their disagreements, especially in big families, but it seemed that the Hart clan had exponentially more than their fair share. I always felt it probably had a lot to do with the fact that everyone was in the same business: wrestling. Instead of being happy for each other's successes, as they should have been, being in the same industry bred a competitive environment in which jealousy and backstabbing ran rampant. It would intensify as time went on, which was a real shame given they had all grown up being taught to stick up for one another through thick and thin.

Without telling anyone, we had started building our house long before the wedding. We were really proud of it and, following a honeymoon in Hawaii, we invited the family over with hopes we could all just get along. It sparked another wave of shocking disrespect as it quickly became obvious they couldn't handle our happiness and success.

I wanted a nice home and family—not to keep up with the Joneses or for anyone else. I wanted it for Owen and for me. Still, Helen walked into the house and started crying because she and Stu never had a warranty on their house or a proper laundry room like we did. I knew she had always wanted the white picket fence–type life.

Georgia's husband, B.J. Annis, didn't even want to come into the house. He reluctantly decided to storm through the place, neglecting to take off his shoes, before leaving. Georgia, forever the sensitive one, was teary-eyed because she never had a house. They've always lived atop their gym, BJ's. She was also upset because her husband had walked out and was sitting in the car waiting for her. I felt sorry for her but I just wanted people to come in, enjoy the afternoon and have a piece of pie. B.J. couldn't wait to get out. It seemed to be the common theme among the family.

Bret came over and said, "Yeah, Mom told me to brace myself."

What did that mean? Why weren't they happy for us? We weren't competing with anyone. We were supposed to be family.

On top of all that, instead of being praised for all of our hard work and how much we had accomplished at such a young age—I was twenty-two years old and Owen was twenty-four—the whispers revolved around how cheap we must be to have enough money for such a nice home. I couldn't believe it, especially considering how generous I had been with them in every way.

That was the last straw. I knew I couldn't count on those people for anything. There was no support—like a net with a bunch of holes in it. If they couldn't be happy for us in the good times, Lord knows they sure wouldn't be there for us in the bad times. We decided then it was us against the world in this family and we obviously gave ourselves priority. From that point they became a secondary concern.

Months later we tried being cordial by inviting Stu and Helen over for weekend breakfasts, which they'd be several hours late for. It infuriated Owen and embarrassed him immensely.

But that was the way the Harts were—always late. They didn't mean anything by it but Owen would get upset. I had long stopped expecting anything from them—that way they couldn't disappoint me anymore. But for Owen it wasn't that easy—their actions really hurt him. They acted inconsiderately and that was that.

From then on we always remained kind to them but never allowed them to be emotionally close to us again.

Shortly after the honeymoon, Owen returned to *Stampede Wrestling* where he once again received top billing. Over the course of the next year he was also making frequent trips to wrestle in Japan while I stayed in Calgary working. I had left the bank and was employed with an oil company.

In April 1990, a call from a German promoter came with an enticing offer that would allow him to continue making lucrative trips to Japan and Mexico while wrestling in Germany. Unsure how long he'd go for, we decided I should go with him. We were home in Calgary for mere days that year, including a three-hour layover in town to check on the house and switch suitcases en route from Mexico City to Bremen, Germany. In many ways it was the most normal year of our marriage and the most exciting of my life, as I had a husband with me every day.

While wrestling abroad, Owen was known as the Canadian Superstar. He wore basic red and white gear with a maple leaf prominently displayed in front. He was a draw everywhere we went because he was a good-looking foreigner with talent to burn. Adapting well to the smaller, high-flying opponents in Japan, he was a huge crowd favorite.

The Mexican fighters were equally diminutive, often incorporating a beautiful high-flying, acrobatic style called *lucha libre* that Owen quickly added to his repertoire. In Mexico the matches were held in old bull fighting arenas and attended by abnormally bloodthirsty fans. After one match Owen was lightly slashed across the chest by a crazed, knife-wielding fan. It was the first of two such slashing incidents he had in Mexico. I hated it there—it wasn't safe at all and we couldn't wait to leave.

It was customary for Mexican wrestlers to wear masks concealing the participants' identities—paying tribute to the ancient Aztec tradition of masked warriors. However, once it was clear we were leaving and never coming back, Owen agreed to let them unmask him in his final match. It was a big deal, as losing your mask was considered the ultimate humiliation a wrestler can endure. They also had a "shave your head" match in which the loser winds up getting his hair shaved off by the winner. Owen briefly considered it for the extra money before I put my foot down.

The ensuing discussion we had about how far he'd go in the ring to entertain set the groundwork for similar conversations we'd have later in life when his employers started getting out of control.

Paid per match, he generally made between $450 and $600 Canadian a week. Paychecks fluctuated as the shows in Vienna were in an outdoor stadium, and when it rained the show was canceled and nobody got paid.

In January 1991, Owen hooked up with World Championship Wrestling, an upstart competitor of the WWF's that had just been purchased by media mogul Ted Turner. After a four-month stint, we looked into the possibility of Owen signing on full-time. Problem was, they were reluctant to sign him unless he moved to Atlanta, where the company was based. I went as far as to get the ball rolling on a green card application before we decided we wanted Calgary to remain our home.

We had lived several places around the world and we always kept coming back to Calgary. There was just no better place in our eyes. A quaint city approaching a population of one million, Calgary had plenty of things to see and do without the crime or expense of most major U.S. cities. There were plenty of good flight connections for Owen to make use of and it was a phenomenal place to raise children. We loved the seasons too, as we were an hour's drive from the Rocky Mountain playgrounds of Banff and Lake Louise. In our eyes Calgary had the best of everything, including the support of our friends and some family.

Bolstered by a thriving oil patch sector and an NHL franchise that won the Stanley Cup in 1989, Calgary also happened to be home to the world's most celebrated rodeo, the Calgary Stampede. Attracting visitors from around the world for its annual ten-day celebration of our western heritage, the Stampede routinely brought out the best in a trusting community bustling with pride. Wherever he wrestled, Owen was proud to be announced as a Canadian from Calgary, Alberta.

So in the summer of '91 we decided we'd had enough of the travel and returned to Calgary. Owen took time off to rest his body and put all his efforts into being hired by the fire department his brother Keith worked for and raved about for years. Owen was always so envious of Keith as he had both a steady, normal job as well as a family.

Thrilled to find out I was pregnant with our first child, Owen felt now was the time to break away from the wrestling game and start the normal family life we both craved.

That summer Owen had eye surgery twice to correct near-sightedness and was holed up for many weeks while recovering. To bolster his qualifications he took a few courses at local Mount Royal College as well as a First Aid, CPR and a CB radio course. He even did a roofing job to help him get used to heights.

Upon hearing his most talented son was planning on hanging up his wrestling gear for good, Stu was furious. Helen stood by Stu and said it was my fault, then accused me of robbing Owen of his career. I was surprised by Helen's response as she always indicated how much she hated her sons wrestling. One would have thought Helen would have been happy Owen was getting out of it, but she wasn't. She may not have liked wrestling, per se, but I think she liked the status and high profile it gave her children, which was understandable.

However, it was Owen who was making the decisions about his career, not me. I was just supporting him. I was helping him fill out applications and assemble his driving record, high school transcripts and other pertinent information. When he asked his mother to type up his resume, she refused. She wouldn't play any part whatsoever in helping her son follow his dream of getting a normal job.

Physically, he could easily pass the fire department's grueling tests. Mentally, he was sharp enough too. However, he was never given the opportunity to write the firefighter's aptitude test. Those hired ahead of him seemed to have the university or college degrees Owen was missing.

Disappointed at being overlooked on three separate occasions, Owen wanted so badly to escape the wrestling world that he typed a two-page letter to Calgary Fire Chief Wayne Morris. "I am not bitter or jealous [of the successful applicants]," he wrote in the letter dated Aug. 31, 1991. "I do envy them and hope one day I can get a chance to write the exam to prove myself and be judged on my test results. Although I am discouraged I am hopeful you can inform me of what other requirements I should obtain in my quest to be a firefighter." He signed the letter, "Discouraged Applicant."

He never heard back from the fire chief and never applied again.

In the meantime, we knew wrestling would still be able to support us. I didn't have a big fear of Owen staying in wrestling because I didn't think he would. He hated the travel and stress on the body and he wanted to be close to home, especially now that we were going to be parents.

He dreamed of a day when he'd be home every night for dinner at 5 P.M. Although the fire department wouldn't have provided the normal nine-to-five job he craved, it still would have been better than the alternative.

Owen thought about going back to university to finish his degree, but at the same time we felt we needed money to support our soon-to-be-born child.

Once again, the door was open for Owen to return to Germany, so we packed up and headed to Hannover. There we lodged on the fairgrounds next to the arena. We lived in a cramped metal container that had two single prison beds and rats living underneath the structure. We had no running water and the only time I could shower was at night after all the wrestlers had cleared out of their dressing room. We'd walk down to the showers where Owen would guard the entrance of the dressing room while I doused myself with the ice-cold water. Afterwards we filled up our buckets so we could cook and wash our clothes in our shoddy shack. I couldn't even sleep on the same tiny bed as my husband, so we tried pushing them together. It was horrible. The shockingly primitive living conditions gave us a real appetite for returning to North America.

Although we'd definitely reached a low in our lives, Owen's sense of humor did well to make light of a horrible situation. We had to trust and support one another through some very trying times, but it brought us even closer together and helped us appreciate all we had later in life. Years later we chalked it up as an adventure.

In November 1991, we got word through a German promoter that Bret was looking to speak with Owen. Apparently the WWF really wanted Owen back.

Standing outside at midnight, using candles to illuminate the keypad on a smashed up outdoor pay phone, Owen dialed up a WWF official. Ten days later he was on a plane while I stayed behind in Germany, alone and six months pregnant.

Owen flew to WWF headquarters in Stamford, Connecticut, where he felt he entered the negotiating process on solid ground. He knew his previous departure from the WWF bolstered his stock in a strange sort of way. They knew Owen wouldn't put up with the same bottom-feeder treatment he had been afforded earlier.

Signing a deal to start in the WWF a month later, he was confident this time they wouldn't waste his talent.

WRESTLING WITH DEMONS: LIFE IN THE WWF

"Any resemblance to the ancient sport is purely coincidental."
—STEVE ALLEN

When Owen returned to the WWF in 1991 there was little doubt he had hit the big time. Although the popularity of wrestling had slipped from the '80s when Hulk Hogan emerged as the biggest kids' hero in America, the WWF was still a noticeable force on the mainstream sports entertainment landscape.

With the WCW pushing hard to overtake the WWF in popularity by stealing its stars, wrestlers were still being pitched as live action superheroes battling evil. Not only had wrestling become a part of American pop culture but most stars now enjoyed an international exposure never before afforded to wrestlers.

It was a movement Owen enjoyed being part of—for a little while anyway.

Reintroduced to WWF fans as the tag-team partner of brother-in-law Jim "The Anvil" Neidhart, Owen was made to wear an MC Hammer–type outfit with baggy purple pants and a checked green, black and blue top. Known as the New Foundation, they were playing off the highly successful

Hart Foundation that had elevated Jim Neidhart and Bret to fame years earlier. However, their duo was dissolved a month later when the WWF and Neidhart parted ways.

A similarly gaudy outfit was introduced with Owen's new partner, Koko B. Ware, as part of the tag team High Energy. (Ware's gimmick included carrying a live parrot on his shoulder.) High Energy too was soon disbanded as Owen began a seven-and-a-half-year association with the WWF that would see his character continually revamped by writers struggling to place him into the proper role.

Growing up in a business known for constantly reinventing itself and pushing the envelope on social acceptance, Owen knew better than anyone his success as a wrestler depended on finding the right gimmick and storylines to appease the masses.

Although I knew little about wrestling throughout his career, it was only after I looked into the history of the sport that I could truly understand its evolution into a modern-day soap opera, or "rope opera," if you will.

Ever since five-time champion Ed "The Strangler" Lewis took a dive against college football player Wayne Munn in 1925, the world's oldest "sport" had changed into little more than a choreographed ritual. Stripped of the honor and purity that enveloped wrestling when men like Plato, George Washington and Abe Lincoln embraced the age-old sport, wrestling was thrust into a world of disrepute in which no one knew what was fake and what was real.

Devoid of any sort of competitive aspects like scoring, rules, time limits or legitimate winners and losers, wrestling allowed its promoters to aim solely at putting on a show. This opened the door for any number of wacky angles and theatrics that have spiraled out of control today.

From the day Lewis "tanked," wearing a championship belt meant more for a man's charisma and drawing power than his ability to wrestle. Those who could tell a story in the ring dominated as headliners.

Handsome Jim Londos became one of wrestling's first real showmen in the 1930s, introducing a beauty versus beast concept that would see him match up against the ugliest wrestlers he could find. Despite being a borderline wrestler, pretty boy Londos took part in a match with Lewis at

Chicago's Wrigley Field that drew a record gate of close to $100,000 at the height of the Depression. The fight was refereed by heavyweight boxing champ Jack Dempsey, one of the first of many big name personalities to lend his celebrity status to the wrestling world.

Wrestling as a spectacle sport had truly arrived.

While traveling carnies began showcasing wrestlers with colorful costumes and trumped up biographies, a promoter named Joseph "Toots" Mondt, who later gave Stu Hart his first wrestling job, developed the concept of a packaged show by introducing time limits and popular moves that became a wrestler's trademark.

Waning in popularity during the '40s, wrestling was saved in 1948 when it was given a perfect forum in which to parade its stars—television.

A man named Gorgeous George (George Wagner) stole the wrestling spotlight soon thereafter with the type of brilliant pre-match routine that has become standard in today's WWF. Shortly after a female valet would enter the arena sprinkling rose petals and spraying perfume, the effeminate Wagner would prance into the ring wearing a long robe and bleach blond hair. Tossing golden bobby pins and tiny mirrors into the audience, he got the crowd going by informing several ladies in the audience they were ugly. Forever remembered for the refrain, "Get your filthy paws off me," people loved to hate him, making George one of the first superstar heels in wrestling lore.

"Nature Boy" Buddy Rogers, another arrogant blond with an annoying strut, was also capable of whipping crowds into a frenzy with his outrageous pre-match interviews. He set the standard for today's ring monologues that now have fans reciting catch-phrase lines along with the wrestlers.

Wrestling continued to push the envelope in the '50s with the introduction of women and midget wrestlers, followed by a horde of politically incorrect characters representing racial stereotypes. Less than a decade after World War II, Hans Schmidt played the role of a Nazi German who infuriated crowds with anti-American rants. (Truth was, he was French Canadian.) Among others grabbing attention with their cultural shtick were Russian Nicolai Volkoff, Japan's Mr. Moto, Argentinian Antonino Rocca and High Chief Peter Maiva, whose grandson, The Rock, is one of today's biggest stars.

Continually reinventing itself to keep up with rapidly changing social attitudes, wrestling took on a decidedly inhumane face through the '60s as menaces like "Dick the Bruiser" (former NFL star Dick Afflis) introduced a hardcore element that saw him use any means possible—including foreign objects—to decimate local stars. The ever-present folding chair was suddenly a weapon of choice.

One of the biggest influences on wrestling in the '60s and '70s was the seven-foot-four-inch, 525-pound Frenchman Andre the Giant (Andre Rene Rusinoff). Dubbed the Eighth Wonder of the World, the man with size twenty-two feet and limited wrestling skills was one of the first to transcend wrestling, having been featured in *Sports Illustrated*.

Shortly before dying of a heart attack in the '80s, Andre handed wrestling's reins to the charismatic Hulk Hogan (Terry Bollea), who urged kids to drink their milk and do their homework as part of his lead role in transforming wrestling into mainstream family entertainment.

However, as Hulkamania swept the land, it was a promoter's son, named Vince McMahon Jr., who slowly assumed control of the modern day wrestling scene after buying out his father's northeastern based Capitol Wrestling Corporation in 1982.

Growing up with his mother and abusive stepfather in a North Carolina trailer park, McMahon didn't meet his father until age twelve. It wasn't until years later he began working for him at the wrestling shows.

Turning heads with his acquisition of several other local wrestling promotions, including Stu Hart's *Stampede* in 1984, McMahon infuriated local wrestling promoters across the country by breaking tradition and invading their territories with his nationally televised shows. Expanding on his father's successful regional model, McMahon built a national network of stations by sending them his pre-taped shows, which he often paid to have aired.

Within a handful of years, his national broadcast attracted so much interest that most regional wrestling loops had folded. Almost overnight, his WWF stole the interest of wrestling fans who abandoned the local shows.

Doubling as a ringside announcer, McMahon oversaw a slick new way of producing wrestling shows that garnered huge TV ratings across the United States. He drew in millions of viewers weekly through the '80s with his unique storylines and outrageous characters, and advertisers jumped on board his network of stations, giving him the money to steal remaining stars from existing satellite promotions.

Using Hogan as his pitchman, McMahon sought to spread the word that wrestling was a controlled, entertaining form of cartoonish violence providing excellent family entertainment. America bought in.

McMahon was in the business of making stars, and nobody was better at it. He soon introduced the Super Bowl of wrestling, Wrestlemania, which later attracted 93,000 fans to the Pontiac Silverdome in 1987, making it the largest live audience in wrestling lore. It was at shows like these he'd routinely pay huge money for celebrities like Muhammad Ali, Mr. T, Mike Tyson, Liberace, Pete Rose and Dennis Rodman to take part in some capacity. In 1987 alone the WWF sold $80 million in tickets to live events, according to *Forbes* magazine.

Thanks to McMahon, America had rediscovered wrestling as the hip, cool thing that could suddenly be found on prime time TV for the first time in three decades. Once a month it aired in lieu of *Saturday Night Live.*

Confirming the whispers of generations, McMahon was the first to declare wrestling was indeed scripted, adding the term "sports entertainment" to Hollywood's lexicon. The bold announcement was primarily made to shed state athletic commissions, which wanted a piece of the massive pay-per-view revenues WWF shows began accruing. Although it was little more than a way around taxes, fans seemed to appreciate his honesty and regularly filled arenas.

Seeing the phenomenal impact that wrestling as pop culture was having on the American public, media mogul Ted Turner jumped into the fray by purchasing the National Wrestling Alliance and turning it into World Championship Wrestling in 1991. Airing it live on his cable stations TNT and TBS, the competition for wrestlers, fans and television ratings quickly became intense. The fight was on.

McMahon and Turner constantly tried outdoing one another with their touring shows, complete with Hollywood-quality light, sound and pyrotechnics. The big stars got richer, as did the creative storylines that continuously introduced new characters and reshaped old ones.

Having stolen several of the WWF's biggest names, including Hogan and Randy "Macho Man" Savage, the WCW quickly established itself as a legitimate alternative for wrestling fans. Eventually, both rival loops aired Monday night shows that regularly outdrew the American broadcast fixture *Monday Night Football* among young male viewers.

Following his brief stint with the WCW, Owen's return to the WWF coincided with a massive ratings war the WWF would slowly start to lose. The WWF was further weakened when McMahon was essentially dragged away from his business to answer to a federal grand jury indictment on charges of possession with intent to distribute steroids during the late '80s and conspiring to defraud the Food and Drug Administration. Several former WWF wrestlers, including Hogan, admitted to using the drugs, which had been declared illegal in 1988.

While McMahon also admitted to past steroid use, he was cleared on both charges. Upon his full-time return to business he found the WWF struggling.

In 1993, the WWF introduced its *Monday Night Raw* show that proved to be a hit. Two years later the WCW countered with *Monday Nitro* and soon began a ratings dominance that prompted both massive WWF losses and a new direction spearheaded by raunch, porn and a reduced amount of actual wrestling.

It was then the storied transformation from the world's simplest form of competition to its heavily scripted theatrics began heading towards an all-time moral low. McMahon's response to sagging ratings revolved around shocking viewers.

Catering to the lowest common denominator in society, McMahon thrust the WWF into a dark, seedy world in which good guys were bad and bad was better. Using Texan "Stone Cold" Steve Austin as his new poster boy for disrespect, McMahon took dead aim at adolescents and began introducing sexual plotlines, increased violence and vulgarity.

Owen hated it.

Due to our struggles in Germany, combined with the disappointment of not being hired by the fire department, Owen was happy his first couple years to simply have a job making decent money. Even though it was far from being his choice employment, he was good at what he did and was respected by his peers.

Oje, our first child, was born on March 5, 1992, and Owen was fortunate enough to be there with me despite pressure from the WWF to get back on the road. A day later he brought me home from the hospital and almost immediately raced off to the airport for a lengthy tour. It was hard being a new mother left alone, although it was something I had to learn to cope with.

Unhappy himself with having to leave us for weeks on end, less than two years into his second WWF stint, he made another serious attempt at gaining employment far from the ring. Among other things, he applied for a job as a United States Customs officer, for which he submitted a letter Sept. 24, 1993, that explained his situation.

"I am presently employed as a professional wrestler with Titan Sports Inc. (WWF) and I have been very successful in my present career," wrote Owen, who held dual citizenship by virtue of his American mother. "However, it lacks what I desire most, which is stability and job security. Leaving wrestling is a sacrifice that I've thought over extensively as I have devoted most of my adult life to it but I feel strongly that I could achieve the same excellence in a new career as I have in my present one."

Under reasons for wanting to leave current job, he wrote, "lack of stability—desire a career with a future."

Again, his applications were sent out in vain.

In 1993, Owen tore the anterior cruciate ligament in his left knee in a match with Bam Bam Bigalow. Though unable to walk, he completed the match, was carried out on a stretcher, and immediately returned home to Calgary.

Clearly a serious injury, what hurt more than the knee itself was the fact Vince McMahon didn't even call. It was hardly surprising Vince didn't seem to care about one of his best young athletes. However, Owen wanted Vince to know he was furious so he complained to Bret, who passed his feelings along to Vince. Days later the phone rang. It was Vince.

Owen had strong words for him and Vince responded by throwing him a few crumbs to the tune of a couple hundred dollars a week. It was a token gesture.

Years later Owen would sign a five-year contract with McMahon guaranteeing his wages. But at the time he was working for a company in which wrestlers were paid strictly on a per match basis. There was no compensation for injuries and no one had insurance or a union of any sort to protect them or their livelihood. You had to look after yourself because no one else would.

While the WWF demanded you give it your all in the ring to entertain the fans, just one miscalculated maneuver or slip by your opponent and you could blow a knee, bust a leg, suffer a concussion or worse. As cold-hearted and ugly as the business was, Owen knew how important it was to get back into the ring. If you didn't, your standing on the card was at risk. So, instead of having surgery as recommended by doctors, he pulled on a knee wrap and wrestled again just over a month later.

For years his knee bothered him to the point he couldn't run down stairs or play with his kids without extreme caution or without wrapping it with a roll of tape first. He suffered from chronic back and elbow problems and knew one day he'd have to have the knee surgically repaired.

By 1993, Bret had reached superstar status as a solo wrestler. He helped give Owen's career a boost when the two were matched up for the first time at a big event called Survivor Series. Brothers Keith and Bruce were also brought in for the four-on-four match, as was father Stu, who sat ringside.

As part of an angle that got plenty of mileage and attention, Owen wound up turning on his family, setting up a 1994 match at New York's Madison Square Garden that Owen won at *Wrestlemania X*.

Re-enacting the type of high-flying match the two brothers lived out many times growing up, their opening match is considered by some to be one of the greatest bouts in WWF history. It was a real art form that did well to open the door for smaller, technical wrestlers to showcase their talents in a world of giants.

While WWF writers were worried the crowds wouldn't buy Owen's act as a heel, he proved to be deliciously naughty. By carrying on the brother feud with Bret, Owen was elevated to top-notch status and won the King of the Ring event in June 1994.

Losing to Bret in one of the best cage matches in pay-per-view history that August, Owen kept the feud alive when he talked his mother Helen into throwing in the towel for Bret and costing him the WWF title in November 1994.

Owen enjoyed wrestling his brother and did his part to play up the feud wherever he was on the road. "If the two of us were seated together on a plane, I'd move," Owen would tell inquisitive fans.

Obviously it was all a ruse. They were actually becoming closer friends on the road and counted on one another to watch each other's back in a world where no one could be trusted.

Owen was content with his placement on the roster, as he wasn't hungry for the power or glory of being a so-called "champion." He wanted to get off the road and get home. Fan adulation was not something he craved but he liked it if he had a good spot and felt he was contributing to the show and climbing the ranks. If he was bumped to a match early in the show he'd embrace it as it meant he could go home earlier.

Although he never felt he had job security, it was a paycheck.

Racking up more than 300,000 air miles a year moving from city to city, working for the WWF was far from glamorous. However, life on the road was something Owen had down to a science. Combining an immense knowledge of flight schedules across North America with a monthly skyguide he ordered from the airlines, he routinely re-organized and rebooked the flying itinerary sent to him from WWF headquarters in Connecticut. He'd change his tickets to ensure he had the best connecting flights to reduce travel time and avoid unnecessary layovers. He wanted to spend every minute he could at home.

For the sake of expediency, he never checked his luggage. Packing lightly to make travel easier, he had one small carry-on full of his wrestling gear and a black leather duffle bag which often contained no more than a pair of jeans and a few essentials. On long trips he'd do laundry on the road—anything to avoid packing large, heavy suitcases.

Unlike other wrestlers, he rarely needed to dress up to head out on the town. Following most shows he'd duck out the back door and head to the hotel to watch television, have a swim or read the paper. He'd wrap up every day by calling me.

It was then he'd often write touching love letters to me on hotel stationery. Sometimes he'd mail them to me, and other times he'd save them until he got home and would slip them into my purse or tuck them under my pillow.

He wrote hundreds of letters, and I've kept every one of them. I reciprocated by sliding tiny notes into his wrestling boots, lunch bag or pocket to be found mid-flight or while unpacking in some remote hotel room. Concerned he wouldn't have the opportunity to eat while rushing to or from a show in some of the smaller cities, I often baked him cookies, banana bread or other treats to take as emergency snacks. I loved cooking for him and he always made a point of telling me how much he appreciated the gesture.

We both did whatever we could to bring happiness to one another.

Owen was one of only a few WWF wrestlers living in Canada. Because of this, he generally spent twice as many hours as other wrestlers getting to American cities from home. While the WWF paid all flight costs incurred as employees criss-crossed the United States and Europe for various tapings and shows, wrestlers otherwise ran their affairs like small businesses.

Responsible for booking hotels and paying for rooms, car rentals, taxis and meals out of his own pocket, Owen had to manage his money and keep receipts at all times. Keeping such documents in a tiny expense book, Owen was relatively organized but would give me fits every spring when it came time for me to file his taxes in both Canada and the U.S.

Although he was ribbed constantly by his pals for being "cheap," the reality of it was that Owen was smart with his money. We had long taught one another the virtues of short-term sacrifices for long-term gain, and by our mid-twenties had a fully paid home to show for it.

Owen's typical schedule included leaving on a Friday morning for a ten-day stretch until the following Sunday. He'd be home Monday through Wednesday before flying out Thursday or Friday for another four- or five-day tour.

When leaving Calgary for any number of possible destinations, Owen was always the last one through the departure gate. Everyone at the Calgary airport knew him and his system. They even held the plane for him once or twice.

Since they were performing in a different city every night, it became second nature for Owen and most of his colleagues to dash to the airport every morning, fly to another town, rent a car or grab a taxi, get to the hotel, find the gym for a workout, eat and get to the arena for the show. On occasion he'd be asked to make promotional appearances, which served to further tighten his schedule. Every month he'd be issued booking sheets detailing his itinerary and would often be contacted at home by WWF writers who wanted to go over his upcoming storyline.

A typical show required wrestlers to check in an hour before start time or be fined $100, depending on the mood of the agent in charge. However, TV tapings often involved two shows in one night and required much more preparation time. On those days the wrestlers were asked to be at the venue by lunch hour, where a full catering service fed them. For the rest of the afternoon the talent went over scripts, taped interviews, had their hair cut by an in-house stylist or dealt with other details like their wrestling gear.

Three sisters acted as the WWF's seamstresses and would fly in for tapings to design and make outfits for the performers. They generally took weeks to complete. There were only a few places in the U.S. you could get wrestling boots. They were light and spongy and made with patent leather and plenty of ankle support. They all had bottoms made of taupe, which was a special rubber with no treads or grip. They wore down like pencil erasers so the boots often had to be remade.

The TV tapings typically began at 5 P.M. and ended around midnight. Occasionally if a match wasn't as good as they wanted, they'd do it again or edit it heavily for TV. Wrestlers were free to leave the arena after their match although they were occasionally scripted to stay for a "run in" to disrupt another match.

The shows were generaly run like a traveling circus, with the same matches and finishes staged for several weeks of non-televised bouts. Only for TV tapings or live televised shows would things change. The wrestlers had a feel for whom they'd be pitted against and how the matches would be run. The spontaneity of it all had long disappeared.

Outside of the rare WWF junkets to England, Germany and Japan, living out of a suitcase for most of his adult life provided little in the way of excitement for Owen. Unlike most others in the wrestling world, he tried hard to see the sights worth seeing, like the Statue of Liberty or Empire State Building in New York City, Pearl Harbor in Hawaii or the Taj Mahal in India.

I forever urged him to scout out various tourist destinations with an eye to picking a place where the kids and I would enjoy meeting him on a future trip. His favorite place was Sun City, South Africa, and he wanted so badly to take me and the kids there someday to show us how beautiful Africa was.

To ease the burden his travel schedule had put on our relationship, I would join him for a quick visit every six weeks or so. We'd scout out a "good run" in his schedule, which meant he'd be in one general area for a handful of days, and the kids would join me for a short vacation.

Otherwise, being a WWF wrestler was a very empty, lonely existence for Owen. You go to the show as a big star in a make-believe world only to return to the hotel alone. Owen and I always pitied the handful of decent guys with the company who didn't have someone important to call at night or see on days off. While many were content to simply fill their free time with incessant womanizing, drug use or drinking, Owen always told me how happy he was to have the kids and me supporting him at all times.

In his letters he'd express such sadness and loneliness. Despite being a big, muscular man who needed double-XXL dress shirts to fit his neck and upper body, he was very sensitive and gentle.

I, too, felt empty when he was on the road though I had the kids to keep me company. When he'd call, sometimes I could hear *Barney, The Magic School Bus* or another children's show in the background. He would often flip the hotel television on to watch the very shows he knew Oje and Athena enjoyed.

Reminders from home came in various forms. Oje's underwear was once mistakenly placed in Owen's drawer and taken on the road. Needless to say, Owen got a huge laugh out of pulling his son's tiny undies out while dressing one morning.

Always thinking of his family, Owen would bring something home for us almost every time he traveled, even if it was just a cookie from the flight for Athena, a good buff puff from the hotel for me or a toy train for Oje.

Owen made a point of never missing Oje's birthday party. He also had an adorable way of marking Mother's Day. While it always seemed he'd have to leave on the previous Friday, he'd go for a little walk and put a Mother's Day card and small gift in our mailbox located a block down the street. I would retrieve the mail on Monday to find a wonderful "surprise" even though it became a regular routine every year.

The last card he wrote me was so sweet it brought me to tears. "I'm not perfect, but when I'm with you that's the closest I feel to it," he wrote.

We had some hard times, brought on largely by his travel schedule, but we never gave up. There were tremendous highs and lows depending on his whereabouts and, in many ways, I think that's what kept our relationship so fresh. Because our time together was limited, we made the most of it, enjoying every moment as a family. Forever demonstrating to one another how happy we were, we found that such simple gestures seemed to make it all worthwhile.

Owen was rarely home on the weekends, so it was unusual for us to join the Harts for their traditional Sunday dinners. When we did make an appearance, we typically left early, as the conversation always turned to the only thing they knew—wrestling. They were all so wrapped up in it and Owen just hated that.

I guess it was the one thing we, as the Hart family, had in common, but Owen's job didn't represent who he was. He often got up in the middle of a family wrestling conversation and starting packing up our stuff to leave. It was the last thing he wanted to talk about during his precious little time at home.

While Owen enjoyed entertaining people both in and out of the ring, he tried his best to go from city to city incognito. Although he wore a baseball cap pulled down to hide his face, it often failed to conceal his identity. Perhaps it was his golden blond, shoulder-length hair, his well-toned frame or his baby face that gave him away. Nevertheless, it prompted wrestling fans of all ages to approach him for an autograph and quick chat. Polite to all, he understood the celebrity status involved with his high-profile job. He even took the extra step of carrying an autograph marker and promotional photos of himself whenever he traveled so he could brighten the day of some of the nicer people he ran into along the way. Not many WWF performers did that.

The only time stardom bothered him was when we were out as a family and people would shout things at him at the mall or ask for autographs while he was eating. If he signed one, waves of fans would follow.

Once, in Germany, a pack of about a hundred kids followed us at the zoo for more than three hours. We had a tour guide who tried asking the kids to respect our privacy but they continued to mob us right up until we got into our rental car and drove off. I felt like a gorilla in the zoo but Owen thought it was hilarious. He knew it was part of the gig. In fact, unless he was with the kids and me, he actually quite enjoyed meeting various people.

Ever the comedian, he liked to joke with the fans. He relished the fact he could entertain people, but he also enjoyed his home and private life too. He didn't crave or feed off the attention. He was secure. He had gone to university, had always played sports and was a member of a relatively famous family, so he knew how to handle notoriety. He accepted it but it never went to his head. He didn't abuse his status and often used it to help others. It humbled him to go to the children's hospital and made him feel extremely good to do it. He would gravitate to handicapped or disabled people and was always generous with his time and money when charities came calling.

When he occasionally found himself with too much time on his hands, one of Owen's favorite ways to pass the time was by playing harmless jokes on his colleagues. He was, without question, the ultimate ribber. Fellow wrestlers rarely played a joke on him, though, for fear they'd endure the wrath of his wildly creative mind.

One night he ordered a pizza long before his roommate, Ken Patera, had returned from the bar. Upon Ken's arrival, Owen said, "I'm hungry. Let's order pizza."

Ken agreed and Owen picked up the phone pretending to place the order. To Ken's amazement, the food arrived five minutes later, prompting the thoroughly puzzled Patera to ask the delivery man, "What did you do, brother, cook it in the car?"

There weren't many in the WWF who hadn't played victim to some sort of prank phone call, room service at 3 A.M. or a misguided directive from head office courtesy of Owen.

A master of imitating other wrestlers, Owen's best impression was always that of his dad, which created plenty of interesting phone calls to wrestlers who had long admired Stu.

Even Stu himself wasn't safe from Owen's antics, once fielding a call in a hotel room from a long-time friend he hadn't heard from in years. While several others overheard Stu's side of the conversation, they were surprised when it took a turn for the worse and a clearly agitated Stu became involved in a heated exchange with his old pal. After saying a few choice words, Stu slammed down the phone, looked up at the roomful of puzzled family members and shook his head.

"That lousy Owen got me again," he said.

One of the not-so-nice tricks other wrestlers took pleasure in was known as "shooflying" someone. Often performed at hotel bars where a lot of wrestlers convened late into the night, it involved throwing a sleep-inducing drug in someone's drink when they weren't looking. Some also called it Mooshie-Mooshie.

They'd do it to fans who came up to them in the bar, taking advantage of people who were being generous or unaware, and would sometimes even rip them off in the process. They'd also even stoop to shooflying other wrestlers.

Owen rarely joined the guys at the bar, but in some cities there simply wasn't anything else to do and nowhere else to grab a bite. He enjoyed the odd beer but was by no means a drinker. He did everything he could to avoid situations where some drunk would come up to him with false courage to start trouble.

Unlike many others in the wrestling world, Owen was a classy family man, content to do his job and call it a day. A devoted husband and father, he was not impressed by the spousal cheating, illicit drug use, rampant alcoholism and incessant womanizing that punctuated most evenings on tour. Instead, he would often enjoy running into decent types like Al Snow, Mick Foley or Jeff Jarrett at the hotel following an event.

He'd tell me stories of what some of his sick, lost co-workers were up to. I had long ago lost any respect for most of the people he called colleagues. Weeks later I'd run into the wives of these cheating scumbags and wonder how they could either not know or put up with their husbands' infidelity.

When in a situation where his colleagues were up to no good, Owen was the kind of person who would take these hangers-on aside and warn them to keep an eye on their drink. Owen was thankful for the support he received from his fans. Instead of ignoring or walking all over the generous souls who took time to write some of the thousands of letters Owen received every year, he forged relationships with some of them. They'd pick him up at the airport in their city, take him to the hotel and to the arena. Sometimes he stayed at their houses. They loved it. He'd return the favor by treating them with respect, getting them great tickets to the event, buying them dinner or getting them backstage to meet some of the other wrestlers. It also gave Owen a nice break from the cast and crew he spent so much time around.

Drug use was rampant among WWF wrestlers. They took various substances for everything from insomnia to nagging injuries, as well as illicit street drugs, all in an attempt to battle depression and deal with the stark reality of their lives. Owen's brother-in-law Davey Boy walked around like a zombie for many years while addicted to prescription and non-prescription drugs.

Owen resisted even the mildest of prescriptions many of the other wrestlers used to fight sleep problems. Instead, Owen always carried a small baggie of pills ranging from anti-inflammatory drugs for his damaged knee to dietary supplements. He wasn't into steroids like many of the others. He was simply blessed with a large frame that he worked hard to keep in top shape. Still, the pressure was certainly ever present to have all WWF wrestlers bulk up as much as was humanly possible.

In his first incarnation with the WWF (1988–89), Owen was routinely pressured to "get on the juice," which was one of the many reasons he left. It was back then many gathered in hotel rooms nightly to do cocaine, heroin, crack or simply smoke marijuana. Owen happily declined and kept to himself.

I saw first-hand just how shady these guys could be during a visit with Owen in Hartford, Connecticut, for *Wrestlemania* in 1995. Owen had suffered a concussion in his match and was at the hospital. Meanwhile, I sat in our hotel room watching TV as three-year-old Oje slept. In the room next door I overheard a heated twenty-minute argument between four wrestlers whom I recognized by their voices. One of them had brought a woman back to the room with an eye to having sex with her.

Another wrestler was none too pleased with the situation and I could hear him yelling, "Get her out of here! You're not f—ing her in here."

They argued back and forth for quite some time before I suddenly heard their door open and she was literally thrown out. I opened my door to see if she was okay and she shook herself off and hurried down the hall, clearly humiliated.

As Owen often said, there was never a dull moment around those guys.

The same could be said for overseas flights, which Owen dreaded for having to travel alongside the immature and often unsavory hordes he called colleagues. Owen got along with everybody but only counted a few as good friends. Problem was, it only took one goofball to ruin a trip.

It was on those transcontinental group flights that no one was safe from the twisted hijinks of his fellow man. Anyone sleeping could easily have their eyebrows shaved, as happened to Classy Freddie Blassie on one trip. Others could wake up with shaving cream on their head or much worse. On one commuter flight from Halifax to Moncton I had the misfortune of being on with baby Oje, the 1-2-3 Kid thought it would be a scream to light a stink bomb in the lavatory and ruin everyone's flight. He did it to impress his buddies—I'm sure they just thought the world of him after that. The whole plane reeked.

Owen's status as king ribber likely saved him from plenty of targeted attacks, but even he had to be alert at all times. Often unable to sleep during flights anyway, he'd thumb through magazines and catalogues of all sorts, tearing out pictures of furniture, appliances or wacky knick-knacks he wanted me to check out or buy. On long journeys he'd bring the odd novel to read.

Given the rough and tumble nature of his job and his rigorous schedule on the ground, flights would have been the perfect time to catch up on some sleep. However, Owen's large frame often made the tiny seats uncomfortable and he had a hard time nodding off. On long flights he'd occasionally upgrade to first class at his own expense. He also got his share of the royal treatment in first class when he'd use frequent flyer coupons or the check-in people would recognize him as one of their wrestling heroes.

No matter how far back in the plane Owen sat, when he was flying home for a few days of family time he would always stow his carry-ons in the overhead bins at the front of the plane so he could be the first off. He would dart to the front of the aircraft as the plane was being taxied in, much to the dismay of the flight crew. He couldn't wait to zip through customs and jump into the arms of his waiting children, who I'd often bring to the airport with me. So anxious to get home at the end of a road trip, he'd sometimes dash from an arena to the airport in his wrestling gear to catch the last flight of the evening. In those cases, he'd change on the plane without showering. I doubt his fellow passengers appreciated that, but I sure did.

Throughout the late '80s and early '90s the WWF paid Owen anywhere from $200 to $2,000 US per match, depending on his spot on each card and his role in the event. Vince told his staff payment depended on the size of the crowd, but the feeling was it likely had just as much to do with Vince's temperament on that day. None of the wrestlers knew on a weekly basis what their checks would be. You could kind of guesstimate but when they arrived you either liked it or lumped it.

Once Bret got to a certain status, he got up the courage to hand back one of his checks to Vince and demand it be augmented. Vince obliged, but most others would've been terrified to try such a tactic. The bottom line was that most of the pawns in the WWF were simply happy to have a job. They were being made famous and had very few other employment opportunities outside of bouncing at bars. McMahon knew this and used it to his advantage.

Pre-recorded television tapings were the worst. Vince only paid $50 for those, his rationale being the wrestlers were privileged to be on his show. The goal for every wrestler was to appear on the big shows like *Wrestlemania*, where you were generally expected to get at least $10,000 US for one match. At one *Wrestlemania*, Bret got close to $200,000 for being a headliner and biggest part of the show. He would later sign a contract for close to $1.2 million a year before his split with the WWF allowed him to accept more than twice as much offered by the WCW.

From 1991 to 1995, Owen's pay increased from $100,000 to $200,000 US, which included a small percentage of merchandising proceeds. For years Owen felt the WWF didn't market him properly. It wasn't until late in his career, when he was featured in a video game and a line of figurines, that his share of merchandise sales started to really climb.

On the morning of September 23, 1995, Athena was born and I was thrilled Owen was once again able to stave off his bosses long enough to be by my side. However, Owen still had to fly out of town on the redeye while I spent the night at the hospital. He called me the next day and I was an emotional wreck. Oje was a handful at three-and-a-half years old and he didn't know what to make of having a sister. I had to drive myself home from the hospital the next day and felt so terribly alone.

I thought, "If you're not here now when I need you, then when will you be?"

Obviously it wasn't his choice to leave, but then, it wasn't his choice to be a wrestler either. That was just the way it was. It was tough on both of us.

Athena was christened on Easter weekend, 1996, and among the small group of family and friends who joined us that sunny day was Georgia's son Matthew. Months later we'd all be shaken by the sudden passing of this happy, pleasant boy after he quickly succumbed to a strain of a flesh-eating disease.

The Hart family Christmas photo, 1969. Top row (from left): Smith, Wayne, Owen's father Stu and mother Helen, Keith; middle row: four-year-old Owen, Bruce; bottom row: Dean, Bret, Ellie, Diana, Georgia, Alison, Ross.

Owen Hart, ringside on the Stampede Wrestling float in the 1972 Calgary Stampede parade.

Owen in 1979, fourteen years old, in front of his parents' home.

Martha and Owen at Martha's house in 1982, soon after they started dating.

Martha and Owen's wedding day, July 1, 1989, at the Hart family home. From left: Owen's brother Bruce, Owen, Martha, Martha's sister Virginia.

Martha and Owen in love in Paris, 1990.

Owen in 1990 in one of the squalid
caravans where Martha and he lived
in Germany.

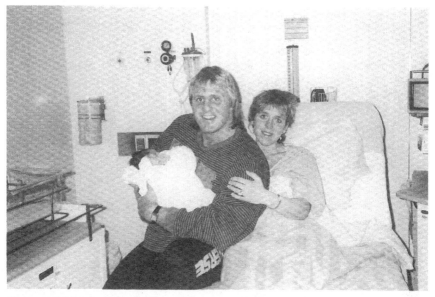

Owen and Martha with their newborn son, Oje, on March 5, 1992. Oje was Owen's nickname.

Owen holding newborn daughter Athena, only four weeks old, in October 1995.

Stu Hart with his sons in May 1992. From left: Wayne, Bruce, Stu, Keith (on knee), Smith, Bret, Owen and Ross.

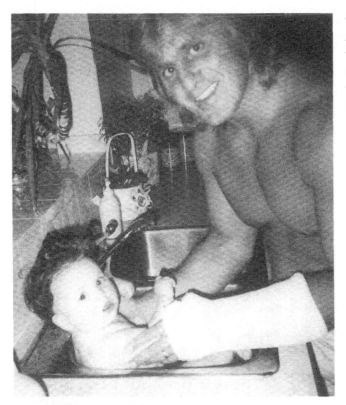

Owen gives Athena a bath, wearing a cast on his injured wrist, in early 1996.

Owen and Oje, dressed as Superman, on Halloween in 1996.

Owen's favorite family Christmas photo from 1997.
He had this photograph in his bag when he died.

The Hart family Christmas photo from after Owen's death in 1999, in his memory.

Owen had visited Matt a few days into his hospital stay and was devastated when he heard Matt had passed away. Owen flew home immediately to support his sister.

"It's just wrong—he was just such a healthy boy," Owen said in his documentary. "It killed me to think just a week before he was perfectly healthy and strong ... the epitome of what a perfect young boy should be. It kind of makes you realize you're living on borrowed time—walking along one day and doing nothing wrong, playing by the rules, being a good person, doing everything right and it doesn't guarantee you anything."

After years of living paycheck to paycheck, always concerned about the possibility his employment could be terminated with one injury or disagreement, Owen finally achieved a level of security in 1996 when Vince signed him to a contract. The rise of the WCW had forced McMahon to lock up his biggest assets to ensure they wouldn't be lured over as part of Turner's massive talent raid.

The deal on the table was five years at $250,000 US a year. It also included approximately $50,000 US annually in merchandising.

What Owen really wanted was to sign on for two years and then retire from wrestling altogether. He had ideas of moving onto other interests, like running a bike shop, after he retired. However, McMahon wouldn't budge so Owen signed a contract that wouldn't release him until he was thirty-six years old. It was then we finally had to accept wrestling was his career, like it or not.

The deal did give us one obvious advantage—a level of financial security. We knew it enabled us to better plan for the future. It was then we first starting talking about having a third child. This led to our decision that we'd need a bigger home, so in 1998 we purchased our two beautiful acres of land, and later that year got the ball rolling on the construction.

Designed entirely by Owen and me, the house was expected to cost $800,000 Cdn to build. In addition, we'd soon be facing landscaping bills, higher taxes and other increased costs. All of this meant he'd have to tough it out with the WWF for at least a few more years, regardless of how insufferable it got.

However, by 1996 the WWF was losing the ratings war and plenty of money.

Owen had spent the last couple years as a tag team partner with 700-pound Samoan wrestler Yokozuna (Rodney Anoia) and later with Davey Boy.

The Owen and Bret feud had long since died down, and the two brothers banded together in 1997 as part of an anti-American shtick that increased their popularity in Canada but made them public enemy number one stateside. Spit on routinely as they waved their Canadian flags, their mock disregard for Americans helped give rise to the popularity of redneck Texan "Stone Cold" Steve Austin.

Gone were the days of Hulk Hogan and Randy "Macho Man" Savage, when wrestling was a clean-cut passion play revolving around the never-ending conflict between good and evil. Replacing them were degenerates like Austin. He crushed beer cans on his head, swore at every turn, disrespected his employer, gave the finger to the audience and was a poster boy for everything that was wrong with society. Naturally, he became the WWF's star attraction.

Although Owen got along with pretty much all of his colleagues, he disliked Austin on a personal level. Owen thought he just wasn't a very nice person. Besides, he was one of those wrestlers who started believing he really was a world champion.

Their relationship soured even more during a match in August 1997. Owen administered a routine "tombstone piledriver"—a move that is made by picking up an opponent, flipping him upside down and placing his head near your lower thighs before dropping to your knees.

It was suggested Owen placed Austin's head too low before dropping him. As a result, Austin was left lying on the canvas claiming to be temporarily paralyzed.

The incident kept Austin out of action for an extended period of time and Owen took a lot of heat from the fans.

Being a seasoned, extremely cautious wrestler, Owen told me he executed the move properly. He would have felt horrible if he had hurt anyone, but he would have owned up if he'd done something wrong. In this case he suspected Austin was being dishonest. He even told me weeks beforehand he thought Austin might fake an injury. Either Austin was using the incident as an excuse for some time off or, if he truly injured his neck, which surgery would indicate, Owen figured the damage had been done prior to their routine match.

Either way, the idea that he injured the WWF's biggest superstar didn't help Owen's popularity. A feud was scripted for the two that involved a ridiculous shirt sold at the events that read, "Owen 3:16—I just broke your neck." Owen became one of the most hated heels in wrestling.

Three months later, in November 1997, Bret ended a fourteen-year association with the WWF in a disturbing fashion. Almost a year after rejecting a much more lucrative offer from the WCW and signing a long-term WWF contract, Bret was told by McMahon he could no longer afford to pay him. Low ratings continued to plague the WWF in their TV battle with WCW and Bret was told to sign on with the rival circuit. Problem was, Bret still had the WWF title belt and couldn't possibly be allowed to leave with it.

Unable to agree on how he'd surrender his precious title, Bret and McMahon argued back and forth how it would shake down. Hours before a pay-per-view match in Montreal they agreed to have that match end in disqualification. It meant the belt wouldn't change hands that night. Their conversation was captured on video and audiotape as part of a documentary being filmed on Bret.

Although concerned about being jobbed in some fashion, Bret was sure that after all his years of loyalty he wouldn't have to really worry about McMahon trying anything underhanded. However, Vince changed the dynamics of the match against Shawn Michaels mid-stream and ordered the ringside official to ring the bell prematurely, declaring Michaels the new titleholder.

Well aware Bret's longtime employer had masterminded such a dishonorable discharge, Owen sprinted to the ring to be by the side of his distraught brother. He knew how much Bret's wrestling career meant to him and knew he'd be devastated. Davey Boy followed.

Furious with being double-crossed after fourteen years of dedication, Bret stood in disbelief while Owen tried to console him and calm him down. Bret stared down at McMahon ringside before spitting in his face.

Bret then smashed several ringside TV monitors. He later broke a bone in his hand, as well as McMahon's jaw, when the two met afterwards in the dressing room. Owen was one of a handful who helped separate the two during the ugly melee but immediately wanted nothing to do with the man who deceived his brother.

In his best-selling book, Mick Foley ("Mankind") called it "the most controversial night in the history of the business."

Returning home for a few weeks to contemplate his future with the WWF, Owen soon asked Vince for his outright release. He figured he'd be able to join Bret in the WCW. Willing to forego a contract that was to pay close to $300,000 US each of the next three years, Owen felt he simply could no longer work for a man he couldn't trust. However, McMahon refused to let Owen out of his contract.

Suddenly Owen felt like a prisoner, caught between his love for his brother and his livelihood. McMahon's hard stand caused friction between Bret and Owen for a short time. Owen assured Bret he fully supported him regardless of whether he worked for McMahon or not and it wasn't long before their relationship resumed the status quo.

Vince did what repairs he could by upping Owen's contract to $400,000 US annually plus an expected $50,000 in merchandising. McMahon went a step further by offering to backdate the pay hike to the beginning of the contract year. As Owen's contract stipulated, he either wrestled for Vince or no one. With really no other option but to leave the wrestling game altogether, Owen accepted.

This new deal put Owen among the top ten salary-earners in the WWF and solidified his position as one of their staple wrestlers.

Owen always said he'd be out of the business before his son grew up, as he didn't want Oje subjected to the same schoolyard taunts and funny looks Owen endured for years. "You're father's a phoney wrestler," they'd say.

When Owen started in the business he quickly developed a passion for performing. He enjoyed it in the sense that if he could get a reaction from the crowd he was doing his job well and that was important. However, such sentiments had long since disappeared, replaced by his concern for a family that meant everything to him.

In his last few years he would often comment that he was getting older and felt he no longer fit into this new, filthy world of wrestling.

He was right, so very right.

"Owen was the most spectacular performer in wrestling until wrestling changed," said Dave Meltzer, editor of *The Wrestling Observer* and a wrestling historian. "He wasn't this flamboyant, outrageous character … he didn't fit in with the new style."

Just before Bret left, things were getting stupid. For instance, Brian Pillman was made to wear a dress on one show. Everything about the WWF and its new crude direction made both Owen and Bret uncomfortable.

Increasingly unhappy with the direction wrestling was taking, Owen found himself constantly refusing scripts as outlined by McMahon and his twisted writers. There was one finish where WWF writers wanted Mankind to gag him with his trademark sock-puppet finish. While other wrestlers agreed it was part of the shtick, Owen refused. He thought it held sexual connotations.

They then wanted Owen to have a scripted affair with Debra the valet, a buxom blonde (are there any other kind in wrestling?) who was supposedly dating Owen's new tag team partner, Jeff Jarrett. The idea was that it would pit the two partners against one another. They went as low as to suggest I get involved by doing an interview for their monthly magazine with reactions to Owen's "infidelity." It was sick. Owen didn't consider it for a minute and demanded the entire idea be scrapped.

Owen liked Debra on a personal level, telling me many times what a nice girl she was despite the hard life she'd had. However, he disliked having to do any angles with her or any valet.

Owen also shot down discussions about an effeminate wrestler named Goldust (Dustin Runnells), who was to put his hand on Owen's crotch while in the ring. Such scenarios may have been fine for other wrestlers who figured anything goes in the name of entertainment. After all, some of them were just unskilled muscleheads who loved the party life, the fan adulation, the fame. They'd do anything to shock the crowd.

Not Owen. The older he got, the more he could see the impact wrestlers had on other people. Through his children and his friends around the world, Owen could see that people were looking to him as a role model. He didn't want to abuse that privilege by degrading women, condoning immoral behavior or being rude. He was open-minded but didn't want anything to do with many of the vulgar angles the WWF was now building to try to win a losing ratings war.

A study completed in 1999 by Indiana University's Walter Gantz drew attention to just how bad things were getting. He found that during 100 hours of WWF programming the wrestlers grabbed or pointed to their crotches 1,658 times, used obscene phrases and gestures 591 times, simulated sexual acts 128 times, simulated satanic activity 47 times and simulated drug use 42 times. It prompted several major advertisers to temporarily pull their ads until the publicity wound up improving ratings.

Despite the fact Owen was an educated athlete who knew how to tell a story in the ring, the WWF writers still had a lot of difficulty scripting Owen effectively. They once tried him in a hardcore match, where anything goes—foreign objects of any kind are used.

"I tried one hardcore match like that ... I got hit with a guitar and it cut me for a bunch of stitches," Owen told the *Calgary Sun*. "So I spoke up about it and said, 'I don't want any part of that anymore.' I'm a good technical wrestler, I'm under contract and I wrestle for the WWF but I'm not going to risk myself to become popular with the fans with a bunch of gimmick matches where I could get seriously injured. I just want to finish my contract and enjoy spending time with my family."

Every TV taping Owen would attend, he'd hold his breath wondering what was next. He never minded the increased acting roles that eventually began dwarfing the actual wrestling segments. He loved to ad lib and act. In fact, one of his favorite projects was an appearance on the television show *Honey I Shrunk the Kids* that was taped in Calgary. He teamed up with Bret for an episode in which they played wrestlers. Owen had a blast doing it as it was clean and it was fun—two things foreign to his job in the WWF.

Ironically, one of his lines in the show was, "Wrestling promoters aren't the most understanding people you'll ever meet." No kidding.

As the WWF continued to shift to an extreme, hardcore mentality where the more disgusting you are, the better, Owen struggled with being surrounded by filth. He didn't have a lot of respect for Vince or anyone running the WWF shows. The way Bret was discarded left a bad taste in his mouth. Despite a sweetened-up contract from McMahon, Owen knew he couldn't trust him in any way. McMahon was a great marketer and brilliant entrepreneur—he built his father's regional wrestling circuit into a billion dollar business. But he saw McMahon as both greedy and dishonest. Owen always figured the bottom line for McMahon was the almighty dollar and that he had little regard for the people that made him that money.

Owen's wrestling colleagues soon started entering the ring pointing to their crotches and screaming words like "suck it." Another scenario saw one wrestler sleeping with another wrestler's wife. Vince and his wife Linda, who helped him run the WWF, refused to apologize for the obscene, graphic nature of their shows, suggesting those who didn't like it should turn it off.

Meanwhile, here Owen was trying to keep his moral beliefs intact while at the same time trying to keep a job that paid extremely well. This proved a difficult struggle. While there was a façade that the WWF was promoting itself to adults, it was the kids who were being targeted for most of their merchandise sales. That bothered Owen, who knew how impressionable kids can be. We heard the odd story where a kid would manhandle his sister while wrestling and accidentally hurt, paralyze or even kill her.

Owen was now ashamed of his profession. The days when he felt good about being a wrestler were over.

"We are pushing the risqué button," said a diplomatic Owen when asked by TSN's Dan Gallagher on December 9, 1998, if wrestling had gone too far. "It's getting violent and a little cruder than I want. I make sure what I do as a pro athlete both in and out of the ring is acceptable to my family and my friends. I want to uphold the Hart reputation of being a true professional."

Admittedly, it was getting harder and harder for the WWF to cast Owen as it proceeded to market itself in a degrading manner. It seemed the more scandalous, outrageous and sexually explicit the characters and storylines got, the higher the ratings.

Nicknamed "The Black Hart" for a while, Owen was made to do in-ring rants that would revolve around his catchphrase "Enough is Enough." He'd reiterate, "It's time for a change. I tried to be a nice guy …" His persona was greeted with ridicule by the fans.

Running out of ideas on how to incorporate Owen into the WWF's madness, the brass decided he'd slowly evolve into the vintage Blue Blazer character he played almost a decade earlier during his initial incarnation with the WWF.

Because he was Mr. Goody Two Shoes in real life, they figured they'd make him a cheesy do-gooder who the crowd would hate. In some ways he was relieved because he wouldn't have to keep fighting with his bosses over everything. If that's what it took, he could live with it.

It was once again a parody of the super-hero, action-figure-type wrestlers that ruled the WWF in its '80s heyday—a spoof on wrestlers from the golden age. Mocking old-school, good-guy wrestling icons like Hulk Hogan and Bret, the Blue Blazer would swoop into the ring wearing a humiliating blue, feather-lined outfit, flapping his arms and sending fans into fits of hysterics. Wrestling fans had become so putrid and tainted thanks to the angry mob mentality bred by Vince McMahon, that Blue Blazer was spit upon and degraded on a nightly basis. Still, it was just part of the job.

Armed with a shtick in which he promised to right the wrongs of a horrible wrestling world run by a nefarious crop of foul-mouthed sexual deviants and scum, Owen peppered almost every interview with a comical reminder for children: "Say your prayers, eat your vitamins and drink your milk," he said, before letting loose with a trademark "Whooo!" Still, Owen was saddened to think children were watching at all.

Once unhappy with a bit role that concealed his identity, he was now relatively content to be left alone playing a part much like the one he played in real life—a good guy. Instead of going to every TV taping worried about the next lurid storyline they'd inevitably try writing him into, he could now function without concern for the constant maneuvering necessary to carefully preserve his job while at the same time standing by his moral beliefs. It wasn't perfect, but we both had to admit that wrestling had given us a lot in life. It was only realistic that we'd have to take the good with the bad.

In April 1999, the WWF sold out a show in Calgary's 18,000-seat Saddle-dome and Owen wanted the kids and me to see him perform. Although he was now embarrassed by his profession, he was proud to have been a part of the reason for the sell-out. Besides, his kids had rarely seen him wrestle. More importantly, he wanted to show off the two kids he was constantly talking about to his colleagues.

I agreed, but only on certain conditions. I agreed to watch his match only and I wanted to keep the kids shielded from the busty valets who always wore high-cut skirts and had their breasts hanging out of their tops. Nevertheless, Debra and several others came over before the show to say hi to me and the kids wearing their skimpy outfits. They were very sweet but I still felt uncomfortable.

Owen's fellow wrestlers all knew his kids and I would be in attendance for his match and promised not to do anything lewd or outrageous, which Owen and I appreciated. Owen was very well liked by his colleagues so they were happy to respect his wishes. Despite their differences in lifestyles, Owen befriended all of them and accepted them the way they were. He could see redeeming qualities in virtually everyone.

In the late '90s more than 30 million viewers were tuning into wrestling on a weekly basis, and the battle between the WWF and WCW was still intense as they fought for viewers in more than 110 countries, watching in eleven different languages.

The WWF and WCW split nearly $1 billion US in revenues annually through an arsenal of apparel, publishing, recording, pay-per view and toy ventures related to wrestling. In 1997, pay-per-view revenues alone topped $140 million and rose to $178 million in 1998. In the first quarter of 1999, they had already exceeded $84 million. Bigger was definitely better, and writers in both companies continually dreamed up ways to out-do or make fun of the other.

It was through this competition the WWF decided to add a stunt element to Owen's introduction at an upcoming pay-per-view event in Kansas City in May 1999. They decided the show would be enhanced with an aerial descent from the rafters that would see Owen, as the Blue Blazer, comically flapping his arms as if he were flying into the ring.

It could have been a spoof on the WCW's Sting, who did a similar stunt. They wanted to be off the wall, constantly in search of a magic show or anything to get a rise out of the fans. After all, this was entertainment.

Informed of the stunt less than a week before it was to occur, Owen was nervous about it. He had done two aerial entrances before, but both times they had involved riggers that set him up to rappel in on a slide wire, only to be pulled back up. At all times he could hold onto a line that was fastened. Never before was he to release himself from the secured line.

This was different. There'd be no safety line to hang on to and it would be a straight vertical drop from eight stories.

Owen wasn't afraid of heights but he was concerned about the safety issue. When he did the stunt before he talked about how frightening it was and how he almost lost his footing up there.

He always tried to be conservative and cautious in every area of his life. Although he didn't like the idea one bit, he put his faith in who he was told were top rigging experts and decided he'd lump it. A job was a job.

6

THE FALL

"An event has happened, upon which it is difficult to speak, and impossible to be silent."
—EDMUND BURKE

Writing this book has been an emotional experience as it forced me to relive the horror surrounding Owen's death on a daily basis. Having spent more than a year and a half painstakingly collecting information about what happened that fateful night in Kansas City, I'm satisfied I can accurately relay the events surrounding his fall. Days after laying him to rest I even went as far as to stand high atop Kemper Arena on the catwalk from which Owen took his final step.

Based on all accounts, reports and research compiled by my lawyers, myself, police, witnesses and various other sources, and with the help of periodicals and videos, I have pieced together what I believe happened on the last day of Owen's life.

Arriving at Kansas City International Airport shortly after 10:30 A.M. on Sunday, May 23, Owen was picked up by fan Treigh Lindstrom as was the drill whenever the WWF stormed through Missouri. Owen befriended fans in various cities. While many wrestlers scoffed at the notion of getting involved with their fans on a personal level, Owen quite enjoyed their company and treated them with respect.

After checking Owen into his hotel, the two arrived at Kemper Arena at lunchtime on a beautiful sunny day. Dubbed mid-America's premier venue for concerts, sporting events, touring shows and national conventions, the 19,500-seat facility was located in the heart of Kansas City's stockyards. It was there cattlemen from across the midwest used to gather at the Kansas City Stock Exchange building to buy and sell cattle for slaughter. It seemed an appropriate place for the WWF to frequent, given the way Vince McMahon had treated his beefy talent like chattel over the years. (As he was overheard saying on numerous occasions, "Talent can be replaced.")

Eating lunch at Kemper six hours before show time, the two were approached by Bobby Talbert, a rigger out of Orlando, Florida, hired by the WWF to coordinate the stunt that would lower Owen into the ring from the rafters. After introducing himself to Owen, Talbert boasted that he was the one who had overseen the exact same stunt several times with Sting, the wrestler from the rival World Championship Wrestling loop.

Alluding to the fact Vince McMahon was unhappy with the speed and fumbling that occurred with a somewhat similar drop-in entrance made by Owen in St. Louis six months earlier, Talbert said the addition of a quick-release snap shackle would make all the difference in the world. Once he was lowered to the canvas, Owen would simply have to tug lightly on a release cord that would disengage the rappelling line from his harness. Within a split second he would be free to move around the ring.

Having spent the morning rigging up the elaborate setup of racks and rope in the rafters of the arena with two city riggers and his assistant Matt Allmen, Talbert had allegedly already run two clean tests of the system. The first was done with a 250-pound sand bag, the second with Allmen strapped into the harness. It's unclear to this day whether these tests were run with the quick release snap shackle to be used with Owen or a locking carabiner, which is the industry's safety standard.

Either way, Talbert was very luck that both descents were made cleanly and efficiently while he manually controlled the pressure applied to the nylon rappelling rope as it ran through the rescue rack.

Everything seemed fine to Talbert, so it was time for a dry run with Owen in the harness. Owen politely declined. "I've done it before, it's no big deal," shrugged Owen, continuing to eat his lunch.

Extremely uncomfortable with the vertical drop and the heights involved, Owen simply did not want to subject himself to any more terrifying experiences than he absolutely had to. In one of his two previous high-level stunts he told me he almost fell, compounding his fears. He hated every minute of these stunts whether it was for rehearsal or the real thing. If at all possible, he wanted to limit the number of descents he'd have to endure.

Talbert sensed Owen wasn't being cocky about it—he just seemed disinterested in rehearsing. Informed it was a different setup than he had ever used before, Owen was urged again by Talbert to familiarize himself with the equipment. As well, they had never worked together so it was in everybody's best interest for them to go over everything first.

Steve Taylor, the WWF's VP of Event Operations, got involved in the conversation, again asking Owen to try the entrance at least once before show time. After all, tonight was the night Owen's Blue Blazer character was to win the Intercontinental title over a colorful, pimp-like character named The Godfather.

Asked earlier in the week for his jacket measurements and informed he'd be making an aerial entrance, Owen had been assured by the WWF that top rigging experts from Los Angeles had been hired to ensure the stunt was done safely.

Still, it was no secret Owen did not want to do the stunt. He wondered aloud on several occasions why he couldn't just stick to wrestling and the interviews.

However, having argued with script writers so often of late over his insistence on being excluded from lurid storylines, he felt he could ill afford to continue butting heads with WWF brass much longer. Despite his stature on the talent roster, there was an inherent job risk every time you begged off of a storyline or stunt. Everyone knew it. He didn't want to lose his job so he said nothing to anyone of consequence.

What added to Owen's discomfort, though, were plans to have him descend into the ring with a midget wrestler named Max Mini attached to his harness. As part of the spoof, the midget would be wearing an identical Blue Blazer outfit.

Owen made it clear at that point he didn't want anything to do with the added responsibility of a second stuntman dangling from his beltline. "I've got enough to worry about myself, getting into the ring and undoing myself," he said.

Although WWF officials had plans to continue with the double drop-in, Owen figured at that point the issue had been dropped. He was wrong.

Owen's motive for begging out of the rehearsal had as much to do with inconvenience as fear. Acutely aware of how incredibly disorganized and rushed rehearsals typically were the day of an event, he didn't want to waste time waiting around for people to get their act together. However, feeling pressured to appease the powers that be, he reluctantly agreed to rehearse the aerial entrance at 2 P.M., when he said he'd return from his workout.

Two o'clock came and went and there was no sign of Owen. Extremely organized and generally quite prompt, Owen simply hoped his deliberate, extended absence would ensure he could opt out of the rehearsal. As time ticked away, several WWF officials began asking around for Owen, anxious to see how the stunt's speed would translate on television monitors.

As Talbert, Allmen and several others waited around for Owen, unsure when he might grace them with his presence, the call was made to scrap that evening's plans to include the midget in the stunt. It was decided time was getting desperately short and things would be too chaotic to try dropping them both in at the same time. Complicating matters was the fact Max Mini didn't speak English and required the help of a translator to explain the particulars of the stunt and the danger involved if he were to pull his release cord too early.

They decided they'd try the dual drop the next night in St. Louis.

As Talbert would later say, "Call it an act of God." Owen's deliberate stall tactics wound up saving Max Mini's life.

Upon Owen's return to the arena at 3:30 P.M. he tried again to pass off rehearsal, saying, "Oh, I'll be all right." It didn't work.

Climbing to the rafters mere feet below the eighty-five-foot–high roof, Owen white-knuckled his way along a steel grated catwalk that was ill-designed for pedestrians. High atop the southwest corner of the ring, he stood on the catwalk with Talbert, staring down at the large scoreboard below that he'd soon slide past on his way to the ring. As he assembled his harness, Talbert later claimed to have briefed Owen on the importance of not touching the quick release cord before landing in the ring.

"As long as you don't put your hands on this, nothing's going to happen," Talbert allegedly reassured him. "When you get to the floor, you grab it and give it a deliberate pull upwards so it gives me a visual cue to pull the rope back up."

Despite having difficulty in trying to keep his cape from interfering with his arm movement, the test went relatively well. However, upon landing, Owen forgot to pull the release cord, prompting several WWF officials to scream and yell at him as he moved around the ring with the rope still attached to him. Asked if he wanted to try it a second time, the answer was a quick, "No, I got it."

Like most wrestling pay-per-views, action in the ring began long before the show was broadcast to the masses. During one of the preliminary warm-up matches, Vince McMahon was mugged by a group of wrestlers dubbing themselves Corporate Ministry and led by Vince's son Shane McMahon. In an effort to prevent him from being a special guest referee later in the night, one of the wrestlers smashed a steel chair over Vince's leg. The crowd went wild. To play up the seriousness of the staged injury, the WWF had requested in advance the use of an ambulance and two paramedics for a segment showing McMahon being treated and transported out of the arena to the hospital. Records show the WWF had never before asked the Metropolitan Ambulance Services Trust to attend the Kansas City shows. It simply wasn't necessary, as wrestlers were rarely hurt seriously in the ring.

As the early matches progressed, Owen sat in the bowels of the arena changing into his Blue Blazer singlet and electric blue tights. He laced up his patent blue and white wrestling boots and prepared for his match.

Earlier in the evening he had picked up the vest he was to wear for the stunt and angrily hurled it across the dressing room in frustration. Several wrestlers saw his rare display of emotion and discussed with him how much he hated the idea of the stunt. He was worried about the new setup, as well as the fact his cape kept getting in the way.

Some tried joking with him to ease his fears but Owen wasn't responding in his typically light-hearted way. He appeared gravely concerned. However, being the consummate professional he was, he hyped himself up for a backstage interview to be aired later in the show. It went well.

At 7 P.M. the Over the Edge pay-per-view show opened appropriately with the Undertaker, featured in an eerie, graveyard segment. He promised, "Tonight, darkness will seize the land, destroy all you hold dear …" The death and destruction theme would continue through the night.

Amidst a shower of pyrotechnics, wrestlers Kane and X-Pac entered the ring to defend their tag team championship belts against Sexual Chocolate and D'Lo Brown for the first match of the pay-per-view.

Noticeably quiet as he made final preparations, Owen paced back and forth, prompting longtime colleague Dustin Runnells, a.k.a. Goldust, to ask if he was nervous. Owen admitted he was before Runnells assured him, "It will be all right."

Owen placed his cape and mask into a duffle bag. To help conceal his identity for the walk through the crowd to the rafters, he put on prison-like coveralls and wore a baseball cap pulled down over his face.

Leaving his dressing room with the bag slung over his shoulder, Owen bumped into former wrestler Harley Race. Told by Owen he was very uncomfortable with the upcoming stunt, Race tried to put him at ease by joking, "Be careful that rope doesn't break."

Harley's wife, B.J., offered up a hug to comfort him and asked if he felt better. "The only thing that makes me feel better is your cooking," said Owen.

Owen proceeded down the hall to an elevator that took him from the basement of the arena to the main concourse. Walking briskly past hundreds of wrestling fans, he stared towards the ground of the gray brick concourse, hoping to remain anonymous as he headed for Section 221. He hurried up several flights of stairs to the last row of nosebleeds in the building, then climbed a rickety wooden ladder to the catwalk.

The catwalk obviously wasn't designed for heavy traffic. At first Owen had to negotiate slowly around a floor beam as well as a series of beams overhead. Holding tightly to the railings on either side of the narrow catwalk, he then took a right-hand turn and white-knuckled it thirty feet past a series of light standards that would fully illuminate the building upon his spectacular entrance. His careful steps along the narrow catwalk were further complicated by the dozens of plugs sticking out of electrical sockets, the fact he had his bag in tow and his size nine-and-a-half wrestling boots. Still, he continued his path towards the center of the arena's roof. Careful not to look down at the sea of blue seats and patrons below, whose movement had a dizzying effect on Owen when he had peeked down in his few previous stunts, he made a left turn back towards the center of the arena. Now at the center point of the arena's catwalk system, he turned towards the massive scoreboard that hung well below him. He climbed under an electrical pipe, up a slight incline and over a structure beam. The final stretch was particularly tough to negotiate due to the more than 100 feet of black nylon rappelling rope placed all along the grated floor. It was the same rope Owen would soon attach himself to.

It was there, just south of the center of the arena, that he was greeted by Talbert at 7:10 P.M., half an hour before the stunt was to occur.

Having said that he had worked in the stunt business for seven years, Talbert was hired by the WWF as an independent contractor to design and set up the riggings for Owen's descent. Describing himself as a stunt coordinator and special rigger for Universal Studios in Florida, Talbert landed this job, his first with the WWF, based largely on the fact that he told the WWF he had two years of experience setting up the stunt for Sting. Given the fact that Owen's stunt was meant to be a parody of WCW's silly entrances, who better to hire than Talbert, who had originally executed the stunt for them? However, we later found out he was merely an assistant to Sting's stunt coordinator.

A trusting soul who grew up in a house that never had the doors locked, Owen never questioned Talbert's abilities or qualifications—and why would he? Afterall, he was working for a billion-dollar company that had assured him the best in the business had been hired to rig him.

Despite meeting earlier in the day for the dry run, Talbert went over the stunt once more while Owen took off his coveralls and baseball cap. The only other men on the catwalk were city riggers James Williams and Jim Vinzant from Local 31 of the Teamsters. Earlier in the day they had assembled various span sets and bridles in the arena's ceiling as part of the rigging setup laid out by Talbert. During the show, their job was to simply monitor the stunt. Matt Allmen was positioned ringside.

The railings and floor surrounding them had been covered by black cloth to conceal them as they prepared for the entrance.

The second match of the night was a hardcore title fight showdown between Hardcore Holly and Al Snow (who typically enters the ring holding the severed head of a woman featuring the words "Help Me" scrawled backwards across her forehead—a prime example of how tasteless and insensitive the WWF had become).

In these matches anything goes. Peering down on the action, Owen would have seen the two hammering away on one another with a fire extinguisher, steel chair, a broken table, a metal pan and the severed head of a deer, which doubles as Snow's imaginary friend Pierre.

Vinzant assisted preparations by shining a flashlight on Owen while Talbert helped him put on his rappelling harness. Featuring three straps across the front and plenty of reinforcement to prevent tearing of any sort, the black harness fit much like a sleeveless life jacket. It also had straps that wrapped around his legs to further stabilize him while being lowered.

With Owen securely fastened, Talbert then grabbed the end of the rope and attached the snap shackle device to the metal ring on the back of the harness. He pulled on the snap shackle device several times—once almost lifting Owen off his feet—to ensure it was properly secured. Owen then put on his silly-looking blue, silver and red mask. Featuring holes cut out for his eyes, nose and mouth, the mask had laces in the back used to secure it in place.

With his movements somewhat limited in the confined space, Owen needed help from Talbert to put on his bright blue and red sequined cape.

The sides of the cape, lined with white feathers, were attached to Owen's hands by way of elastic bands he continually readjusted throughout final preparations.

The release cord, designed to quickly separate Owen from the rope upon ring entry, was then brought to the front of Owen's harness and secured on the upper right side of his chest using black gaff tape, similar to electrical tape. As designed, one quick tug on the cord would trigger the snap shackle and allow Owen free range in the ring. It only took six pounds of pressure to rid himself of the rope and Talbert explained that Owen should pull it in a deliberate, upward fashion, cuing Talbert to pull the rope back up. It was the same cord Owen forgot to pull during rehearsal, drawing the chorus of shouts from frustrated WWF officials, angry at Owen's failure to execute the stunt fluidly.

Minutes from his cue, Owen apparently moved his arms out and away from his body several times to reposition his cape in an effort to try to conceal his harness. The awkward cape was heavy and had a tendency to choke him if not positioned properly.

The hardcore slugfest below had finally been won by Al Snow, eliciting a roar from what was said to be a crowd of 18,244 fans. While the event had indeed sold out in one day, capacity on this night hovered more realistically around the 16,500 mark, based on the size of the wrestlers' elaborate entrance ramp, shrouded by metal girders and light stands.

As the two exhausted combatants stumbled from the ring, there was a backstage broadcast interview updating fans on the physical condition of Vince McMahon, suggesting he had likely suffered a broken ankle and would be transported to hospital once an ambulance arrived. In fact, the ambulance was already waiting in-house.

The lights were then dimmed—the cue for Owen to steady himself for his descent. It was now forty minutes into the show.

Talbert instructed Owen to climb over the four-foot hand railing and position himself on the outside of the scaffolding. Owen had trouble negotiating the maneuver, so Vinzant facilitated things by lifting Owen's cape. The city rigger then retreated to ensure the rope would not get snagged anywhere on the catwalk's floor when Owen was to begin his manual descent.

At first facing away from Talbert, Owen turned and held onto the railing, trying not to look down. Talbert checked the tension of the equipment by lowering Owen a few feet, at which point the caped crusader let go of the railing. Dangling with his shoulders parallel to the catwalk floor, Owen placed his hands on his harness and was ready to be lowered. He hung there for a few minutes. Everything seemed fine to Talbert.

Down in the ring, a referee was clearing debris from the hardcore match. On the Jumbotron was a forty-second profile of the Blue Blazer.

Perhaps being somewhat choked by the cumbersome cape, Owen extended his elbows out and away from his body in an effort to make a subtle adjustment. It was then the three riggers were horrified to hear the distinct sound of the snap shackle's release.

Talbert looked down immediately to see Owen plunging towards the ring, falling backwards and in a slight clockwise spiral before landing violently 78 feet below. Several fans heard him scream in terror all the way down.

For most who were glued to the video montage on the Jumbotron, the first they saw of the Blue Blazer live that night was the split second before he savagely met the top rope of the wrestling ring. Narrowly missing the metal post that supported the turnbuckle in the southwest corner of the ring, Owen's upper left side absorbed the violent impact of his plunge.

Shattering his left arm just above the elbow and causing massive internal injuries upon initial contact, Owen was flipped backwards by the highly strung cable. His 229-pound body caromed into the ring, where it sprang a foot off the canvas before settling in the corner. Lying motionless on his back, with his feet pointing towards the center of the ring and his head mere feet from the apron, it took several seconds for his rubbery arms to rest at his side after bouncing off the spring-like canvas.

In a wrestling world in which Vince McMahon delights in thrilling audiences with shock and the element of surprise, the rag-doll figure hurtling into the ring drew a loud cheer from the crowd. Unable to grasp the seriousness of the moment, the majority of fans briefly mistook Owen's horrific fall for a spectacular entrance. Others figured it was perhaps a mannequin. At least that's what they hoped.

It quickly became clear something had gone terribly wrong.

Unconscious due to the violent impact that tore his aorta and instantly began filling his lungs with blood, an innate survival reflex prompted the muscles and nerves of a wide-eyed Owen to attempt to sit up. Described by one man as looking like someone struggling to finish off a set of 100 abdomen crunches with one final, desperate attempt, Owen was unable to do much more than lift his masked head a few inches off the mat. His attempt at one final, desperate breath finished with him returning his head to the mat and turning towards a ringside photographer, his eyes staring blankly ahead.

As people tried figuring out what they had just seen, it became clear Owen wasn't the only one hurt. At the same time Owen's plunging body made contact with the ring rope, one of his flailing legs had struck the referee clearing the ring, sending him sprawling to the canvas in pain. Several witnesses actually suggested Owen's screams were aimed at the ref, warning him to get out of the way.

Confused by the shocking collision, the referee scampered out of the ring. He was one of several people who summoned immediate help for Owen, and would later be taken to the hospital himself with back injuries.

The crowd was quiet. A low murmur blanketed the arena. Another WWF referee stood over Owen, holding his head in disbelief. On the scoreboard Jumbotron, which Owen had just passed at 45 miles per hour, the Blue Blazer video rolled on, featuring brief footage of him descending into the ring via cable.

Off-duty police officers Todd Bryant and Joe Daneff were working security twenty feet from the ring when Owen hit the mat. The frantic ringside cameraman sprinted over to summon the two uniformed men and told them Owen was hurt. Quickly convincing them the scenario was not staged or fake in any way, the two scaled a three-foot retaining wall separating spectators from ringside and were the first to tend to Owen less than a minute after his fall.

Bryant clambered up the metal stairs and into the ring while Daneff positioned himself ringside alongside stunned commentator Jerry Lawler. Lawler, a former wrestler, had sprung from behind his TV monitor mere feet away to help out. Putting his hand over Owen's mouth, he said, "He's not breathing."

Both Lawler and Daneff stabilized Owen's head by tilting it back towards the rafters from which he had plummeted. Bryant confirmed Owen was not breathing and had no pulse. Without wasting time in trying to remove Owen's vest, Bryant immediately began chest compressions.

As several others joined the scene seconds later, Owen's tight-fitting mask was cut up the right side by scissors and removed. Bryant turned his efforts towards mouth-to-mouth resuscitation, using the mask's thin material as a barrier device.

Another uniformed off-duty officer, Jeffrey Cowdrey, entered the ring and took over chest compressions. He had been backstage watching Owen do a pre-match interview less than an hour earlier and was sure it was all some sort of wrestling angle until he saw Owen's lifeless glare.

Backstage, Todd Coleman, one of the two ambulance attendants on hand to take part in McMahon's staged injury, was summoned to the ring. A member of the Kansas City Fire Department, Coleman worked part time for Emergency Providers Inc., which sent him and partner Stephen Underhill to be part of the show. Having just finished filming the second take of the mock McMahon injury seconds earlier, the two sprinted immediately from the south tunnel to the ring.

The crowd was stunned, as were the two referees who paced nervously around the ring, running their hands through their hair and periodically huddling over medics to survey the scene. A ringside cameraman stood five feet from the ring capturing the rescue efforts on a tape never to be released to the public.

The Blue Blazer introductory montage soon ended on the Jumbotron with Owen raising his arms in triumph and parading out of the interview with one of his comical whoops.

The arena was filled with little more than a low hum of voices. The sea of crude and comical signs that have become the trademark of raucous wrestling crowds were parked at peoples' feet while most stood in silence. It didn't take long for them to identify it was indeed Owen Hart in the ring, not a mannequin, and he was apparently clinging to life.

Those watching on TV were oblivious to what had just transpired and were welcomed back from the Blue Blazer video intro by ringside commentator Jim Ross, who was sitting mere feet from Owen's lifeless body.

As several other medical personnel rushed to join Bryant, Daneff, Coleman and Lawler at the scene, Ross scrambled to divert the pay-per-view audience to an interview with the Blue Blazer taped earlier in the day. Clearly stunned by the shockingly violent entrance Owen made seconds earlier, Ross punctuated his brief cut-in by saying, "We've got big problems out here."

It was a huge understatement.

As the short, hokey interview entertained puzzled viewers, chest compressions continued. Seconds after his medic bag arrived in the ring, Coleman prepared to intubate. At the very same time, Coleman's wife was taping the pay-per-view, oblivious as to what had transpired minutes earlier.

With the show coming to a screeching halt, the fans were now very much aware of the seriousness of the situation. The only sound, other than the buzz of horrified wrestling fans, was a smattering of well-intended catcalls bellowing out Owen's name.

Meanwhile, TV viewers saw the taped interview with Owen wrap up with the Blue Blazer's trademark sign off, "One last thing in closing to all my little Blue Blazers: Take your vitamins, say your prayers and drink your milk."

Television viewers were then shown a live, wide shot of the Kemper Arena audience aimed far from the ring itself. With spectators standing to see several more medical personnel join in the rescue efforts, the camera turned to Ross who explained the dire situation to millions of viewers the best way he could.

"Ladies and gentleman, when you're doing live television a lot of things can happen and sometimes they are not good," said a suddenly pale-looking Ross, wearing a black cowboy hat, black WWF wrestling button up and headset with a mic extension.

"The Blue Blazer, as we know is Owen Hart, was going to make a very spectacular superhero-like entrance from the rafters and something went terribly wrong here. This is a very serious situation here. This is not a part of the entertainment here tonight. This is as real as real can be here.

"The EMTs are tending to Owen in the ring now. We are at a little bit of a loss in this situation. I have been doing this for more years than I would like to admit and this is one of the most shocking things I've ever seen. This is not your typical wrestling storyline. This is a real situation.

"I don't know if the harness broke or what the malfunction was. We're going to keep our cameras on the crowd at this point in time simply because we are hoping to move on as best we can."

Obviously directed by his production truck producer to fill in during this most awkward and serious situation, a shaken Ross proceeded to throw to a two-minute preview of a mixed tag-team match featuring Owen's former partner Jeff Jarrett and his sidekick Debra.

When the preview ended, Ross was once again handed the burden of trying to hold the broadcast together despite the horrific gravity of the situation.

"The paramedics are working on Owen Hart," repeated Ross, as several attention-seeking fans behind him disregarded the seriousness of the moment by hoisting their beers and happily waving into the cameras.

"This is not a wrestling angle, this is real life. We are not going to put this on television—it is not a sensationalistic attempt to leave a mark here on this event. We will have the rest of this broadcast, but the bigger issue now is that a human being, Owen Hart, has been terribly injured here on this live broadcast. Something has gone wrong with the equipment as he was being lowered. We don't know what malfunctioned. Obviously something in the apparatus—we assume—went wrong, unless Owen inadvertently released himself before he was near the ring.

"Right now nothing is more important than the health and the welfare of not only a great athlete but a very unique and good human being."

Visibly shaken, Lawler returned to Ross from ringside. "No, it doesn't look good at all," was all he said.

Several minutes after his fall, Owen's body began to change color. His systems had shut down, turning his skin an ashen gray. There were no vital signs and Owen wouldn't respond in any way to the efforts of paramedics. His eyes remained open, staring blankly ahead.

Underhill arrived in the ring with a fiberglass spine board. Coleman's efforts then turned to the intubation, which was complicated by the musculature of Owen's neck. It was a task made even more difficult as a man who identified himself as a WWF doctor began hampering the rescue efforts. Unable to speak fluent English, the man reached into Coleman's paramedic bag and grabbed monitor paddles used to shock patients with bad heart rhythms. However, with no monitorable heartbeat, an agitated Coleman insisted the man put the paddles down. The man reacted by trying to pull Owen's chest harness off. Coleman demanded the man stop what he was doing and step away. The man refused to move and wound up doing some brief chest compressions on Owen.

Once the airway was established minutes later by way of a rigid stylette used to form the tube, air was hand pumped to his lungs while Owen was carefully log-rolled onto the spine board. With so many medics milling around the ring, causing a disruptive amount of movement, it was decided further treatment could not be administered on site. It wasn't safe, it was chaotic.

Owen's limp body was then pulled under the ropes and placed on a cot, prompting a loud cheer from the stunned audience. Cowdrey immediately jumped aboard the gurney, straddled Owen and continued chest compressions while being wheeled along the ramp.

As the growing number of emergency personnel escorted him out of the arena, chants of "Owen, Owen," filled the arena air.

By this time, eight minutes had elapsed since Owen's fall and there were no signs of medical progress. Owen's lips had turned blue as cyanosis progressed and his body was depleted of oxygen. Time was getting desperately short.

As the entourage of medical personnel wheeled Owen from the ring, Cowdrey heard one disgusted fan yell, "This is f——ing fake." Many others, however, had tears in their eyes and offered up words of encouragement for their fallen hero.

Meanwhile, the pay-per view coverage returned to the massive stadium screens, as Debra and Owen's tag team partner Jeff Jarrett struggled to hold back tears during a live, backstage interview aimed at hyping their upcoming match.

Wheeled out of the arena to the building's south loading dock, Owen and the rescue workers breezed by a group of teary-eyed wrestlers who had been watching the scene backstage, consoling one another. Several wrestlers, including The Rock, Dwayne Johnson, desperately wanted to rush the ring to try helping Owen. They were ordered to remain behind the entrance curtains for fear their emergence would have sent the crowd into a frenzy, and might have led many to believe the fall was part of the show.

As several wrestlers offered their own words of encouragement for their wounded warrior, Owen was taken to the waiting ambulance.

His emotional wrestling colleagues mobbed the area where the ambulance had been parked. Coleman and crew hauled Owen past the horde and climbed into the ambulance with Cowdrey, who continued his CPR efforts while dripping with sweat.

The alleged WWF doctor continued to get in the way by somehow gaining entrance to the vehicle. After bellowing ridiculously inappropriate instructions to "watch his arm, watch his arm," the stranger was finally removed by Underhill. Demanding he be allowed to stay because he was a doctor, Underhill asked him if he'd sign a doctor intervention form. When he refused, he was pulled from the ambulance and the back doors were closed to keep wrestlers out and allow medics to continue their work unimpeded. It was also done to prevent further videotaping of the incident by a roving WWF cameraman intent on capturing the ugly scene on film.

Coleman and Cowdrey continued trying to get solid CPR established and force oxygen into Owen's system. Owen and his cot were secured, a cervical collar was placed on him and he was hooked up to a monitor. It was then Coleman established Owen still had electrical activity in his heart but the heart wasn't actually beating. It was deemed an "agonal" or "dying heart rhythm," meaning he had yet to flatline. A shot of atropine was administered in an effort to raise his heart rate—it had no response. Owen's eyes remained fixed and dilated.

Since the ambulance had been hired to act as standby for Vince's fake injury, company policy for Emergency Providers Inc. dictated that the paramedics wait for another ambulance to transport Owen to the hospital. The first ambulance was supposed to stay for the duration of the hire. However, as precious time ticked away, several distraught wrestlers began to demand that Owen be transported immediately.

At one point The Rock leaned into the driver's side of the cab and began yelling, "Who is driving this motherf——er?" At the same time, another wrestler jumped into the passenger side.

Underhill tried explaining to The Rock they had to wait for another ambulance and that Owen was being stabilized for transport. This statement was met with increased anger. Underhill also told the unidentified grappler to leave the ambulance immediately. He complied. At this point, Underhill and Coleman agreed the mob surrounding the ambulance had grown too hostile, too emotional. Things were getting out of hand. With no one attempting to control the emotional group clustered around the vehicle, it provided too much of a distraction for ambulance attendants to fully focus on Owen. A judgment call was made to leave the building.

En route to the Truman Medical Center just three miles away, epinephrine was administered into Owen's airway tube. He was also hooked up to an IV seconds before he was taken out of the ambulance at Truman. In Coleman's opinion, however, Owen was already clinically dead.

When any fall greater than twenty feet occurs in the Kansas City area, there is an automatic activation of the hospital's trauma team, which consists of four top doctors. They quickly assembled for Owen's arrival and the CAT scan technician was also put on alert.

It had now been slightly more than twenty minutes since his fall. With Owen's arrival at 7:59 P.M., the team, headed up by Dr. Micheal Rush, wheeled him into the trauma room for a final, desperate attempt to save his life. However, they were well aware of Owen's grave condition via radio transmissions. His Glasco Coma Scale—a measure of neurological function—was listed as a three out of fifteen. It obviously wasn't looking good. Two units of O-negative blood were at the ready for possible transfusion. Nurse Michael Tucker was brought up to date on the situation by paramedics as Owen was wheeled through the emergency entrance doors and into Truman Medical Center. After transferring Owen's body from ambulance cot to the bed in Trauma Room 1, several attendants had problems removing Owen's vest. With help from Tucker, who had to cut a shoulder strap and several belts off the garment, it was removed. The laces of his boots were also cut right up the middle.

Electrocardiogram pads were immediately placed on Owen's chest in search of any recordable heart rhythm. The initial reading from the cardiac monitor indicated he was asystole, meaning he had no sign of heart activity whatsoever. However, seconds later there were signs of a light PEA (pulseless electrical activity). It meant the heart was not beating but faint electrical activity was still apparent. He was still fighting for his life. This offered a brief moment of hope. As dire as the situation appeared, reviving patients from PEA to a shockable rhythm wasn't beyond the realm of possibility. Both Tucker and Rush had seen it happen before.

At this point all those who transported Owen to hospital, except Cowdrey, had left the room. He stood in the doorway, sadly anticipating what was to come.

Nurses began calling out observations to Tucker, who recorded the findings. Owen's skin was blue, his lips were colorless and his skin was cold to the touch. Nurses reported he had no bowel sounds and his abdomen was soft. One aide noted there was no sign of alcohol on his breath, which was listed as bilateral and equal, maintained only by tireless CPR efforts.

Owen's eyes remained open and fixed ahead, revealing no sign of life whatsoever. That his pupils dilated to five millimeters—nearly twice normal—was yet another ominous sign.

Owen had an open fracture above his left elbow and a cut below, but these wounds were of little concern. A large bruise on his left lateral chest was further proof his heart had quite likely suffered from irreversible damage. While fears escalated that he had, by now, suffered brain damage, the only thing that mattered was that he regain consciousness.

Four minutes later, in an effort to stimulate the heart, a 16-gauge IV catheter inserted earlier in his left arm by paramedics was used to feed Owen's unresponsive body with epinephrine. It immediately blew the vein. A minute later, another amp of epinephrine was administered through an endotracheal tube, then at 8:06 P.M. a large IV was placed in the right groin to pump in more epinephrine and atropine.

Still, monitors recorded no signs of progress. No pulse. His heart continued to show slight electrical activity, but nothing of significance. Very little hope remained as the precious minutes ticked away.

Outside in the waiting room, retired wrestler Harley Race paced anxiously, awaiting word on his longtime pal. He would later be joined by Jeff Jarrett, still in full wrestling gear, and a host of concerned wrestlers who numbered close to two dozen by night's end.

At 8:07 a final amp of epinephrine and atropine went into Owen's right femoral line.

Four minutes later he was still unresponsive. CPR continued for a final few minutes until doctors determined all resuscitation efforts were futile.

Thirteen minutes after arriving at the hospital—thirty-three minutes since the fall—all work on Owen was stopped. At 8:12 P.M. Central Standard Time the supervising doctor called Code.

At age thirty-four my Owen was dead.

Eye drops were placed in Owen's eyes by Tucker for the purposes of possible donation. Unfortunately the request for organ donation was never made, as I certainly would have consented as per Owen's wishes.

His belongings were collected by Detective Cowdrey for the criminal investigation that began immediately. The medical examiner was called. The doctors were interviewed by police, and detectives were dispatched to Kemper to secure the scene in an effort to piece together what went wrong.

Wearing nothing but a pair of white socks, Owen's naked, lifeless body was covered with a white sheet.

Meanwhile, the show went on …

THE CALL

"They don't even realize their little lives are changed forever."
—MARTHA HART

In preparation for the move to our new house, I spent the day dismantling the home we'd happily lived in for almost ten years. It had been a long day of packing, and I had been plagued by a looming, inexplicable sadness.

Owen traveled so much that loneliness was no stranger to me. This feeling was different, though. It was a puzzling emptiness and despair that suddenly intruded on a very happy time in my life. It gnawed at me all day long.

Owen's routine, no matter where he was, often included frequent calls home to see how we were all doing. On this strange day I longed to hear his voice. Only he could pick up my spirits with a simple "Hello."

It was the Sunday of a long weekend and so many of the families on the block were enjoying the beautiful sunshine and the company of loved ones. The kids were outside playing with the neighbors' two daughters and seemed content to do their own thing. Owen was gone most weekends so we had our family time when we could. It seemed like we were never on the same cycle as the rest of the world, but even though our setup was a little bit out of the ordinary, we weren't. The only thing that made us different from any other normal family was the fact Owen traveled a great deal. We looked forward to a day that would all change, but for now we did well to maintain a regular routine of sorts.

As I stowed and cleaned, I filled my mind with thoughts of what our lives were going to be like after we moved. I looked forward to our big yard as I loved gardening. I thought about the front porch swing Owen had painted just before he left and I pictured us sitting on it on cool summer nights with a blanket and a hot cup of tea. It would all be so wonderful.

I saw with my mind's eye how I was going to decorate the house. I would make it such a haven. The kitchen would always be filled with the aroma of fresh baked goodies, and I thought of some interesting recipes that would surprise Owen and the kids. I loved to please all of them any way I could. After all, my life revolved around my three bright stars.

Yet through all these thoughts, my mind continually drifted back to this darkness that was lurking. There seemed to be no escaping this awful feeling. By mid-afternoon I could take the nagging sensation no longer. To ease my troubled mind I stopped packing and called my sister Virginia. Virginia and I had walked the line together all our lives, growing up in difficult circumstances with only each other to lean on. No matter what the situation, we rallied behind one another. I rang her and was grateful she answered.

After several minutes of idle chit-chat she asked, "What's wrong?"

I told her I wasn't sure, but that I felt awful and wanted Owen to call. She told me I was feeling jittery because we were taking a big step. Our new house meant a new life in a lot of ways. Financially we'd be more strapped, and because the house was much bigger there'd be more upkeep. We had also decided to have a new baby—another responsibility to add to the list. I had been enrolled at the University of Calgary for three years now and desperately wanted to finish my psychology degree while also juggling motherhood with my part-time jobs at the post office and the pool. All of these issues weighed on my mind.

I also knew that while I loved my family life, I had dreams of my own that I wanted to realize. I tried to do the things I wanted without stepping on anyone's toes, but was aware that all the added duties would rest largely on my shoulders since Owen would continue to travel frequently for at least the next few years.

Virginia suggested I try contacting Owen so I grabbed his booking sheet, which listed his destinations. In some cities, like Chicago and L.A., he always had the same accommodation arrangements. If he had been in one of these cities, I might have been able to contact him. However, seeing as he was in Kansas City, Missouri, I had no idea which hotels to check. I ended my conversation with Virginia by repeating, "I just wish so badly that Owen would phone me."

An hour later the kids were restless and begging to go out somewhere. I decided to take them with me for a few errands. Owen had suggested I go to the hardware store to buy two industrial garbage pails with wheels. He figured I would need the wheels because we were going to be living on an acreage with a long driveway. I laughed to myself at his backhanded form of thoughtfulness.

Off I went, kids in tow, to the hardware store. I made a few other runs then stopped at the park to give Oje and Athena some quality time with me.

Still thinking ahead to our nightly call, I couldn't wait for him to charge me up with the encouragement I so sorely needed. I returned home with the kids, the pails, and the hollow feeling I left with.

Just as I started the kids' dinner, the phone rang. The call display indicated the call was "Out of Area," which was known in our house as "Owen Abroad." Thank God! I grabbed it after the first ring with great excitement.

"Martha," said the deep voice that followed my cheery hello.

"Owen!" I gasped.

"This isn't Owen. This is Vince McMahon," he said.

I was so sure it was Owen's voice, I would have bet my life on it. Owen was such a joker, I thought for a second he was playing some sort of trick on me.

"Vince McMahon?" I repeated hesitantly. "Why are you calling me?"

Still unconvinced it was Vince, his response rattled me. "Owen has fallen from above the ring and he's hurt."

With my suspicions it was Owen pulling a crank call, I quickly grew perturbed. It wasn't unusual for Owen to get under your skin with a prank but they were generally harmless ones. "Is this a serious call? Because I don't appreciate being upset for nothing," I said.

"Yes, this is a very serious call," was the response.

At that point I realized it really was Vince McMahon. I became moderately alarmed but still wasn't completely convinced. "Is this really a serious call? Or is this a part of your production?" Vince was doing such ridiculous things in the world of wrestling I thought it might be some gimmick to get a reaction.

He seemed a bit stunned by my demeanor. "No, it's not," was his response.

A pensive solemnness was taking shape between us. I sensed this truly was a legitimate call and now we were talking about my husband's well-being. Suddenly, I became deeply worried. I could feel goose bumps tingle over my entire body.

"Is he conscious?" I asked.

When the answer was a quick, "No," my heart sank.

A panic ensued as I peppered him with rapid-fire questions.

"How far did he fall? Did he break anything? How is he now? Who's taking care of him?"

Over and over he repeated his simple response: "I don't know."

There was a moment of silence. I thought he was acting peculiar—nervous and evasive.

"I know how much you and Owen meant to each other," said McMahon.

This sent me into a state of hysteria. I begged him to tell me this was just some sort of sick joke.

"Were you watching the show?" he asked.

I had no idea what he was talking about. What show? It was so early in the evening. It had slipped my mind Owen was wrestling in a late afternoon pay-per-view that day.

Right after I told him I wasn't, he offered up more chilling information. "The paramedics worked on him and took him to the hospital."

I snapped. "Paramedics! Are these real, qualified, paramedics, or are they uncertified quack doctors that you have sit at ringside?" I yelled.

"No, they are real—we had real paramedics on hand today," said McMahon. "They cared for Owen and took him to the hospital."

When asked what hospital, he reverted once again to his standard, "I don't know." Annoyed, and with my head swimming, I told him I needed to talk to someone who had some answers.

"Someone will call you soon," he said sheepishly to end the call.

That was it, no good-byes. We both just hung up. I began pacing around the house. I looked out the window to check on the kids who were still happily playing with the neighbor's daughters.

I didn't know what to do with myself. The doom that plagued me all day was engulfing me. I felt like I was drowning, it was hard to breathe. Were my worst fears going to be realized? Ever since we had laid down the groundwork for our new dream home I had this impinging fear that something dreadful was going to happen. Owen shared this mild fear with me. We were both afraid tragedy might strike because our lives were too good to be true. We were too content, too happy together.

I knew something inside me was going to give so I quickly called my mother. I didn't want to tie up the line so I briefly explained something dreadful had happened to Owen and that I would need her to come right away to look after the children. I figured I might have to jump on a plane. I really didn't have any details, just a feeling that everything was going to break loose shortly. I called the Hart house, too, but they knew nothing so I hung up.

I waited anxiously for an update. It seemed as though I was left suspended for a long time. Mercifully, the phone rang minutes later and I lunged for it. It was only Stu calling back. I explained I had no new information and that I had to get off the phone. I only had one line and didn't want to tie it up. I told him I would call as soon as I heard something—anything.

Again, I waited in an agitated, disturbed state. Gazing around my sitting room I noticed all of our beautiful family Christmas pictures that still hung on the walls. Why hadn't I taken them down yet as part of the move? I had taken everything else down.

Once again, the phone rang. Looking down at the call display. I saw it was from Out of Area. Inundated with mixed emotions, I answered.

It was the doctor from the hospital where Owen was being treated. He identified himself and asked if I was alone. He started describing the particulars of the incident, explaining the fall Owen had and the severity of the injuries he had sustained. Overwhelmed with anticipation I interrupted him.

"Doctor, please just tell me the end result," I said, convinced I could deal with any injury at all, as long as my Owen was still alive.

"Normally you should be flown down here to receive such news," he began. "I am so sorry, I did everything I could to save him, but his injuries were fatal. There was nothing more I could do. Your husband has died."

With tears bursting out of my eyes, I doubled over and screamed out loud, "NO, NO, NO. Please, please, oh God, no."

Waiting patiently for me to catch my breath, he reiterated how sorry he was.

"Would you like to speak to Harley Race?" he asked. "He is one of the wrestlers that accompanied your husband to the hospital."

Through my tears I said, "No, I don't even know him." I hung up, sat back and melted into my chair.

Oh my God, I couldn't believe it! A million thoughts raced through my mind. A battle was being waged inside my head. One side of my brain said, "No this didn't happen, it couldn't happen, it's not true." The other side of my brain was saying, "It must be true. Who would be so cruel as to tell such a grave lie?"

Devastated, I quietly stared at the ceiling of my dismantled room. What just happened? The reality of it all was slowly sinking in and it felt like the weight of a thousand ships heaped on top of my chest. I could barely breathe. I felt all at once sick, nauseous. My head hurt, the walls were closing in, the room was spinning. I was going to throw up. With my hand on my heart, I thought I was going to collapse right there in my sitting room.

I quickly called my mother back, saying simply, "He died."

Minutes later, an eerie calm consoled me for a brief moment. I was in the eye of the storm. It was a moment of truth. I could see clearer than I ever had before. I saw before me two distinct paths, one of destruction and one of construction. I knew exactly what my situation was. Which road would I take? Would I choose to live for those who loved me, or lie down in a whirlpool of defeat? The unknown was ahead and I was left to navigate through this dense fog alone. Either way, all I could do was batten down the hatches and wait for the devastation to hit.

Then the short-lived calm disappeared, replaced by a chaos that began swirling around me. Owen no longer existed? How was that possible? Where did he go? I felt extremely ill. There was a thick knot at the base of my throat, and I wondered if I was even capable of talking. I had to find a way to gather my senses, my thoughts. People needed to be told, didn't they? How was I going to do that when I denied it myself?

I felt obligated to inform Owen's parents. They should hear it from me, I thought. But how would I tell them when I couldn't get my own head around it? I dialed each digit with great trepidation, unsure of what I should say.

Helen answered.

"Helen, I am sorry to have to tell you, your son has died," I said.

Somewhat prepared for the news thanks to my frantic call minutes earlier, she nevertheless pleaded sorrowfully. "No, not Owen, he can't be gone."

Shocked at having to confirm something I had yet to fully believe, I reiterated he was indeed dead.

She let out a horrific scream as the receiver dropped to the floor. I could hear her bellowing, "Owen is dead! Owen is dead!" She must have been running because her voice grew fainter and fainter. I listened until there was silence. Nobody returned to pick up the phone.

A numbness swept over me. The waves were starting to crash. Owen's death was going to rock everyone's foundation to the core.

Someone was pounding on my front door. Logically, I thought it must be Oje or Athena. Oh my God, I had forgotten about them. I ran over and swung the door open. There stood my sister Virginia. Dumbfounded, I looked at her sideways. Her watery eyes glistened, her skin was colorless. She appeared drawn, her spirit drained. She knew. But how?

"Is it true?" she asked in a meek, somber tone.

My silence answered her question as we embraced, wet tears streaming down our cheeks.

"How did you know?" I asked.

She explained they announced it on television.

"On TV?" I said, surprised.

"Yes, on the WWF pay-per-view show," she confirmed.

Her seventeen-year-old son, Michael, was watching with some of his friends and called Virginia as soon as word broke of the fall.

Then it came flooding back to me—the pay-per-view show. That's what Vince was talking about. That's why he asked me if I was watching the show. Right, of course, it was televised. Our eyes locked.

"Oh, no," I said, suddenly grasping the scenario. "That stunt, it was that stunt!"

The puzzle was being pieced together now. I had been in such a state of shock I had not understood Owen was working in front of an audience. Even when the doctor was describing Owen's fall I didn't realize he was doing *that* stunt. How could I have missed it? I knew it was coming up soon but I hadn't realized it was today.

"That stupid stunt," I said. The one he talked about. The one he said he didn't want to do. The one we had talked about the night before he left. Of course, of course, that stupid, meaningless stunt!

I stood speechless with my sister, the door still wide open as we contemplated the shock of it all. She walked into the house, her arm around my waist, and we kind of held each other up.

Inside the house it was quiet. But outside, there was much laughter and joy. As we entered the kitchen I walked straight to the window and watched as Athena playfully chased Oje in the back yard. They were having so much fun together.

"They don't even realize their little lives are changed forever," I said.

With my heart broken into a million shards I covered my face with both hands and broke down crying. Virginia gently guided me to the kitchen table where we both sat, staring aimlessly into space.

Our quiet reflections were momentary, as the noise would soon begin to escalate and wouldn't stop for days on end.

At 7:40 P.M. Calgary time, announcer Jim Ross had apparently informed the pay-per view audience that Owen had been pronounced dead. This prompted a flood of phone calls from friends and relatives who wondered if it was part of a strange wrestling angle. No one could believe it was true.

I rushed outside to check on the kids and saw our neighbor, Bill, who was one of Owen's favorite people. I thought he could tell by my expression something terrible had happened so I called him over and quietly told him what happened. We hugged and he started to shake and cry, saying, "Oh my God. Oh my God."

By 8 P.M. my mother had arrived, just as news of Owen's death had made its way to mainstream media outlets. Suddenly my house had turned into information headquarters. The phone was ringing off the hook and a steady flow of people arrived into the evening to lend support. Everybody wanted to know what happened and they all wanted to hear it from me. I felt compelled to oblige so I composed myself as best I could and repeated what few details I had.

Owen was the baby of twelve children and I was the baby of eleven, so when all the relatives began to arrive the house was packed. Most of Owen's family was there, except for Bret. He was flying from Ottawa to Los Angeles to make an appearance on *The Tonight Show* with Jay Leno the following evening. Mid-flight he was handed a note by the pilot informing him of a family emergency. He called home right away, learning of Owen's death sitting among strangers on the plane. He called me as soon as he landed and asked if he should come home. He already knew the answer but I confirmed he was needed immediately.

Everyone at my house was telling me I would be okay because I was such a strong person, yet I didn't feel that way at all.

"What am I going to do?" I asked Bret in a whisper. "Everyone thinks I'm so strong but I'm not."

His words were reassuring. "Don't worry, hold on. I'll come home right away. I will be there as soon as I can."

We hung up and I returned to a living room and front hall full of disheartened family members who stood among the boxes I had been packing all day. The place was a mess and the atmosphere was prickly and uncomfortable. The conversation was not flowing. No one knew what to say.

I could feel all of their eyes on me and I could sense the pity they felt for me. All of us were wallowing in anguish and yet there was no warmth among us. I knew Owen's family must have felt terrible for me and for Owen, but we weren't that close to them. In a way it felt like I was in a room full of strangers.

I never realized how little his family knew me and how little I knew them. I knew what they were like from their patterns of behavior but I never knew them intimately. Owen and I had always been cordial and respectful to everyone. Occasionally we dropped by the Hart house for birthdays, Christmas or the odd Sunday dinner. But our relationship with them was mainly superficial. Our distance from the family was an evolutionary process, not a spontaneous shift. As we grew older we differed in our value system and our philosophy of life, which slowly separated us. It had been almost ten years since our wedding when the separation began. We weren't the only ones who distanced themselves from the family. Bret, Keith, Wayne and Alison had detached themselves too.

With few words left to be spoken and no action to take, my visitors soon began to leave. I appreciated their efforts that night and felt disappointed we weren't a closer family. We feebly hugged good-bye and I closed the door.

At 9 P.M. my phone was still ringing off the hook and only my side of the family remained in the house. Virginia was receiving all the calls and taking messages. She addressed each call politely and thanked each caller on my behalf for his or her condolences. I took the odd call from the media as I hoped they could help shed more light on what happened.

Oje and Athena were uncertain what was going on. They had seen the parade of people marching through our house, some shaking their heads, some shedding tears. I hadn't told them yet because I thought I should wait until we were alone. Oje knew something was wrong and asked me if we were having some sort of party. I told him something very sad happened and that I would tell him and his sister once everyone had left.

Being children they still had unavoidable needs that had to be filled. They were hungry and dirty. Virginia helped me feed and bathe them. Once they were clean and dressed in their pajamas, I took them into my room and sat them on the side of the bed. I knew I had to tell them at that moment—it was only fair they be told on the day their father died. I knelt on the floor and looked into their big blue eyes, which were filled with anticipation. I had thought earlier about how to relay this gruesome material to them without frightening them so I closed my eyes and started to speak. It took all the strength I had not to break down and cry. Their mental wellness depended on me not showing weakness right now. I would save my agony for later.

I explained in the simplest terms Daddy had been hurt and that was why all the people at our house were so sad. I explained God didn't want Daddy to feel the pain. God thought it would be too much for Daddy to live with, so he took him to heaven so they could live together. I told them that Daddy was very happy to be with God and that he wouldn't want them to cry too much or be too sad that he wasn't coming home again. I told them not to worry because I was going to take good care of them. I told them we were going to be just fine.

They trustingly looked at me and said, "Okay, mom." They were very serious.

I gave them both a hug as I was proud of their brave reaction. At age three and seven they were clearly too young to grasp how their lives had just been so horribly altered.

I asked if they wanted to sleep with me and they both nodded yes. After they crawled under the blankets with their teddy bears I kissed them good-night, told them I loved them, turned out the lights and walked out the door with the world's heaviest heart.

I had just delivered the most horrible news a child could ever hear. Winded by the hopelessness that lingered inside of me, I was glad the children had been put to bed as I had one less thing to worry about. Still, how was I going to raise good children, especially a good son without a father?

The sun had long set, and outside it was as dark as my soul.

Things were beginning to die down around the house. The telephone still rang every few minutes but for the first time I was able to think rationally. I was in great distress but my wits were razor sharp. I couldn't wait for the eleven o'clock news to come on so I could hear more about what really happened. My head would not allow me to accept that Owen was dead until I had concrete proof. Even though I knew he was, a part of me still clung to the silly hope that maybe this was all a bad dream or a sick mistake. Seeing it on the news would be the confirmation I was searching for.

My mind raced as I started thinking about Owen's fall from the very top of the arena. How could this have happened? A man can't just fall all that way without tremendous error. In the midst of my review I had a very scary thought: There is negligence here. There must be major, major negligence here, I thought.

Owen was the most cautious person I knew. He would never take an uncalculated risk. He was not a thrill-seeker or an extreme person in any way. The thought that there must be negligence was a disturbing revelation to me. I didn't know how or in what form the negligence was. I just knew I needed to investigate it further. But how? As different scenarios played out in my imagination the phone rang as it had all night. I decided to answer it.

It was Bret calling back.

He explained no flights were available out of L.A. and doubted he could get back home until the next day. I barely paid attention to what he was saying as a voice in my head kept repeating, "There's negligence." I wanted to tell him so badly what was on the tip of my tongue, but could I trust him? Would he think I'd gone mad? I decided to take a chance.

"I think there's negligence," I said to Bret, holding my breath.

"I'm sure there is," was his response.

What a relief, I thought. He believes it too. We talked for a few minutes then he ended the call by telling me the company he worked for (WCW) was trying to arrange for a private jet to bring him home. He told me not to worry, he would come to my house as soon as possible.

Unfortunately, I could not take his advice—I had much to worry about. The news would be broadcast shortly and waiting for it was the only thing holding me together.

Finally, it was eleven o'clock. I waited with the channel changer in my hand so I could surf back and forth. I didn't want to miss any of it. It was the top story on every station. They splashed still photos of Owen lying dead in the ring, being worked on by paramedics. I felt like the wind had been knocked out of me. All the reports described the fall in graphic detail. Every report included pictures of me, Oje and Athena and was punctuated by the catchphrase, "He leaves behind a wife and two young children." I was amazed at the footage and wondered where they got the family photos.

It was official, I was a widow at age thirty-two.

It was all so surreal. I felt hollow, like an empty vessel stripped of all vital parts. For everyone else the world kept turning. Sure, they would feel very sad and speak of how tragic it was. But everyone could shut their TV off and go to bed unaffected. The life I took seventeen years to build with Owen had just been violently ripped away from me. Where was I supposed to go? How could I live in a world without Owen? I turned the television off. For a moment I was oblivious to the people around me.

Poor Owen, I thought.

My pain was intense, not only for my loss, but also for his pain and his loss of life. I thought about him up on the catwalk eight stories above the ground. Did he know what had happened? Did he know he was going to die? That bloody wrestling, I thought. He would be so mad that he died this way. He had confided in my sister years earlier that he had a fear of dying in the ring, surrounded by strangers. He would be so displeased to be remembered only as a professional wrestler, especially because the industry had become so slimy.

Out of the blue, I blurted out, "I have to do the eulogy."

My sister and mother were aghast. It was unheard of. They all shook their heads indicating they didn't approve.

"You don't understand," I shot back. "I am the only one who really knew him. I have to do it. He was more than the stereotypical wrestler and

I have to let everyone know that. Everyone has to know he was different—we were different. I can't let anyone think otherwise."

My family glanced at each other. I'm sure they thought I was delirious. But no one wanted to upset me—I was already upset enough. I'm sure they all thought I would change my mind after I gave it a little more thought.

It was getting late and I was tired. In fact, I had never experienced such exhaustion. It was as if someone had sucked the life out of me and left every cell in my body sagging. I was greasy with sweat, my hair was stringy, my skin was gray, my face was stinging from the tears I smudged away and my clothes were dusty from packing our stuff earlier in the day.

I hadn't eaten since lunch, which was a good thing. I wouldn't have been able to keep anything down. I decided I should go to bed, even if I couldn't sleep. I had to lie down to stop my head from pounding. I left everyone and dragged myself upstairs.

Without a doubt, it was the darkest night of my life. A thick cloud of gloom hovered heavily above the house. I entered my bedroom and looked at the kids sleeping so peacefully. I had to shower because I couldn't stand the way I felt. When I was finished I slipped into bed beside my two angels.

I hadn't really cried in front of anyone all day except for my sister Virginia. Ever since I could remember I found it awkward to cry and fully express my emotions with others around. It was like I could package up my fears and tuck them away in a box, then leave them until I could safely open up the box and sort them out. This was why people always thought I was strong. It wasn't that I didn't have to deal with the turmoil. I did. But I could postpone it for what I perceived a more appropriate time.

Now, for the first time since I had received the news of Owen's passing, I was alone with my thoughts. I started to cry softly. No sobbing sounds escaped, just a surge of tears. I squeezed my eyes shut in an effort to stop the flow, but soon my pillow was soaked and I had to flip it over. My heart raced so fast I thought I might have a heart attack. Episodes were popping into my mind and I kept thinking, "Oh, I'll have to tell Owen that." "Owen would be interested to hear …" Then I'd remember that I wouldn't be able to tell him anything anymore.

I thought I was going crazy. My nerves were zapped, as if I had been hit by lightning. Was I going to have a nervous breakdown? I calmed and reassured myself I was okay. Just relax and breathe, I told myself.

At 3 A.M. every fiber was tingling but I was not asleep. My heart continued to race as quickly as my mind.

I reflected on the events of the day over and over. I recalled that Linda McMahon, Vince McMahon's wife, had called me moments after I had received the doctor's call. She worked with Vince and helped run his company. We spoke briefly. I remembered asking her, "What am I going to do?"

As I lay quietly among the shadows of my dim room a thought struck me. Why had Linda called me rather than Vince? I re-enacted my earlier telephone conversation with Vince word for word. Then it hit me: He knew. He knew Owen was already dead when he phoned me. What a coward! I got out of bed and started walking around my room, but my legs couldn't catch up to the thoughts that zoomed through my mind.

Of course no one would want to tell a wife her husband had died, especially if they were in some way responsible. But he should have called me back, not have his wife do it. It was his company that was ultimately responsible for my husband's well-being while he was on the job.

It then occurred to me he was positioning himself for a lawsuit. I bet he called his lawyers. I figured he was the type of man who would be more worried about his own well-being than that of the man who had just died under his watch or of the people it affected. My fists were clenched as I felt a vehement anger welling up inside me. I had to stop myself and refrain from judging anyone right then. I didn't have all the facts and it wasn't fair to assume anything or point any fingers of blame. Regardless of what kind of person Vince was, he was still a human being who merited some consideration. He must feel terrible too, I thought.

I got back into bed and tried to rest, knowing what the morning would bring. I would have the hardest challenges of my life ahead of me.

I thought about Owen. He was the best person I ever knew. Planning his funeral would be a grisly operation, but as morbid as the thought was I still wanted to give him the most beautiful funeral the city of Calgary could offer up. I would make sure his funeral mirrored the degree of love and respect I had for him. He deserved that much and he would have it at any cost. I would see to that.

In a sacred prayer, I vowed to Owen, with God as my witness, I would get to the bottom of what really happened. I would get justice for him, if there was any justice to be had. He could count on me, I wouldn't let him down.

I lay awake sleeplessly frozen, waiting for day to break.

HEAVEN AND HELL

"Was ever grief like mine?"
—GEORGE HERBERT

My bedroom window faced west, keeping the morning sun from seeping in. It was still quite dark but I could tell the night sky was receding. I quietly got out of bed, careful not to wake the children, who had slept soundly all night.

I hadn't slept one single minute. Instead, I suffered throughout the night, tortured by thoughts of the gruesome reality I faced.

My sister had stayed over, across the hall in Oje's room. As soon as she heard my door open she sprang to her feet and met me in the hallway. She told me she hadn't slept all night either.

With morning upon us it seemed so unfair to me that the sun would even rise on an Earth that didn't include Owen anymore, but it had. How dare there be any warmth or light of any kind, for my soul was the coldest, darkest place on the planet.

My mind continued to race, as it had all night.

My life was ruined. All the building, all the work, all of our dreams—everything I believed in was gone.

Any time I'd struggle with his extended road trips or loneliness over the years, Owen would always remind me, "It's for our future." He'd been wrong.

Seventeen years of memories—what was the point of it all? Had we been fools all this time believing we had something tangible, when in a blink of an eye it had been snatched away? What kind of cruel world was this anyway? None of it made sense. Owen was a healthy, productive person who brought a lot of good to people's lives. He wasn't supposed to die from some ridiculously meaningless stunt. He was meant to live and help make this world a better place.

Without Owen, the path of life seemed a worthless, desolate stroll into oblivion. All that kept me going was a fierce inner drive to show the world how much Owen meant to the children and me. I decided I'd put my heart into organizing the classiest of funeral arrangements. I needed to do that for him, as he had brought such incredible joy to my life. I loved him so much. Maybe too much.

I vowed my final duties as his wife would be to uncover the truth behind his death and to ensure his time on earth was recognized in a permanent, meaningful way.

As I walked down the stairs with my sister, I knew today would begin the most important mission of my life and I would not fail Owen on either accounts.

Downstairs, my sister and I greeted our mother, who lay on the sofa wide-eyed—she had also stayed the night. We all wore the same pained look, and no one knew exactly what to say. There was now a gaping hole in our lives, as if our hearts had been ripped out.

Exhausted, we moved around the kitchen lethargically, discussing the roles each of us would play for the day. We were like three robots going through the motions of living. I was to get ready and go to the funeral home to make the appropriate preparations. Virginia was going to deal with all callers and visitors to the house, and my mom was going to keep Oje and Athena occupied with an eye on shielding them somewhat from the somber goings-on.

Having dispersed from the kitchen, it wasn't long before we were in full swing. The phones were ringing again, Oje and Athena were up demanding attention and I was busy thinking about what to do first.

As I stood in front of the bathroom mirror, struggling to pull myself together in an effort to look presentable, I couldn't get away from thoughts there was severe negligence involved in Owen's demise. It haunted me all morning.

Dozens and dozens of calls from friends, acquaintances and well-wishers had flooded the house and Virginia was doing a good job weeding through them. Calgary Mayor Al Duerr, Alberta Premier Ralph Klein, Canadian hockey icon Wayne Gretzky, Stan Schwartz from the Calgary Stampeders football club, Ron Bremner from the Calgary Flames hockey team and a host of wrestlers and their wives either called or sent flowers. Even the Governor of Missouri, Mel Carnahan, was in the midst of preparing a letter of condolence. Boxer Lennox Lewis, who had met Owen previously, even called just days before fighting for the heavyweight crown.

Owen's tag team partner and good friend Jeff Jarrett called five times a day and proceeded to send food, books and other gifts throughout the week. He and his wife were truly crushed by it all.

I couldn't possibly deal with everyone who called to extend their condolences and offer support so I only accepted the most critical of calls. Anyone who could help provide me with answers or information was immediately passed to me.

When I finished dressing, I took a deep breath, wiped the tears from my eyes and headed downstairs. It was there, at the bottom of the stairs, Virginia told me Pam Fischer was on the line and handed me the phone.

Pam was a dear friend of ours who had recently had Owen and I over to her house for dinner. She and her husband Charles were both lawyers and had a son, Peter, who was good friends with Oje. Charles was shocked to read about Owen's death in the morning paper and after breaking the news to Pam she pushed past him to call me immediately.

As we spoke, I kept thinking about her profession. Pam specialized in cases involving personal injury and negligence, with Pipella Warren, one of the city's most prestigious firms in that area of the law. I desperately wanted to ask for her help but she was calling as a friend and I didn't want to put her on the spot. We were talking about Oje and Athena and about childcare when she said, "If there's anything I can do to help ..."

I knew she was referring to the possibility of helping out with the children but I jumped in with my troubling thought immediately. "Pam, I think there's negligence," I said.

I sensed it caught her off guard. "Oh no," she gasped. "I haven't read the paper yet, what do you know?"

I told her I didn't know much at all about what happened but I had a bad feeling about it.

"All I can tell you is that if there is negligence you will need to get a private investigator in Kansas City on it right away," she said. She explained that as time passed, crucial evidence could disappear, so it was imperative I retained an investigator immediately.

"How do I do that?" I asked. "It happened in Kansas City, Missouri— I barely know where that is."

Answering my own question, I suggested it might be wise to call the Kansas City Police Department. She agreed that would be a good place to start.

I immediately began trying to get a hold of the proper police official. This took quite some time as I had to painfully explain to every new person I talked to why I was calling. Eventually I was directed to Detective Kevin Kilkenny, who had first-hand knowledge of the police investigation that was being conducted. I listened intently to every word he said. He disclosed all the evidence the police department had accumulated to that point and said all preliminary reports indicated it was an accident. There were no signs of intent or foul play but the case was by no means closed.

I told him of my burning suspicion negligence was involved.

He informed me that according to the law he could not confirm or deny my suspicions.

However, something in his voice told me to press on. I asked him straight out if I should hire a private investigator to pry into it further. He reiterated he could not advise me either way, but more or less expressed I should go on my instinct and follow it.

I knew right away more work needed to be done so I thanked him for his time and consideration and disconnected.

I suddenly felt extremely pressed for time. Before Pam's call I had made arrangements to meet the director of McInnis and Holloway Funeral Home in the city's southwest. It was located by our children's school, and Owen and I often drove by it.

The grounds of the funeral home were well kept with beautiful gardens and a lovely fountain that made it look so warm and welcoming. Owen and I had commented on how pretty it was, especially for a funeral home. Even though I knew Owen was dead, it was important to me he be well taken care of. I felt good knowing he would be somewhere we both liked.

Running late, I was seconds from walking out the door when Pam phoned a second time. I relayed all the information from the police and told her the funeral home was expecting me.

She offered one piece of advice before we ended our call. "Tell your family to quit talking to the press," she said. "I read the paper and they're making off-the-cuff remarks while they shouldn't be saying anything."

I agreed and left it at that. I hadn't seen any of the newspapers at all. I had no idea what I was in for. Later, Pam would comment that trying to keep the Hart family away from the press was like trying to stop an avalanche.

Against the wishes of everyone at my house, I elected to go to the funeral home alone to plan the funeral. I explained I needed to do this by myself because I wanted everything done a certain way. Only I could do it.

As I backed out of my driveway and circled around the meridian I caught a glimpse of the two local newspaper boxes placed by the bus stop across the street from my house. I gasped when I saw them. Oh my God, Owen was on the cover of both! I slowed down to get a better look.

The *Calgary Sun* had a large close up of Owen's face with the caption "DEAD" at the top. The *Calgary Herald* had a photo of Owen lying dead in the ring while the paramedics were working on him.

Although anything involving the Harts got huge media attention, it blew me away. The reality of the situation intensified. There I was, his widow, driving to the funeral home to plan his funeral. What kind of a nightmare was I in?

I sat in my Jeep, horrified to see what I was seeing. Everyone else in the city would read all about it but it was me who was living with it. With my head feeling like it was in a vice and ready to explode, I drove myself to the funeral home in a complete state of shock.

Meanwhile, Owen's lifeless body lay in the Kansas City morgue. They hadn't made plans to fly him home yet because we weren't sure if we were going to have an autopsy performed on him.

I didn't want anyone dissecting my husband until I was sure it was necessary. If police investigators believed there was negligence involved in the deadly stunt, then an autopsy would be key. Vince was already trying to direct the blame on Owen and an autopsy would quash any implications he might have been on drugs and fell as a result. It also would have eliminated any concerns over whether some medical condition contributed to his fate.

I had no doubt that if I was to go after Vince and the WWF they would stop at nothing to defend themselves, including trying to paint Owen in an unfavorable light. I knew that was impossible, as Owen was the cleanest guy in every way, but I couldn't afford to take any chances. After a brief consultation with Pam, I gave them the go ahead for the autopsy.

It really bothered me to think he was lying in some darkened refrigerated drawer wearing nothing but a toe tag. I desperately wanted him back in Calgary where he belonged. I didn't want to think about Owen lying on a cold slab while they cut and sawed away at him, removing tissue, blood and urine. It was hard to think it had come to this, but I could hear him telling me, "Do whatever it takes to get me some justice."

I would have to deal with accepting it as a medical procedure, reminding myself he couldn't feel anything anyway. It was just another gruesome reality I would have to come to grips with.

I arrived at the funeral home and reluctantly went inside. To my surprise the inside was as picturesque as the exterior. It was hardly the morbid environment I somehow assumed it would be. Instead it was bright, well decorated and inviting. Shaking hands with the director, I walked with him through the foyer and up a magnificent staircase leading to a vaulted upper floor.

Sitting me down in one of the consulting rooms, the director was a very pleasant and considerate young man who seemed sensitive and understanding of the difficult task I was about to undertake. He told me it was most unusual I had elected to come alone. I explained that I had clear instructions on how the entire funeral should be conducted and that I didn't want anyone else to interfere in any way.

When Owen's brother Dean had died nine years earlier from a kidney malfunction caused by Bright's Disease, Owen and I both felt the way his family handled the burial arrangements was less than desirable. We were very disappointed. Neglecting to give him a proper funeral, the family had Dean cremated and his ashes were left uncollected at the crematorium for some time. They were finally picked up after a series of calls were made to the Hart house. The Hart family then conducted their own private gathering at their home devoid of a minister or the deliverance of last rites.

Dean's ashes, which were housed in a cardboard box provided by the crematorium, were then scattered across a field in front of the Harts' hillside acreage. Owen and I found it disheartening that there was no special spot marked for his grave.

In our opinion, there seemed to be little respect for the dead. Owen felt his parents were too cheap to bury Dean properly so they just did it "the Hart way"—a derogatory term which Owen often used.

Dean was a bit of an odd character, so maybe his parents had their reasons for doing things the way they did, but somehow Owen and I couldn't help but feel so sad about the way it was handled.

So the way I saw it, I had no options but to orchestrate Owen's funeral plans alone. I felt I had nowhere to turn, even if I wanted advice. Although Bret later offered to pay for Owen's funeral, I wouldn't hear of it. This was my way of saying goodbye.

Owen's funeral would exude respect and honor. I would have it no other way, regardless of cost. I relayed my wishes to the funeral director and we began the dreadful preparations.

I told the director I wanted Owen to remain in the funeral home for viewing as long as possible. I dearly wanted to spend as much time with him as I could before burying him and explained how important it was I delay burial as long as was permissible. Solemnly, I told the director how much I loved my husband and how difficult it would be for me to let him go.

He informed me eight days represented an extended period of time and thought it unwise to wait much longer than that, especially since I refused to have Owen embalmed. (The thought of having Owen's blood drained and replaced with chemicals horrified me.) We decided the funeral would be held the morning of Monday, May 31, 1999—eight days after his death.

We then discussed the travel agenda as Owen still needed to be transported from the Kansas City morgue to Calgary. I wasn't sure at that point just how that was going to be arranged but I speculated it would be by private jet.

I wrote the obituary, which I instructed to be run in all Calgary newspapers every day leading up to the funeral. I also announced to the director I would be delivering the eulogy.

He gazed at me with a well-meaning smile and put his hand on my shoulder. "That is not a very good idea," he said. "You will probably change your mind later about that, but let's not worry about it right now."

I complied but assured him I would not change my mind.

We moved on by designing the pamphlets containing the schedule of the funeral. Two days later we added a poem I wrote about a lighthouse, which I thought encapsulated Owen's giving spirit.

With much of the paperwork done and the funeral plans underway, the most unpleasant requirement of the process still awaited me—the selection of the coffin. The director warned me to brace myself as he slowly opened the door to a hidden, windowless room—almost like a secret chamber—filled with a sea of open coffins.

He began rhyming off the redeeming qualities of each model but I instantly gravitated to a beautiful, deluxe cherry wood coffin. I explained that our new home, the one Owen and I would sadly never enjoy together, was decorated in cherry wood, our favorite.

As odd as it sounded, I told him I wanted the cherry wood coffin so Owen would feel at home.

How stupid I must have come across to him. How could Owen feel anything? He was dead. Yet, to me everything I did carried a deep, profound meaning unfamiliar to anyone except me.

I didn't care what anyone else thought. I wanted it all done a certain way. I would think however I wanted to, whatever it took to get me through it. Every single aspect of Owen's funeral would be done with the utmost love, care and consideration, just as every area of our life together had been.

The director and I were becoming weary. We had spent hours together and there was still so much to plan. However, we had accomplished a great deal and agreed to break for the day, with plans on staying in constant contact.

I stepped out of the room and was stunned to see Pam sitting in the chair in front of me. Her blue eyes were red and her face was draped in sorrow.

"What are you doing here alone?" she asked.

Again, I didn't care to explain so I shrugged it off. More important issues were on the horizon for Pam and me. We needed to talk in detail about what my next move should be. She suggested we go to her home nearby, where we could speak in confidence. I knew where she lived but she was worried about my mental state and insisted I follow her.

When we arrived at her home we sat at her dining room table—the same one we all sat at as happy couples when Owen was still alive. Visions of the last evening spent there flickered in and out of my mind. Neither Pam nor I could have imagined then that the next time we sat in these seats Owen would be dead.

We proceeded to sift through every shred of information I had, which wasn't a whole lot. Equipped with her pen and yellow notepad, she wrote feverishly as I spoke.

The first thing I did was identify the WWF as Owen's employer.

"What does that stand for?" asked Pam. I was shocked by her ignorance.

Only then did it occur to me she had never heard of the WWF because Owen and I rarely, if ever, discussed his occupation with our friends. They all knew he was a professional wrestler but most of them didn't follow his career in any way.

As our discussion deepened, it became clear we'd have to seek out legal counsel in Kansas City to begin a supplemental investigation into the circumstances of Owen's mysterious death. We spoke at length, regurgitating what little information we had.

Finally, I could take no more. I hadn't slept in almost forty hours and I thought I might pass out from the strain and overwhelming pressures the day had brought. I needed to lie down.

Pam probably wasn't thrilled either about being dragged into a potential lawsuit, but she was a good friend and assured me she was on board and willing to help. As she walked me to the door she advised me to limit my comments in the media about Owen to those of my grave personal loss. Further, I was to make no allusions whatsoever to our plans to investigate. She knew the media would be swarming around this story like a bunch of scavengers scrounging for any tidbit. One day in and they had already started.

She told me she would try to get something going in Kansas City and would contact me later in the evening. I left for home apologizing to her for my weak mental state.

Fatigued and dispirited, I drove myself home, wondering what had just happened to my life. In less than a twenty-four-hour span my husband had died, I had planned the basis of his funeral and had given birth to the possible launch of a full-blown lawsuit. Could this be real? On top of all this, I was supposed to be completing our packing, as we were moving in four days.

Depleted and faint, I arrived home to a driveway full of concerned people. With barely an ounce of energy remaining, I staggered through the front door. The floral arrangements were arriving in droves and the smell of them wafted throughout the house. The smell would eventually sicken me, preventing me from enjoying fresh cut flowers for years.

I bypassed everyone and climbed up to my room, tripping over my own feet before I fell limply into my bed. I didn't want to see or speak to anyone. My sister kept coming to my room, announcing so-and-so was here or such-and-such needed to be done. I was oblivious to all of it. Numb, I politely asked her to stop disturbing me.

As I lay in my bed, the demons in my mind were tormenting me. I felt like I was adrift, unreachable, a castaway stranded on a remote island no one could get to. I was stuck in a frightfully unfamiliar place with no one around me, and no one in sight.

I was involuntarily alone in this world and no one understood the depths of despair that engulfed me. I felt myself slipping pitifully into the bleakness of hell, clinging hopelessly to the damp walls of gloom. Please God, please don't leave me, I begged.

Curled into the fetal position on my bed with my back towards the door, I heard a light knock and turned my head to see Bret standing there. Thanks to a private jet, he finally managed to get home to lend his support. I immediately found new life, springing out of bed as he quickly walked towards me. We met in the middle of my room and embraced. We both loved Owen dearly and were similarly devastated. I didn't realize until the moment he hugged me that I had been waiting for him. It marked the first time since this terrible ordeal began that I felt some form of security and safety.

As Owen's brother and a world-renowned professional wrestler, Bret was the closest thing physically to what I had lost. I found great comfort in his company and his embrace. Bret's build was similar to Owen's, as was his deep, soothing voice that provided reassurance with every word.

Their big, strong hands were identical, as were their thick forearms. When he held me I felt like it was an extension of Owen. It was a good place to be.

I knew I needed him to help me get through the trauma of losing Owen. I would also need him to support me if there was going to be a lawsuit. I'd count on him heavily to help me deal with a wrestling business he knew inside out. Specifically, he was all too familiar with Vince McMahon—the man I suspected was ultimately responsible for Owen's death. I was sure Bret wouldn't hesitate in assisting me any way he could to ensure justice was served.

We hugged for a long while in the middle of my room, and when we were done we sat on my bed still clinging to each other. I expounded on every fact and detail I had surrounding the distorted picture I was attempting to put together. Bret listened attentively and offered to help in any way he could. I informed him I already had the wheels in motion on an investigation and that my friend Pam was assisting me legally.

I told him I thought Vince was running scared. It was almost a full twenty-four hours since Owen had died and Vince still hadn't the nerve to call me back. All I wanted was the truth, not some fabricated version from Vince, who was obviously worried about being legally covered. I had seen Vince on the news the night before and he was telling the world that Owen had apparently released himself. Within hours of the incident he was trying to blame Owen for his own death.

It didn't add up in my mind. First of all, how would Vince know Owen released himself? From what I knew of the investigation, that hadn't been determined yet. Even if that were the case, surely no man should be suspended that high off the ground with even the remotest of possibilities of an accidental release without a backup safety system of some sort. In fact, it must be downright criminal to put someone in such imminent danger.

There was no doubt in my mind Vince was already positioning himself for a plea of innocence, using the media to get his point across very quickly. The whole thing stunk of negligence and the more time I had to think about it, the more it became very clear that someone was responsible for Owen's death.

That someone was not Owen. He was just doing his job.

Bret agreed with me on every point. We talked and comforted one another for more than an hour before he left in the early evening to go home.

Returning to my house later that evening, Bret sat down on the couch, hung his head and openly wept. In our attempt to console him, Virginia, my mother and I all ended up sharing his tears. He wound up staying over, providing me with a comfort that allowed me to sleep for a few hours.

I was confident and touched to know Owen was right when he suggested Bret would stand by me if anything ever happened to him. Together we would stand united and strong through the storm sure to come.

The days that followed will forever live vividly in my memory.

After just a few hours sleep, I awoke at 2:30 A.M. Tuesday morning to prepare for a live interview on *Good Morning America* with Charles Gibson. Shortly after that, NBC's Matt Lauer was scheduled to do a live bit with us on his morning show.

Despite a grief and sorrow that made it hard to speak about Owen without choking up, I wanted to bring attention to the fact Owen wasn't just another stereotypical wrestler who was uneducated, hard-living, unsophisticated and foolish or reckless enough to take unnecessary risks. He was an exemplary person and a smart family man who was extremely cautious. The world needed to know it lost a great man.

I decided I would agree to talk to only the most legitimate of news agencies and journalists. After all, Owen was a legitimate person and didn't deserve to be splashed around on the cover of publications like the *National Enquirer*, which offered my sister $10,000 for inside information on Owen's death.

The interview was scheduled for 4 A.M. at the Hart house, and as I drove into their long driveway, I was surprised to see such a large number of cars.

Walking into the house, I was floored to discover almost every one of Owen's ten siblings had arrived. I don't know if they all thought they'd be included in the interviews, but I felt like a complete outsider. I didn't feel accepted or welcome in any way. Although these were people I had known for seventeen years, I felt like I didn't belong there anymore. The hugs were, for the most part, cold. I realized that in their minds I was never truly considered family and now that Owen was gone, I was really out.

Several of them were there with hopes of getting their TV time in and to begin their separate campaigns in search of whatever they could reap from their brother's death. As would be evident the following weeks and months, they were having a hard time realizing Owen's death wasn't about them. Bret really respected that and was the obvious choice to speak on behalf of the family because he was well spoken, knew the situation and was well known.

I asked that he be the only one of the siblings to speak on behalf of the family, a request Diana, Ellie and Smith found hard to follow. They continued talking to the press despite my pleas otherwise.

The ones who really grasped what had happened, Alison, Keith and Bret, had been at my house, helping me grieve. The others considered the Hart house the central grieving place, which I found a strange atmosphere indeed. Wayne, who was distant from his family but was always very decent to me, was nowhere to be seen through most of the ordeal.

Sitting with Stu, Helen and Bret for the *Good Morning America* interview, I struggled for words as Gibson graciously conducted the interview via satellite.

Lauer was equally as respectful, although I began crying when he asked how my children were doing. "My daughter is three and doesn't understand right now, but when she's getting married and she doesn't have her dad to give her away then I'm sure she'll understand the tragedy that's occurred," I said. "My son, I thought he was doing okay but he has just recently started to cave in and cry and ask for his dad and says he wants to sleep with his dad dolls. That's really hard on me."

I remember little else of what we talked about, but after watching the tapes a year later I could see the profound sadness in me. The distress. Watching it still brings tears to my eyes.

In another TV interview, I held up a picture of the house we were supposed to move into. I also clung to a shirt of Owen's I had been hugging because it smelled like him. It reminded me of years earlier when Owen left me alone in Germany while he flew to the States for a week of WWF interviews. I was six months pregnant with Oje and I found great comfort sleeping with his coat.

Whatever I said or did was all simply the product of raw emotion. I was numb. I was lost. And because Owen was so famous, my empty soul was being broadcast around the world for all to see.

Bret told Lauer, "Owen should never have been called upon to be Batman."

Bret also had harsh words for McMahon and the wrestling industry. In another interview we did, he told MSNBC that despite the fact Owen worked in a billion-dollar business, "The wrestlers are treated like circus animals, especially in the WWF." Bret added he was disgusted with bloodthirsty wrestling fans today. "You're called upon to do as the wrestling promoter says or you could very well be out of a job."

On every major network in the U.S. the debate raged around what they said was the first death in the wrestling ring in twenty-three years. It was even debated on Johnnie Cochran's show.

After wrapping up Tuesday morning's interviews, I continued on through another hectic day. The funeral plans continued, as did my search for answers.

Pam and I met again later that day in an effort to try unearthing as much information as possible. The autopsy results had been published in the paper the same day, revealing Owen had died of blunt chest trauma. The medical examiner, Dr. Thomas Young, said Owen's aorta was severed from his heart upon impact. Young labeled it an accidental death, based on his limited knowledge of the events surrounding the fall.

He pointed out there were no head or neck fractures and no sign of head trauma of any kind. Not only did it rule out reports his head had hit the ring's turnbuckle but it also put me at ease. I couldn't bear the thought of him lying in the ring, suffering with the bones of his neck snapped.

As expected, the autopsy also confirmed Owen had no illegal drugs or alcohol in his system.

Along with the medical examiner's reports came a public barrage of finger pointing from the Hart family. Opening their doors to reporters while they mourned Owen and posed for photos, the Harts vented their frustrations. They ignored my meek pleas for silence. While they certainly had every right to comment on their brother's passing, what worried me was that they might say something that would be damaging in any future lawsuit or court battle.

While Smith blamed wrestling's ratings war for his brother's death, Stu told the *Calgary Sun* the tragedy rested ultimately with McMahon. "It's his show and somebody miscued," said Stu. "He's the captain of the ship and you blame the captain when the *Titanic* goes down."

Despite hoping her wrestling husband, Jim Neidhart, would land another high-level wrestling job with the WWF, even Ellie weighed in. "Wrestling has gone too far," she told the *Calgary Herald*. "In their efforts to beat the WCW, the gimmicks and the dangerous stunts just get out of hand. Owen was a sacrifice to the ratings."

Helen, who was always uneasy with the prospect of one of her sons getting injured in the ring, said she was "angry at wrestling itself for relying more and more on shock and outrageous things."

Wrestling expert Dave Meltzer agreed. "The truth of the matter is wrestling itself has sacrificed itself to TV ratings," he said. "That is now what the whole business is about—winning Monday night ratings and going to whatever extent it takes."

Bret blamed the fans. "Wrestling is supposed to be body slams and falls—it's never meant sailing into the ring." He said Owen had no business being pressured into performing the duties of a stunt man. "Owen would have hated this and that's why it's so tragic. Owen was much more a cynic about wrestling than any of us. He was disillusioned about the way wrestling's gone. I see these wrestling fans as rabid dogs frothing at the mouth, looking for the next thrill. They can be so cold. They did not deserve my brother's last seconds."

Although admitting he would immediately put an end to aerial descents, McMahon shamelessly backed the high-risk stunt. "Stunts like this are performed at major sporting events on a routine basis in Hollywood—we compete with Hollywood for entertainment," he said.

Immediately following the accident McMahon also said Owen may have accidentally triggered the release mechanism. It was a theory backed by the Kansas City police, who said their preliminary investigation suggested perhaps Owen was disoriented by the darkness in the rafters, causing him to lose balance and trigger the release himself.

"It would be very convenient, and Owen can't defend himself," Stu told the *Herald*.

Well aware of how legally contentious Owen's death would likely be, Pam's firm agreed to assist us. Despite the likelihood of negligence and the public debate Owen's death sparked concerning the state of wrestling, we still had no idea Ed's firm might need to come on board as representatives in any potential lawsuit. It seemed to me this would be an issue that called strictly for experts in Missouri law. Pam was just a good friend trying to help me in time of crisis.

Pam corresponded with different people in Kansas City, trying to hire private investigators and put together a legal team for me. After plenty of research we narrowed our search for the best Kansas City lawyers to three firms, including Robb & Robb. Our contact with their people was brief. They were well aware of Owen's death and the circumstances surrounding it and they offered to hire a private investigator to get things going at their end. We agreed to let them go ahead with the investigation but made it clear we were not ready to commit to retaining them just yet. As upset as I was, I felt great relief in knowing someone was doing something—anything—to help.

I included Bret in our discussions. He had proven to be an asset, as he was able to provide good background information on the WWF. We were all on the same page and worked well together with one objective in mind: getting to the truth.

To continue life in as normal a manner as possible, I decided the children should go to school the week leading up to the funeral. Too young to fully comprehend how their lives would be forever altered, their little minds didn't need to be subjected to the ongoing pain and confusion that engulfed me every minute of the day.

While I sifted through the damage caused by the bomb that hit our lives, it was important some order be restored. I went as far as to make sure Oje attended his piano lessons. Although I drove the kids almost everywhere and tried my best to maintain a sense of normalcy, they obviously knew something was wrong.

For the first time in their young lives Oje and Athena didn't have my complete attention. Neighbors helped cook for the kids and many others graciously volunteered to help with them in any way, including my good friends Lisa and Wade Hartzell, who took them to soccer and school. The kids were so well behaved through it all.

The funeral home's limos were shuttling me to and from my house throughout the day, prompting me to ask the limo driver one afternoon to pick up the children at school. I even made the driver wait for an hour outside the local college while Oje took his full piano lesson. It was a bizarre arrangement but I felt it was critical for the children to believe that even though their dad was never coming home again, I would still have the same expectations of them.

I also decided we would continue our regular swimming and pizza outings on Friday nights. They would now hold an even greater importance, considering that's what we did the last night we all spent together.

Tributes continued to pour in for Owen, whose popularity around the globe became evident. NHL player Brett Hull, a former Flames forward who knew Owen from his days in Calgary, took to the ice for a playoff game with the initials O.H. on his skates. Theo Fleury, another former Calgary Flame then playing for the Colorado Avalanche, asked *Hockey Night in Canada* to pass on his condolences. Before his game, the Avalanche had a moment of silence for Owen.

Thousands of letters from wrestling fans were sent to the Hart house and my house—some with nothing more than: Owen Hart, Canada on the envelope. Dozens more appeared in the Letters to the Editor section of both local papers. Premier Klein even spoke of naming a park, mountain or river after Owen.

Still, the man at the center of all this, Vince McMahon, had neglected to phone me back. What kind of a man was this? How could he not call me?

Deep down I knew why he hadn't. He was afraid. After all, Owen died in his wrestling ring, under his watch.

There were other issues as well. Vince did not even have the decency to discontinue the show. He let it run to completion, perhaps fearing he would lose money if he didn't. And, despite their emotional state, he ordered the grief-stricken wrestlers to continue performing.

Seconds after Owen was wheeled out of the arena to cheers, the pay-per-view went to a live interview with Jeff Jarrett and Debra, both visibly shaken by the turn of events. Pacing nervously, Jarrett turned to the camera wearing a muscle shirt that read, "Don't piss me off," and told Owen he was in their prayers.

Announcer Jim Ross cut in right after their interview saying, "Unfortunately the show must go on here. We will do our best to keep you updated on the condition of Owen Hart."

At 8:40 P.M., a half hour after Owen was declared dead, Ross told the world of Owen's fate. "Earlier tonight tragedy befell the WWF and all of us," said Ross, who deserved plenty of credit for respectfully handling his regrettable role. "Owen Hart was set to make an entrance from the ceiling and he fell from the ceiling. I have the unfortunate responsibility to let everyone know Owen Hart has died."

The show immediately went to a video involving The Rock and his broken arm. The Rock was locked into a ringside casket and his cast smashed repeatedly with the sledgehammer by Triple-H. Yes, a casket. The Rock would later be shown backstage covered in blood.

Fittingly, the show ended at 9:35 P.M. with Austin taking on The Undertaker as manager Paul Bearer stood ringside.

Unlike the viewers who watched the show on TV, fans in attendance didn't find out about Owen's death until they got home. While the WWF tried disguising this "show must go on" decision as having to do with crowd control, McMahon was vilified by the media. Minutes after the show, he and a reporter didn't see eye to eye on her line of questioning. "Lady, I don't like your tone," he said, staring her down while cameras rolled.

McMahon then issued a statement extending his condolences to the family, adding, "The highest tribute that we can pay is to go on entertaining the fans he loved so much."

In addition to the media, many fans also thought it was distasteful to carry on with the show. Kansas City's Kevin Brice left the arena with his 12-year-old nephew and 10-year-old daughter. "It was disgusting [for them to continue the show]," Brice told the *Kansas City Star*. "For them to continue on as if nothing happened is just sad."

One of the only people who defended Vince's decision was Davey Boy Smith (who wasted little time trying to position himself for future employment with the WWF). "No one knew Owen's condition after it happened," he said, disputing The Rock's claim that all the wrestlers backstage could see Owen was essentially dead and couldn't be revived. "No one knew if it was fatal. You get people saying it was in bad taste that Vince went on with the show, but if you didn't you'd have 18,000 pissed off fans who might riot."

To me, though, no matter how Vince wanted to try justifying it, the decision to go on was an unforgivable act of inhumanity. It showed absolutely no respect for Owen or the people affected by his fall. The sheer nerve of it shocked me. I thought of what an awful person he must be to have such a heart of stone. At least it was mildly comforting to know he would have to answer for his poor judgment—if not to me then to himself. Surely he had a conscience.

However, McMahon's inappropriate behavior didn't stop there. Less than twenty-four hours after my husband had been killed and placed in the protective custody of the Jackson Country Medical Examiner's office, Vince followed through on a Monday night *Raw is War* show scheduled for St. Louis. Rather than postpone or cancel the show, giving his wrestlers time to cope with the loss of their friend and colleague, he used Owen's death as a golden opportunity to bolster ratings in the highly contested viewership battle.

McMahon transformed the show at the Kiel Centre into a tribute card for Owen. Wrestlers stood with tears in their eyes for a ten-bell salute to open the evening. The matches were short and were devoid of risqué behavior or angles of any sort. Throughout the show wrestlers and staff spoke of their favorite memories of Owen in pre-taped segments that aired between regularly scheduled bouts.

Never once have I questioned the profound sadness and loss most of the wrestlers felt in the days and weeks that followed Owen's death. In fact, some, like Jeff Jarrett, continue to stay in touch with me and show their support and respect to Owen to this day.

"This business is cold, callous, selfish, self-serving and unrealistic," said Jarrett, during his emotional tribute. "It's a fantasy world. He did what he did with integrity and integrity in this business is few and far between."

Almost all of them spoke of his pranks, which endeared him to everyone. Dustin Runnells told of how Owen poured a whole bottle of hot sauce into a pot of chili during a wrestling gathering in St. Louis. Debra spoke of how he used to write all over her hands at autograph sessions. Referee Dave Hebner said Owen "used to tie my shoelaces together when I went down for the count."

Perhaps the most touching words came from Jim Ross, who said he hoped he could be "as good a man as Owen, so I can see him again someday."

Jerry Lawler, who held Owen's head seconds after impact, added, "Don't leave home without telling the people you love what you think about them."

Steve Austin and Mark Calloway (The Undertaker) chose not to pay their respects in a recorded segment. (Austin was also one of the only wrestlers not to show for the funeral.)

Although I appreciated the words of many of Owen's colleagues, I still couldn't help seeing the whole show for what it was—a sick way to profit from Owen's death. Indeed, it garnered huge ratings, some of the biggest ever for a Monday night show.

Several days after the accident I received a call from Carl DeMarco, a Canadian WWF representative who also used to double as Bret's agent of sorts. I complained that Vince still hadn't called me, a fact that left Carl admittedly stunned. He made no excuses for Vince and appeared to be disgusted by the news. He said he would contact Vince and find out why.

Twenty minutes later the phone rang. It was Vince.

When I heard his voice I started crying. My voice cracking from a combination of fear, outrage and sorrow, I asked, "Why haven't you called me?"

His response was curt. "What?" was all he could muster.

It was as if he was barely able to tolerate having to listen to me. But if he thought I was a sniveling, weak person who he figured could be easily intimidated, he was wrong. With all my strength I composed myself and repeated in a loud, strong voice, "Why haven't you called me? There, did you hear that?"

He changed his approach immediately. "I didn't call out of respect."

Baffled by his response, I fired back. "Out of respect? You weren't calling out of respect? That's funny, everyone else *is* calling out of respect!"

We argued back and forth. "I think you decided not to call me because you're worried I'm going to take you to the cleaners," I said. "You're just getting yourself ready."

Months later we would discover he had indeed called his lawyer, who was vacationing with his family the night of the accident, to position himself for the likelihood of a lawsuit.

I had to make a conscious effort to calm myself down. I wanted Vince and his entire company to attend Owen's funeral to witness the pain and heartache his death had caused. I wasn't going to achieve that goal if I exploded on him. Regardless of Vince's behavior, I decided I would not let it change me. I would treat him well, just like anyone else. This was not a personality conflict, and whether Vince was a nice person or not was irrelevant. If he did something wrong he would have to stand accountable and adhere to any punishment that might be meted out, but if he wasn't guilty, I didn't want to regret treating him or anyone else in the WWF poorly. From that moment on I pledged to be cordial to Vince, without excusing him of any responsibility.

When I insisted he and the WWF cast attend the funeral he was initially reluctant. However, he quickly realized it was something he had to do.

Once he agreed, I told him I couldn't guarantee how he'd be received by others at the funeral but that I would treat him kindly.

As we concluded our brief conversation, I made it clear he was not to include anything from the funeral on his show. I didn't want him to continue profiting in any way from Owen's death.

"That would be pretty low," I remember telling the *Calgary Sun*.

Early Tuesday evening we got word Owen would be transported home via private jet at the WWF's expense, as per Owen's contract agreement. On the heels of an extremely taxing day that began with the 4 A.M. TV tapings, a limo was dispatched to take me to Calgary International Airport. Bret joined me.

As we approached the airport's private entrance, we were met by a slew of reporters and television crews. The driver of the limo drove past the mob and up to a private area in the hangar. We remained in the car to avoid photographs, but through the dark tinted windows we could see several men remove Owen's body from the plane.

In shocked silence, we watched closely as Owen's body, covered with a Canadian flag, was taken from the airplane on a stretcher and placed gingerly into the hearse. I could see the outline of his face and body through the flag and became weak as my heart raced.

Jay Andronaco, a young man who worked for the productions department in the WWF, was assigned the grisly task of escorting Owen's body back to Calgary. He looked rather shaken. Although attempting to be of help in removing Owen from the plane, he seemed to be more in the way than anything else. He was drenched in sweat and could not control his nervous shaking. I felt so sorry for him.

Moments later we were on our way. We were provided with a police escort all the way to the funeral home, which was half an hour away. News vans followed, as did a media helicopter.

I could tell the news agencies were disappointed, as they hadn't been able to capture much of Owen's arrival. Since none of us got out of the limo, all they could get were shots of our procession to the funeral home. Police officers on Harley-Davidsons surrounded us at all times and traffic was stopped so our small pack of vehicles would not be disturbed. Canadian flags fluttered from the front of our limos. There was a lot of fanfare—I thought Owen deserved as much.

Absolute silence marked the ride to the funeral home as I sat fixated on the silhouette of Owen's frame laying in the hearse ahead. The whole episode felt surreal. I felt like an actor in a play, and this was just some big show everyone wanted a glimpse of.

The stark reality of it was this was my life. And I wasn't at all ready for what was to follow in the days and months ahead. I'm not sure anybody could have been.

We pulled into the private garage of McInnis and Halloway, closing the doors behind us to stymie the hungry media. I got out of the car and walked straight to the hearse, standing directly in front of where Owen lay. It was the closest I had been to him and I wanted desperately to see him for myself. When they opened the doors, he was so close I could touch him. I was expecting to have to identify him on the spot. However, the director was there to greet us and explained they would send for me in a few hours when Owen had been prepared for viewing.

I went home and waited for further notification. For the entire time I couldn't help but wonder what they were doing to him. I had selected one of Owen's finest suits, the suit I liked him in the most, and had given it to the funeral home earlier that day. I sat in my kitchen, tormented by images of him being dressed by complete strangers. I thought of the difficult job that would be considering Owen's size. I was a little surprised the funeral home requested I provide socks and underwear along with the suit. It seemed somewhat pointless to go to all that trouble, but I guess it was standard procedure.

About 8 P.M. I got a call informing me Owen was ready for viewing and that a car was on its way to pick me up. Initially I wanted to go alone, but Bret knew it would be a difficult moment to handle and insisted on joining me.

We arrived at the funeral home and nervously waited for the director to instruct us. Out of the corner of my eye I saw another family sitting in one of the lounge areas, discussing funeral arrangements. Obviously someone they loved had died, reminding me that I wasn't the only one having to deal with death and the hardship it brought. Briefly pulled out of my own despair, I sympathized with this unknown family.

What seemed like a long wait for the director was compounded by the fact I wanted to see Owen so badly. Despite knowing he was dead, I needed to see for myself it was really true. I was growing impatient when the director finally greeted us. He warned me it might be traumatic to see Owen at first and asked if I was ready.

I thought I was. With a nod of my head, he guided us to the viewing room where Owen's body would remain until the funeral. With his hand on the doorknob he asked me a second time, "Are you ready?"

I took a deep breath and signaled affirmatively. He opened the door slowly and as he did I could see the end of the cherrywood coffin I had selected. Then I could see Owen's hands folded one over the other. When the door had been opened completely, at the first sight of his pale, hollowed face, I turned and screamed so loudly that I saw the family in the distant waiting area jump in their seats. Bret clutched me as I tried to run away.

It was too awful. I was horrified. I buried my head in Bret's chest and kept repeating the word, "No."

"I don't want to go in," I said, panicking.

I was using all my force against Bret, trying to get away. Finally, he completely overpowered me and literally wrestled me into the room. Once he got me through the doorway the director quickly shut the door behind us.

As I calmed slightly, Bret slowly inched me towards the coffin. Holding one another tight as we performed a strange shuffling maneuver across the room, we finally stopped a foot away from the man I so dearly thought I wanted to see again.

Although it was frightening to see Owen this way, I looked at him intensely. Lying on his back, with his head resting on a satin lace pillow, he was in much the same position as when he took his final few breaths in the ring.

I was horrified to see it didn't look like him—his features were distorted. The life was gone, like a candle that had been blown out. His eyes were sunk deep into his head. He looked plastic, pasty, just a made-up shell of the man who walked out our door three days earlier. I could see where they had glued his eyes and lips together. I knew it was a common procedure but I didn't like it.

The olive-colored skin of his hands looked nice—he always had a nice complexion—but it was his hair that gave me the most comfort. It was the only thing that truly looked the same. When I looked at how silky and beautiful his blond hair was, I wasn't afraid anymore.

This was the man I loved in life. I didn't need to be fearful of him in death. His appearance would not change the love in my heart, not now, not ever.

I ran my fingers through his hair and held his ice-cold hand. Somehow I hadn't expected rigor mortis to set in already but Owen was rigid and stiff. Bret held his hand too, and patted Owen's arm. "Oh Owen," I said, "look what they've done to you."

Seeing the effects of death on Owen's body was a shock to my system. On top of that, I detected a peculiar, unpleasant odor—a subtle but unmistakable smell. The smell of death.

Bret and I looked at Owen for several intense minutes before retreating to one of the viewing room sofas. Weakened by what we saw, we sat slumped together, speechless.

The room was comfortable, decorated in light red tones. A warm, dim light blanketed the scene while soft, soothing piano music played in the background. Beautiful bouquets of flowers enhanced the room.

I noticed my hair was wet and tangled from the tears I was constantly wiping aside. "What have I done to myself?" I asked Bret.

The words broke the somber silence between us. We started talking about Owen and even laughed a little. It soon became almost comforting to sit in the room with Owen—almost as if he was listening to us.

We stayed for several hours. As we talked I mentioned to Bret how grateful I was he had come with me to the funeral home. Originally thinking I was strong enough to handle it all, I'm not sure how, or if, I could have entered the room if Bret hadn't been there.

Owen was right—I would have support in times of great need. Thank God I didn't have to face this alone.

I don't know how we ended our conversation, but I do know it was close to midnight when we left. Bret continued to stay at my house with me, as I didn't want to be alone. I managed to get about four hours of sleep again that night, which was somehow sufficient to get me through the busy days that followed.

On Wednesday, three days after Owen's death, I had just finished writing a tribute column for the *Calgary Sun* when his luggage arrived from Kansas City.

Staring at his black duffle bag and accompanying carry-on suitcase, I thought of how horrible it was that the bags were still here but he wasn't. It made me angry. I kept thinking that of all the people in the wrestling industry, the best person was killed. How could that happen?

Strange as it may seem, I wanted to see what he packed for his final journey. He always packed his own clothes and I began rummaging through them. I soon turned my efforts towards finding his wedding ring. Police officials told me they didn't have it, which was odd considering he almost always wore it, even occasionally in the wrestling ring.

It was actually his third wedding ring. The first was stolen from the basement of his parents' house. When he lost the second one, he left Oje's birthday party to buy a token band. "I am a father and people need to know I'm married," he said. "I'm not going to be at my son's birthday party and not have my wedding ring."

It was never an issue to me, but I thought it was sweet that even though he didn't like jewelry he thought it was a big deal. With that in mind, I wanted the ring back. I didn't take things out of his bags though. I just skimmed through them.

The first thing that hit me was his smell. He always wore a touch of Caesars for Men cologne, which I'd get my friends to buy when they'd go to Las Vegas. (I still walk by people now and smell his cologne). The suitcase also smelled like "hot stuff," a spray wrestlers use to make them look tanned. In his carry-on bag his clothes were still folded the way I put them in his drawer. There were jeans, a couple T-shirts, a polo shirt and a dress shirt.

In the suitcase I rummaged through personal appearance reports and stacks of airline ticket stubs, memos, awards and credit vouchers. In a side pocket was his coveted Skyguide of flight schedules. On the back of it he had written 12:12 P.M.—the flight time out of Calgary he had switched to Saturday so he could spend more time at home on what was his final day with his family.

Among other things, I found earplugs, his trademark Oakley sun glasses, his black, silver and red wrestling singlet, black boots, a track suit and a gold watch I bought him. I found a tiny pill box with several different supplements and aspirins in it. I knew the police would want the bags back as part of their investigation, so I left it in, knowing he'd have nothing illegal or questionable in it.

In one suitcase pocket there was a purple envelope with his name written on it. Inside was a birthday card signed by Ivory, Debra, Edge, Ken Shamrock and Double J, among other wrestling colleagues. He had turned thirty-four just sixteen days before his death. Next to it was our family's Christmas card photo from two years earlier. The four of us had dressed in traditional garb for a nostalgic photo. He loved the picture and carried it wherever he went.

In his toiletries bag I found a note I had sent with him when he left. It read: "Dear Owen, I think you're really such a wonderful man in every way and I really want to be the best wife to you. Please don't give up on me because I think I can make it. I love you completely, Love Martha."

It referred to a little disagreement we'd had a week earlier regarding the house plans. The tiff had been so unlike us, but we were both stressed. I remember being a little miffed for a few seconds when I saw the tiny, flowered piece of paper had been crumpled up and thrown back into his bag.

We had written each other so many tiny notes over the years, I wondered if perhaps it had become old hat.

I left everything as it was, and at the request of the police I sent the bags back to Kansas City for analysis. It was then they found the wedding ring in one of his pockets. The lawyer delivered it personally to me in a small envelope where it still sits in my bedroom.

My house was still serving as headquarters. Bret, Keith and Alison spent large amounts of time there, which I appreciated. Ross popped in from time to time as well. The Hart house also attracted many, including most of Owen's siblings. I was so busy trying to organize the funeral, uncover the facts of the fall, keep my kids in order and deal with the shock of it all that I barely noticed the newspaper coverage, but several Harts continued to relish the spotlight Owen's death afforded them. However, now their comments were changing to a tone that stopped assigning any blame to Vince.

Bret was the first one to suggest some of his family members were positioning themselves for jobs with McMahon in the WWF. The comments some of the family members were making echoed the stance being taken by McMahon, suggesting Owen was the one responsible and that there was no one to blame. I wondered where they got the nerve to make such remarks before knowing what truly happened.

One of the most sickening stances was taken by Diana's husband, Davey Boy Smith. He told the *Calgary Sun* he'd "fulfill Owen's wish" by attempting a comeback from a back injury in Owen's honor. As part of his veiled attempt to garner kudos and employment from McMahon, he said WWF brass shouldn't take the blame for Owen's death.

"They're running a business and we all do crazy things," said Davey Boy Smith, despite the fact he'd been dumped by WCW while he lay in a hospital bed battling a serious spinal infection. "We're stunt men—we take our own falls, we use harnesses and pulleys. It really makes me mad when they say wrestling's phony."

There was little doubt in my mind all the Harts were genuinely upset over Owen's death, but as the days wore on and the possibility of a lawsuit increased, some of the Hart family members felt threatened—a good job opportunity might be disappearing. It was the first sign of trouble within the family.

I sensed Vince was making them promises left and right to keep them onside. However, if a lawsuit was launched, the Harts probably felt all of Vince's offers would be taken off the table. At the time I was too distracted to care what they were up to.

However, what did bother me was news Diana had a $10,000 US check issued to her by the WWF. After catching wind of it, I confronted her about it and she claimed it was to pay for the brothers' pallbearer suits. I'd later find out the brothers didn't receive any such proceeds. It was clear where she would now stand in any possible legal action against the WWF.

Following our last conversation, Vince began calling me every night, probably on the advice of his lawyers. At first I didn't want to speak to him at all so I cut our conversations short. Then I changed my mind and decided it was best to keep him on the phone as long as possible. I figured he should have to hear how difficult each and every minute was for me.

I described the anguish I felt when I took Oje to see his father lying dead in the coffin. Oje became terrified at the first sight of Owen because he thought Owen didn't have any legs. I had to get the director of the funeral home to open up the bottom half of the coffin so Oje could see his father was still all in one piece. It's funny how a child's mind perceives things.

I told Vince how Athena kept pleading with Owen to wake up. She couldn't understand why her father wouldn't get up. After all, he had always listened to and obeyed her every word.

I felt it important that Vince know the suffering that was taking place in my home—not just my misery, but also that of my children, now and in the future. I knew Oje and Athena didn't totally understand what had happened nor what the repercussions would be. The severity of their loss wouldn't hit them until their daily routine became so glaringly empty without Owen by their side. When Athena grew up and married there would be no father to walk her down the aisle. For Oje, there would be no father to guide him into manhood; no dad in the stands when he played hockey or graduated from high school or university. The thought of it all crushed me.

However, as great as all of our losses were, it was Owen who lost everything. As he told me the last night we spent together, he just wanted to keep living. All the unrealized potential—what a terrible shame it all was. And I was sure to let Vince know, night after night, the measure of heartache and distress we were all living with without our beloved Owen.

I sensed Vince didn't really care. In my mind, his phone calls were just part of a damage control strategy devised by his lawyers. He probably even taped them. Their hope was Vince's transparent show of compassion would lessen the likelihood I would launch a multi-million dollar negligence lawsuit.

Vince kept saying things like, "I will take care of you and your children."

The problem was, this wasn't about the children or me. This was about Owen. The bottom line was that Vince didn't take care of Owen and he knew deep down he'd have to face the consequences. Anyway, I figured Vince's promises to take care of us would only be in effect until the statute of limitations ran out, at which point it was doubtful he'd even remember my name.

I had mixed feelings about speaking with Vince night after night. One part of me felt disgusted with him but another side of me still felt empathy. He was in the worst position of his life and he knew it. Like a trapped animal, he would do whatever he could to escape.

My main mission was to get him to the funeral. I wanted him to see Owen in the coffin—that was very important to me. I figured he didn't truly appreciate what happened to Owen. Vince's wrestling business did a good job of mocking every aspect of life—and death. The Undertaker gimmick was a prime example. The Undertaker played the part of a guy who died then came back to life as a corpse. He often had matches in which he put people into body bags or tried to bury them alive. Even on the night of Owen's death, the Undertaker opened the show with promises of carnage.

My theory was that Vince had lived so long in a fantasy world he had created that, like several members of the Hart family, he didn't know fact from fiction. Owen's death was as real as the pain and suffering I was enduring, and Vince would have to wake up and see it for what it was. Despite the fact he was one of America's wealthiest men and had a great deal of power, there was no way he could weasel out of this one. There was no trap door. Eventually he'd have to face me one on one.

Friday, the day we were to move into our dream home, I drove to the house alone and walked around the empty floors wondering what had happened to my life. So exhausted by it all, I lay down on the floor of my son's empty room-to-be and fell asleep. I don't know exactly why I chose that room. Perhaps it was because at our old house we all seemed to end up in Oje's cozy little room where we would watch TV and play. I didn't wake up until several hours later when I heard a loud pounding on the front door.

It was a neighbor. He must have seen me drive up. Coming to the house of a distraught woman who had just lost her husband, I'm sure he was afraid of what he might have found. I opened the door and explained that everything was fine and that I had accidentally fallen asleep. I could tell he was relieved to hear it.

Returning to the kitchen to collect my thoughts, I couldn't believe that just one week earlier Owen had joined me and the children for our weekly swimming and pizza night. I pledged I would keep Oje and Athena's schedule consistent with what they were used to so I locked up the new house and drove to our old one to pick them up.

When I arrived at the pool that night the look on everyone's face said it all. Shocked at our appearance, several friends met us with hugs. There were many whispers and stares but I managed to keep it together.

We had our regular swim then left. The loneliness I felt was beyond words. All I could think of was that Owen would never join us again. Yet again I couldn't believe our life together was over.

After the kids ate their pizza and went to bed, I went to the funeral home to sit with Owen. I was putting together a video presentation for the funeral, using photos set to the song "Amazed" by Lone Star, a song Owen said reminded him of me. To this day every time I hear it, it's like a message to me to keep going.

I thought that if I was going to present our life to everyone, I wanted to do it in Owen's presence. Although the funeral home had long been closed, I worked into the night with my sister Virginia, assembling the montage of photos.

The director working with us was one of the only staff members left in the building. I told him how much I liked coming to sit with Owen and how I wished I could sleep in the room. I was shocked to hear him say he would arrange it if I was serious. I actually thought about it for a minute before deciding it would be mentally unhealthy.

Throughout the week, time seemed to stand still. The hours on the clock meant nothing to me. I did so much in a day that when evening came it felt as if a week had passed. I had never experienced anything like it. Monday wasn't Monday. Tuesday wasn't Tuesday. No day had felt as it had before. It was all stale, nondescript time. The days all melded into one and before long it was Sunday, the day before the funeral.

I had made arrangements to get my hair and nails done. As silly as it sounds, I wanted to look nice for Owen. I wanted to represent him well. I knew all eyes would be on me just as it had been for our wedding. But this time, instead of kissing him to christen the beginning of our life together, this final kiss would be the last time we'd touch.

Having kept all my appointments, I went home to await the next day—a day I would never forget. I was burying my husband.

My biggest fear was I would live to be an old woman and have to carry this incredible pain to my grave. It had only been a week since Owen had died and the weight of such a burden was already crushing me. Bret was at my house when I got home. Except for the night Owen died, Bret had stayed at the house with me every night since. This night, however, I wanted to be by myself. Bret had been of great comfort to me, but I thought it would be more appropriate for me to stay alone. It would give me a chance to feel it all before I got up to speak about losing Owen.

Bret wouldn't hear of it. He insisted on staying over. I didn't know what his reasons were for not wanting to leave. Maybe he thought I would do something drastic. Deep down I guess I was kind of glad he didn't go.

I barely slept a wink that night. I tried to wake Bret at one point so we could talk, but he was so tired he soon fell back to sleep. My mind was racing, juggling a million thoughts. I was pensive and agitated. My anxiety level was so high that at 4:30 A.M. I went for a long run in the dark. I just ran and ran and ran. I wanted to run away, far from all that lay in front of me.

I was sickened by the turn my life had taken, but as strong as my desire was to abandon everything I ended up right back where I started; at my front door. How could I run away? I had children who needed me, I had responsibilities. I also had to take care of my husband. I had to see to it that he was put to rest properly and that his death was not in vain, that his memory would go on.

As I stood at the bottom of my front steps, I knew the first step would be the hardest. Burying Owen would be the closing of one chapter and the beginning of another. It was not a life I was welcoming, but nevertheless I was stuck with it. The pity of it all was that we spent seventeen years building a life that had just been smashed to pieces, and here I was left to clean up all the debris alone.

Only time would reveal how things would unfold, but it wouldn't be me setting the pace. Time was counting down to the funeral. I entered the house knowing I needed to endure what fate had dealt me and I needed to do it with grace and dignity.

Monday would be the longest, most exhausting day of my life.

THE FUNERAL

"It's a very sad day around here."
—OJE HART

It was 10:15 a.m. and the white stretch limos were parked outside the house waiting to go. My family was downstairs waiting for me, and I was still in my bedroom dressing in black from head to toe. It occurred to me black was the perfect color for mourning because that was how my whole perspective on life felt.

As I placed a black sheer scarf over my upswept hair, I regretted I wasn't able to find a proper widow's hat. I wished I could cover my entire face because I felt so ugly. Inside, I felt the past week had aged me a great deal. I hadn't eaten anything in eight days and it showed. I looked gaunt, and the skin on my stomach was sagging from the sudden weight loss. I was quite frail looking and my chest had almost disappeared. My body, inside and out, seemed like it had gone through a strange metamorphosis.

Here I was, a widow at just thirty-two years of age. It wasn't right. Widows were supposed to be old, not young. This was not the normal cycle of life.

I knew it was time to go, so I exited my room and walked downstairs. It had taken me a long time to get ready, longer than normal anyway, and

I think everyone was worried we would be late. That said, no one wanted to rush me. I was probably stalling myself because subconsciously I didn't want to go.

Earlier, I had dressed the children in their dark formal school uniforms. It was important to me they looked sharp and appropriate. They were relatively playful that morning, but they both had a sense the event was a grim affair. Pam relayed to me a comment Oje had made earlier. "It's a very sad day around here," he'd said. He knew more than his sister about what had happened and was acting very mature for a seven year old. I was very proud of both of them. All week they knew I was immensely distressed yet they never gave me one minute of grief. They both seemed to realize I needed them to behave and that they had to stay in this mature mode for at least one more day. My poor kids. How awful it was they had to experience all this.

We slowly congregated outside, then piled into the limos and were off. The Hart family had also been provided with limos, dispatched to the Hart house. I rode in a limo with Oje, Athena and Bret. Everyone else at my house—mostly my family members and close friends—followed in the remaining limos. The ride was long and silent for the most part as I dealt with a nervousness I had never before experienced. I had never done any public speaking before, and under the circumstances, I was terrified. My one comforting thought was that it would all be over by that evening. Or so I believed.

As we neared the funeral home I reminded the children of how to conduct themselves. I told them they had to be good in order to do their father proud. I said he would expect no less from them. I was a little worried Athena would not respond well to me leaving her when I had to deliver the eulogy. However, I decided I'd deal with that when the time came.

We were only blocks away on Elbow Drive and I could see hundreds of people had already gathered outside the funeral home, as I had invited them to do. While the 300 seats inside were strictly for close friends and family, I didn't want to shut anyone out so I gave the city an open invitation to gather around the funeral home to hear the service. Expecting thousands of fans to attend, city police set up several roadblocks to

Owen Hart, junior heavyweight champion, wearing the International Wrestling Grand Prix belt in 1987.

The first incarnation of Owen Hart's
WWF character the Blue Blazer in 1988.
(courtesy Ted Field)

Owen performing a flying head-butt in Japan in 1988. *(courtesy Bret Hart Fan Club, New Brighton, PA)*

Owen wrestling in Japan in October 1992.

In the wrestling ring on June 26, 1990, in Tokyo Japan, Owen Hart raises his hand with one finger in the air to symbolize his first wedding anniversary. He mailed this photo to Martha, signed "Oje".

(*above*) Owen (left) and Bret
(second from left) on a military
helicopter in Kuwait, April 1997,
on a tour to the site of the Gulf War.

(*right*) Owen Hart at *Summerslam* '93
in Boston.

Owen Hart and Mike Tyson at *Wrestlemania* in March 1998.

Paramedics try to save Owen Hart in the ring after he fell from the rafters of Kemper Arena in Kansas City on May 23, 1999. *(Todd Feeback/Corbis SYGMA/MAGMA)*

The cluttered catwalk at the top of Kemper Arena in Kansas City, which Owen Hart navigated to begin his tragic stunt. *(Police photo)*

The quick-release clip, by which Owen Hart was suspended above the arena, hanging open after his fall. *(Police photo)*

Martha Hart looks to her son Oje (second from right) and daughter Athena (third from right), as they walk to the gravesite in Calgary after her husband's funeral on May 31, 1999. *(CP Photo/Jeff McIntosh)*

Six Hart brothers carry the casket of their brother Owen to his gravesite. *(CP Photo/Jeff McIntosh)*

About 1500 wrestling fans gathered outside the funeral home to listen to Owen Hart's funeral service. *(CP Photo/Mike Ridewood)*

A young girl holds a home-made sign paying tribute to Owen Hart at his funeral. (*CP Photo/Mike Ridewood*)

contain the crowd, and speakers were set up outside the chapel so they could hear the proceedings. I was deeply touched so many people came, as was Bret. Fans and admirers held signs, tributes and flowers throughout the morning, despite cloudy skies that threatened to open up any minute.

I began to get goosebumps.

All eyes would soon be on the children and me. A private person all my life, I found it frightening to be the focus of attention, especially at the weakest moment of my life.

We pulled into the garage of the funeral home and were greeted by respectful staff members. Peeking through an open door into the chapel I could see it was packed. That was when the impact of it all hit me like a ton of bricks. I felt a wave of emotions build up inside of me. I was barely able to pay attention to the director as he explained how he would take us in and seat us.

Meanwhile, three busloads of WWF wrestlers pulled up outside, complete with a black banner reading: "*Owen, you will always be in our hearts.*" One by one the wrestlers and WWF staff members stepped off their buses, wearing suits and black armbands that had "Owen" on them. A host of high-profile wrestlers, including The Rock, Gorilla Monsoon, Sgt. Slaughter, Road Dogg, Chris Jericho, Mankind and Jeff Jarrett, filed slowly into the funeral home while a light drizzle blanketed close to two thousand murmuring wrestling fans outside. They came wearing everything from hockey jerseys and wrestling T-shirts to suits and ties. The odd pocket of fans apparently cheered at the sight of several big name wrestlers before being hushed by respectful elders reminding them it was a funeral, not a performance.

Either way, it was a day of raw emotions. I could hardly blame anyone if they weren't sure exactly how they were to respond to it all.

Many people later commented on the tight red T-shirt wrestler Chyna (Joanie Laurer) wore over her massive, fake breasts. It may have been inappropriate garb for a funeral, but knowing wrestlers the way I do, I knew how hard it was for some of them to step out of character even for such a somber occasion as this. I didn't know Chyna that well, but the few times I met her she was always extremely polite and I wasn't overly concerned by her indiscretion. Owen told me many times she was a friendly person.

When everyone was finally seated inside, we were given the go-ahead to begin what felt like the longest walk of my life. Taking my two children by the hand—Oje to my right, Athena to my left—I walked slowly into the chapel.

Bret led us in, acting like a shield from the hundreds of pairs of eyes that turned towards the children and me. I kept my head down and focused on Bret's feet. I could see all the pairs of legs as I walked by a great many people. I looked up briefly and saw the sad expressions everyone wore on their faces.

I had instructed the funeral home to have Owen in plain view at the back of the room so everyone who entered the chapel would walk by his open coffin. I wanted everyone to see he was really gone. I wanted them all to see what death really looked like, and what had happened to him.

When we approached the coffin I told the children to say a final good-bye to their father and to tell him they loved him. They both did so and touched his carefully folded arm. I don't think they truly understood that they were saying goodbye forever, but I knew they would remember years down the road and be glad they did. I let both of their hands go as it was my turn to say my final good-bye. I reached into the coffin and hugged Owen for what seemed like a long time. I whispered in his ear, as if he could hear me, "Don't worry Owen, I won't let them get away with this. They will pay for what they have done to you. I love you."

Then I kissed him on the lips. Our final kiss good-bye.

Once again I reached for the children's hands and we completed our somber journey to the front of the chapel, where Owen's closed casket would be relocated, adorned with roses. As we filed past rows and rows of friends and supporters, I was careful to keep my head down.

Once we were sitting, Rev. Andrew Risby began the service. I had known Rev. Risby since I was a little girl. He was an Afro-American preacher who conducted his ministry in the church located behind my mother's house. I thought there was no one better to conduct the service than this man. He had performed our wedding service as well as the baptisms of both Oje and Athena. Owen and I both loved him dearly.

Rev. Risby opened the ceremony by introducing country music star Collin Raye. Owen and Collin had developed a friendship largely cultivated by Collin's son Jacob. Jacob was a big fan of Owen's, and Owen really tried to make a big effort for Jacob, often sending him birthday presents. I think Owen even sent him one of his Slammy awards (wrestling's version of a Grammy). Collin mentioned he didn't like his son watching wrestling anymore because it had become so crude, but he didn't mind Jacob watching Owen.

When Collin heard of Owen's passing, he called me right away. When I asked him if he would consider singing at Owen's funeral he didn't hesitate to say yes. He said he hadn't sung at a funeral before, but I reassured him he would be well received. After all, he was Owen's favorite country singer and I knew Owen would have been so pleased. Collin graciously flew up with Jacob and his daughter Britanny at his own expense and I appreciated it immensely.

Collin's voice sounded angelic as he sang two of his own songs "One Boy, One Girl" and "Love, Me." He also sang a stirring version of "Amazing Grace." It was so beautiful. So heavenly.

Following a prayer, the minister introduced me. As I proceeded to the podium, I felt so queasy I thought I was going to pass out. The funeral director took me by the arm to lead me up the three stairs and onto the small stage. As I reached the podium I looked out at the sea of people and took a deep breath to calm myself. I decided I wasn't going to rush. I figured even if I tripped over every word, who would care? Who would judge me? They would all listen respectfully without criticizing. I don't know why, but I took off my scarf. I think it was because I didn't want people to pity me or look at me and say, "Oh that poor widow."

I thought speaking about Owen myself would show I was strong enough to accept my loss even though, at that moment, I was far from that point. Besides, I knew him better than anyone in the world.

I arranged my papers and before I was about to begin I noticed a few faces I wasn't expecting to see. Hulk Hogan (Terry Bollea) was one of them. He was perhaps the most famous wrestler of all time, and Owen truly liked and respected this man, who was largely credited with spearheading wrestling's surge in popularity through the '80s and '90s. I was pleasantly surprised to see him sitting solemnly, dressed in a black suit with his platinum hair poking out of his black bandana. I thought how nice it was that he came all the way from his home in Florida.

I also spotted Alberta Premier Ralph Klein and Calgary Mayor Al Duerr in the large crowd. I noticed Owen's sister Georgia, and my best friend Lisa and her husband Wade sitting to the right of the podium in a private, sectioned-off area. In that same section sat Ed Whalen, the long-time host of *Stampede Wrestling*, as well as his wife Nomi. I also spotted our dear friend Wolfgang Stach, who flew from Germany for the service. All in a matter of seconds, I saw NHL Hall of Famer Lanny McDonald and several other retired hockey players like Joel Otto and Kelly Kisio. Everyone else seemed to blend together.

Apparently McMahon had slipped in a side door with his wife, son and daughter but I didn't see him. Nor was I looking for him.

As I began to speak I was a little worried Athena would cry. I had instructed my sister Virginia to let her join me at the podium if she started to fuss. Sure enough, throughout my speech, I could hear Athena faintly calling, "Mommy, Mommy, Mommy." However, she was not acting out at all so she remained in her seat.

I began the eulogy by stating, "I loved him, I loved him, I loved him," because I felt I loved him at least three times more than most people love their spouses.

I explained how I couldn't sleep the night before, not because I was afraid to get up and speak but because I didn't know how to say good-bye. All week I had been able to visit Owen at the funeral home, and even though he was dead I could still see him and spend time with him. I knew after the funeral I would never see him again and that was hard to take.

I made a point of thanking everyone for coming to celebrate Owen's life because, as awful as it was he had died, he had certainly lived a wonderful life—one worth celebrating.

I told of Owen's school days and of his three best high school buddies, John Esser, Scott Thompson and Darrin Zeer, all of whom were in attendance despite having scattered all over the globe. Each of them turned out to be radically different, but they always maintained their friendship with their buddy Owen. John was an Alberta cattle rancher, Scott was a highly intellectual Ottawa businessman and Darrin was a free spirit who lived in a commune-type arrangement in Los Angeles, writing books on yoga. And then there was Owen the jokester, who turned out to be a wrestler, of all things.

"He was athletic, he was smart, he was cute and he had a car—and that meant something to me at age fifteen," I managed to joke, amidst a speech that had me near tears from start to finish.

I talked about one of my first dates with Owen and how he ran out of gas. I described some of the pranks he played on me. I made it clear Owen was a good everything to everyone—a good husband, father, son, brother, friend and neighbor. He was kind to all. I told of our inseparable attachment and how we hated having to be apart.

I described our life together and the plans and dreams we'd sadly never realize. I spoke of our upcoming plans to celebrate our ten-year anniversary by taking a train ride to Vancouver. I also talked about our plans to return to Europe for our twenty-fifth anniversary, where we'd take the Orient Express and revisit some of the cities and sites we saw as a young couple struggling to get by. This time we'd ride first class.

"We knew what we were doing today, tomorrow, next week, next year, ten years from now ..." I said before having to collect myself. "We had this great life planned, and all we had to do was live it. Now I don't know how to walk over that lonely bridge alone."

Pointing out we were supposed to move into our dream home three days earlier, I talked about reluctantly deciding to move in without him. "Sometimes I feel like a dreamer without a dream. That was our dream together and now I have to move on alone." I told people I didn't want anyone to pity me or my children as we'd rise above this tragedy.

I wasn't going to use my platform as an opportunity to state my plan of action, but I did feel people should be given a prelude of what was to come. I was not going to lie down on this—I would gain some form of restitution for Owen.

"I'm a very forgiving person and I'm not bitter or angry. But there will be a day of reckoning and this is my final promise to Owen," I said, before looking out at the crowd defiantly. "And I won't let him down."

I then read the last letter Owen sent me, just two and half weeks before he died. I felt it acted as a window for all to see just how special our life was together and what we shared in our relationship.

"We're living a dream life," said a portion of the letter, written on hotel stationery May 5, 1999. "When I see so many less fortunate around me on the road, in our families or even on the news, like in Yugoslavia right now, I realize how good we have [it]. As long as we love and take care of each other and our children, we can do anything. We are just starting to reap the benefits of all our hard work. Our new house has been a lot of stress but I'm really anxious to settle down and enjoy it. Sometimes I can't believe all that I have, and as I've told you many times you are the biggest reason my life has gone so well …you keep me always wanting to rush home to see my beautiful family and home."

Thanking my sister Virginia, my mother, Ross, Bret and Alison for their support, I saved my final thanks for Owen, who gave me the best seventeen years of my life. He made me a better person just for having known him.

"I love you Owen, I will love you forever. Thank you."

Somehow I managed to cram a lifetime of love into this thirteen-minute speech that left me feeling all at once weak, exhausted, relieved, heartbroken and proud.

Bret spoke after I did. I asked him to speak because I felt he could best describe the side of his brother that Owen let the wrestlers and the fans see. Bret's part of the eulogy was meant to be light and funny, talking about Owen's humor and practical jokes.

Pointing out his youngest brother was absolutely the best father and husband he ever saw, Bret said it was fitting Owen was remembered for that. He also found it appropriate he be remembered for the harmless pranks that endeared him to everyone.

"He just couldn't avoid a prank and he was always five steps ahead of you," Bret said, relieving tension in the room with laughter. "He could make an outing at a truck stop or airport bathroom into a hilarious moment."

Bret recalled as a kid that Owen often entertained his siblings with a regular wrestling performance he'd orchestrate between their cross-eyed cat, Heathcliffe, and a little stuffed toy. "Owen had this little monkey with real hard plastic hands and feet, and he'd whack that cat on the head a couple times and the cat knew it was game time," Bret said, smiling. "He'd have the cat in a headlock and all sorts of other moves. They were really truly entertaining matches."

Even in the ring Owen would constantly try to crack up his pals, constantly giving goofy thumbs-up to the crowd or administering wet-willies to his Hart Foundation tag-team partners as they entered the ring.

Ross spoke last, on behalf of the family. I knew Ross, the closest brother to Owen in age, would finish up the eulogy on a serious note while nicely describing what Owen meant to his family. It was kind of like a boyhood description from birth of the Owen that his family knew best and missed the most.

"He started going to wrestling at age five, and he always outsold me and the other program sellers and stole the show when he made the lucky ticket draw," recalled Ross. "No matter how good he got you with a prank, you could never stay mad at him because he taught us to laugh at ourselves and never take ourselves too seriously.

"In a profession where there are few real friends, Owen was loved by everyone," concluded Ross.

When Ross stepped down the minister spoke briefly, reminding the congregation we should all be prepared to meet our maker because sometimes that meeting comes without warning. Once he was finished, it was time for Owen's six remaining brothers, Smith, Keith, Bret, Bruce, Wayne and Ross, to act as pallbearers, carrying Owen's coffin to the hearse.

They picked up the heavy coffin and Oje, Athena and I followed behind. As they marched out of the chapel roughly ninety minutes after we entered, I pulled three of the red, long-stemmed roses from the top of Owen's coffin for the children and me to hold onto as a reminder.

Many of the city flower shops reported having difficulties keeping up with the flower orders sent in memory of Owen. The funeral home practically needed a pick-up truck to transport all the flowers from the funeral home to the gravesite. Among the arrangements was a tacky yellow heart-shaped arrangement with the WWF's logo in the middle. Despite the fact it cost $1,000, I ordered the logo—done entirely in flowers—removed, and replaced with Owen's initials.

Everyone else, no matter how well they were known, was discreet in their show of support, but true to form Vince wanted everyone to know what he sent. He wanted credit for his transparent generosity and compassion. It wasn't going to happen under my watch.

The brothers had some difficulty carrying Owen's heavy coffin, and one of them almost fell after tripping over something. Once they got Owen safely to the hearse, they slid the coffin inside. Bret, the children, and I were escorted to the white limo that would follow directly behind. As soon as everyone settled into their assigned limos we slowly formed our procession and began to follow the hearse and motorcade of police officers. As we pulled out, I was once again amazed at the crowd that had gathered outside. We were trailed by close to eighty vehicles. It was a sight so majestic, one broadcaster called it the most celebrated funeral in Calgary history.

As we wound our way to Deerfoot Trail, the main freeway through Calgary, I was shocked to see people were not only stopping, but were getting out of their cars. Some put their right hand over their heart, some bowed their heads, some waved and others doffed their caps in respect. It was an unbelievably powerful show of support. Even on the ramps, which the police escort had sealed off, the people stood outside their cars showing Owen their respect. It was a beautiful sight.

As we approached the entrance of the Queen's Park Cemetery in northwest Calgary, there were more than a dozen motorcycle policemen standing at attention. The most awe-inspiring sight was the appearance of a four star general standing by the seemingly endless line of motorcycle police officers. He was dressed in full uniform and was saluting us as we drove by. I couldn't help but think Owen would be extremely proud of this tribute to him.

We made our way to the spot I had chosen as Owen's final resting place. It was the most beautiful area in the entire cemetery, where a full-grown spruce and a weeping birch provided shade. It also had a lovely, pink-blossomed apple tree like the one in our backyard.

I thought about the trouble I had had getting that perfect spot for Owen. The day I went to the cemetery to pick out the plot, the driver took me to a new part of the cemetery that looked like a construction zone. I started to cry, pointing out I needed Owen to be buried in the nicer, more established part of the cemetery. The director told me they no longer buried people there, but when I persisted he kindly accommodated me, affording Owen the nicest spot I could have imagined. I was glad Owen had such a picturesque resting place.

When we arrived at the plot there was a clean, crisp blue tent and carpeting set up overtop the freshly dug grave. It looked very professional. I noticed the five-foot-high headstone was in place as well, surrounded by a mountain of flowers. I was initially told it would take three months for the stonecutters to finish the tombstone I selected for Owen, but I requested it be done in three days. I knew many of the people attending the funeral would never visit the grave again, and I wanted everyone to see Owen's beautiful monument.

The hearse backed into the spot and the brothers came together again, carrying Owen to the appropriate place. Before leaving the limo, I instructed the children again and confirmed with Oje that once it was folded, he would step up and accept the Canadian flag that blanketed his father's coffin. That flag now sits in a cabinet with the three roses I gathered from his coffin.

Again we followed behind the coffin into the tent. The last rites were read by the minister and we all joined him in saying them out loud. The flag was folded and placed in Oje's tiny hands, while the many red roses were placed back on top of the coffin. I could see down into the dark, six-foot deep hole, and the minister warned me to hold onto Athena, fearing she might slip and fall into the pit. After drawing attention to Owen's headstone, the minister cued the bugle player. As the bugler played "The Last Soldier," Owen's coffin peacefully descended into the crypt where he'd rest eternally. It was devastating to watch him go.

At the ceremony's conclusion, I grabbed Oje's and Athena's hands tightly and slowly led them back to the limo with my head hung low. I didn't want to make direct eye contact with anyone because I wasn't prepared to speak at that particular moment. When we were safely back inside the car I watched all the people through the tinted windows and was relieved I had endured the toughest job of my life. It was over and I was proud of his sendoff. I knew Owen would have been pleased with the way everything was handled.

I asked the limo driver to take me home. I had ripped the back of my dress when I entered the limo and needed to mend it. The kids went with Virginia to the gathering at the Hart house, and I was afforded some time alone to reflect on the week that was. Though tired and drained, I felt a strong sense of accomplishment.

There was food all over the kitchen, on the countertops, on the table and in the living room. I looked at the food and decided that after eight days I needed to eat. My work was done, Owen was at rest and now I needed to stop depriving myself of even the smallest of pleasures, which included eating.

My Asian neighbors, Stan and Ester Oh, had been kind enough to cook Chinese food for the kids every night that week. There were plenty of leftovers so I gathered up some food. It all tasted very good, but I was only able to eat a few bites.

While I was at home, all the other guests were going to the Hart house for the wake. I didn't want to go at all. I didn't want to see all of these people, including Vince McMahon. However, I knew I had to go, if only to say thank you to the many people who traveled so far to pay their respects. My sister was already en route with Oje and Athena, so if for no other reason I had to go to get them.

With my dress repaired, I was off to the Harts' for what I expected would be a short, uncomfortable visit. Upon arriving I reluctantly got out of the car to see hundreds of people in front of the house, mingling and picking away at some food platters. I waded into the fray.

At this point it had already become clear that some of the Hart family members were aligning themselves with Vince and against me. That became very apparent when Owen's sisters Ellie, Diana and Georgia found it appropriate to be hugging, chatting with and milling around Vince McMahon while conveniently avoiding me and my children. It was a powerful preview of things to come.

I wasn't even asking them for their support. I just hoped they weren't working against me. As it turned out, that was too much to expect of them.

I found the atmosphere at the Hart house cold and prickly. I couldn't wait to get out of there. Most of the people who were really close to Owen had opted not to go to the wake. Unfortunately, those were the people I had really wanted to see.

Right away people swarmed me, even those I didn't know that well. Many were from the wrestling world and they informed me they had been good friends with Owen. By all accounts, Owen had good relationships with most of the wrestlers. Jeff Jarrett and the Ultimate Warrior (Jim Hellwig) had had a special place in Owen's heart, but sadly, neither one of them was at the house.

While it was comforting to hear so many of his colleagues pass on their sincere condolences, one wrestler in particular, Chris Jericho (Chris Irvine), showed a degree of class beyond description. Chris had been genuinely touched by his association with Owen over the years. He politely introduced himself, expressed his heartfelt sympathies and handed me an envelope. Upon opening it back at the house, I found a lovely letter and a check for $3,000 he wanted me and the kids to have. Although I did not know this twenty-eight-year-old Winnipeg native (who had trained at the Hart house almost a decade earlier), I knew enough to understand that it was a particularly generous gesture. As he was just a young guy in the midst of breaking through with the WCW, I could not accept the money. However, I called him later to thank him for being the sort of gentleman Owen would've been proud to associate with. He was a little hurt I wouldn't keep the money but I explained to him the gesture meant much more to me than any check could.

I was thrilled to see Collin Raye and his two young children as the parade of well-wishers continued to approach me. When I had thanked everyone I thought I could, I decided it was time to gather up the children and leave.

It was then I saw Vince McMahon waiting in the wings for me. I thought about my promise to him, how I told him on the phone I would be kind and would welcome him. I didn't know what I should say but I knew I had to keep my promise so I allowed him to approach me. I had limited dealings with him in the past and tried hard not to be influenced by all the negative things I had heard about him. I wanted to be fair.

He and his wife Linda, son Shane and daughter Stephanie all walked over for an awkward, uncomfortable exchange. I thanked him and his family for coming and he nervously made some comment about Owen's feet. In my eulogy I had described Owen's funny baby toes and Vince tried to feed off that with a joke none of us were laughing at.

I thanked him again and excused myself when I spotted my old high school teacher, Shirley Schwartz, and her husband, Stan. That was the end of an encounter I had dreaded for days, as I'm sure he had. I later heard he had hired bodyguards to protect him in case I or any other member of the family tried to attack him. If indeed it was true, I wouldn't blame him.

Vince later told local columnist Rick Bell there'd be a day he would have lots to say about all of this but it wouldn't be for a while. I shuddered to think of what that might be.

Soon thereafter, as the Harts gathered for a group photo, I jumped into the limo with the children and drove off with a tremendous sense of relief. I knew one thing I'd never miss was my forced, albeit limited, association with a wrestling world I never liked.

When I returned home I asked my sister if she could watch Oje and Athena while I had a nap. The day had proven to be the most emotionally taxing of my life. I thought I would literally fall over if I did not lie down. The media would be coming shortly and there was no way I could possibly deal with all of that in my present condition. CNN had lined me up for an interview on *Larry King Live* via satellite.

Falling into a deep sleep for close to two hours, Virginia woke me fifteen minutes before I was to appear on a show broadcast around the world. I dozed off again, and she returned five minutes before airtime and brought me downstairs where they sat me beside Bret, fixed me up with a microphone and started the interview before I even had time to brush my hair.

Worried about the legal ramifications of what I might say, Pam Fischer stood behind the cameraman coaching me on what questions I should dance around.

Sure enough, Larry asked if it was safe to assume there would be a lawsuit.

"Well, I don't think it's ever safe to assume anything" was my response, earning a thumbs-up from Pam.

Bret took the opportunity to echo Owen's concerns over the targeting of young wrestling viewers.

"I always thought that it was a shame because I think Vince McMahon almost built his company on the backs of little children. I wouldn't say he exploited it, but he generated a lot of money from kids and then he took this sort of radical direction he's taken. He still sells kids these toys but at the same time the shows are totally unviewable for children."

Within hours of our Larry King interview being aired, McMahon had the audacity to defy my direct request to keep footage of Owen's funeral off his show. Despite promises to the contrary, he opened *Monday Night Raw* with snippets of his wrestlers at the funeral home. It was such a violation. I was devastated. His disrespect had reached new levels.

He later tried to suggest I was so distraught that I might have forgotten about giving the go-ahead to Carl DeMarco. It was pure crap.

Up until that time I had tried so hard to deal with him fairly and with decency, but at that moment it became clear to me my suspicions had been verified—he was scum.

I could see at that point all we had been doing the last week was sizing one another up. Now it was clear the fight was on.

THE LAWSUIT:
The Search for Justice

"And where the offence is, let the great axe fall."
—WILLIAM SHAKESPEARE

Two days after burying Owen, I was on a flight to Kansas City in search of justice. I needed answers.

After sending my children off to school, I was joined mid-morning by Bret, Pam and Ed Pipella, Pam's law partner, for a series of flights that ultimately took me to the city where my husband had died.

Throughout the day I felt like I was traveling into a black hole, especially during the final connecting flight into Kansas City. All I could think about was Owen and how he had been on the same flight ten days earlier with no idea it would be his last. I thought about the arena, the hospital, the morgue—all the places he'd been as part of this nightmare. The overwhelming thought in my mind was that it was here, in a city of strangers, he died alone. He had deserved so much better.

Two weeks earlier I didn't even really know where Kansas City was, and now it represented a place that would forever have a black cloud over it in my eyes. Plagued by a gloom all day long, I just knew that whatever I was embarking on, it was going to be a very long journey. That, in itself, was hard because every day felt like an eternity.

Over the last week it had become inevitable that I would launch a lawsuit so we had set up meetings with three prospective legal representatives to discuss possible strategies. By far the most impressive firm was headed by Gary and Anita Robb, who greeted us at the airport. They had a slew of bodyguards in tow to shield us from the media or distractions of any other kind. We climbed into stretch limos and were taken to our hotel to rest up.

The next morning our entourage of bodyguards, lawyers and officers walked into a large, blandly colored room at the Kansas City police department. All the police officers and paramedics who worked so feverishly in an effort to save Owen's life that horrible night were standing at the back of the room, waiting for our arrival. One by one the chief of police introduced us. After thanking them for their efforts, I hugged every one of them. I was surprised to feel they were all wearing bullet-proof vests. Obviously I wasn't in Calgary anymore.

It was an emotional scene. Several of them almost started crying while telling me how sorry they were and that they had tried their best to save Owen.

Several officers began opening the three brown paper bags of evidence they had. We were warned not to touch anything. They were watching me closely to ensure I didn't grab something and potentially jeopardize the case.

Wearing gloves, several officers laid ropes, rigging equipment and Owen's gear on the tables. It was then I saw the clip—the tiny, teardrop-shaped clip that failed my Owen and ruined my life.

After inspecting it for a few seconds I became enraged. "How could he let them hook him up to that," I spat out loud. Bret and Pam scrambled to calm me.

I quickly realized the blame didn't lie with Owen at all. As ridiculously inadequate as the clip looked, this wasn't his fault. As cautious and careful as he'd always been, he had been given every reason to trust that the riggers were qualified to design and oversee the stunt.

Moving slowly down the table, I came across his wrestling boots with the laces cut up the middle. My God, those boots had just been sitting in my laundry room, getting in the way as they had for years. It seemed I was forever throwing them into the corner. Now here they were on a police table as evidence.

I was disturbed to see some of his gear was bloodstained, something I didn't expect. In fact, for some reason I didn't think he had bled at all—it didn't seem as if he had from the pictures I had seen in the paper.

Throughout these gruesome discoveries, I was numb. The heartache of it all gnawed at me, yet I felt I couldn't allow myself to fall apart. I was in a roomful of men and I didn't want to appear weak. I wanted them to believe I was going to see to it something would be done about this.

Later that night I cried myself to sleep.

Tipped off that I was in town, a horde of reporters and cameramen gathered outside the station. The Robbs had made it clear from day one they wanted little to do with the media until this mess had been resolved in a court of law or otherwise.

Their philosophy was a good one. Once things were said in the press, they couldn't be taken back; they could even give the opposition unnecessary ammunition.

As advised, I made a few brief statements to a *Kansas City Star* reporter before we dashed out of the police garage, avoiding the cameras.

The next day we went to Kemper Arena. I wanted to retrace Owen's final steps with hopes of better understanding what happened that night. The arena's general manager led the way, followed by Pam, Bret, Ed and the Robbs.

I walked up through the seats, climbed a rickety wooden painter's ladder to the catwalk and began traversing the grated metal platform, trying hard not to look down. I'm not afraid of heights but I found it unnerving to walk along a platform that didn't look or feel safe. I noticed my hands were trembling.

I had been warned the catwalk was ill-designed for human traffic and to be careful not to bump my head or trip over cross-beams. Despite such warnings I still found myself bumping into things. I wondered how much harder it would have been if the lights were down and thousands of people below served as distractions. I didn't feel safe.

As I made a series of turns on my way to the center of the arena I looked down into the top of the massive scoreboard and thought how uncomfortable it must've made Owen to be up this high. The roof, which I could almost touch with my hand, was just over 80 feet from the floor.

I walked as far as the railing Owen climbed to prepare for his descent and commented on how close he must have come to hitting the scoreboard. I kept imagining the catwalk opening up beneath me without warning, sending me on a freefall. I wondered what went through Owen's mind when he heard the clip snap open and he began to fall. In the few seconds it took for him to hit the ring he must have known it was hopeless, he was going to die.

How horrible. It was a thought that would haunt me for years. For months I'd lie in bed thinking about it.

They say in situations like that people's lives literally flash before their eyes. If so, I truly believe Owen's last thoughts were of me and the kids.

We stood staring down for close to twenty minutes and I got the feeling they were worried I was going to jump.

Returning to the Robbs' opulent law office, it was clear everything they did was first class. Oriental carpets, bronzed sculptures and chandeliers peppered their spacious thirty-ninth floor perch, which featured pictures of the Robbs with Bill Clinton and Al Gore, among others. They were very well connected. Everything about them and their office exuded wealth and success.

Our initial research told us they were one of the best personal injury firms in the U.S. and that's what I wanted. They had obviously done their research on the situation and provided plenty in the way of information, guidance and support. We soon canceled our appointments with the other two firms.

It was there, in a spacious boardroom highlighted by an impressive library, they presented me with a clip identical to the one we saw in the evidence room. It was made by a British company called Lewmar, and it was expressly designed for the quick release of leisure sailboat masts.

My 229-pound husband had been suspended eight stories above the ground by a flimsy nautical clip. His life—and my happiness—hung in the balance of a four-inch, eight-ounce contraption used by weekend sailors. It retailed for $68.60 US.

What's more, they explained it took only six pounds of pressure to trigger its release, which is roughly equivalent to the pressure required to pull the trigger of a gun.

Holding the clip in my hand, I suddenly felt violently ill. I sprang to my feet and dashed for the door, tripping over Bret's feet on my way. I needed to get to the bathroom.

When I returned ten minutes later my lawyers discussed how disgustingly ill-advised it was to subject Owen to such inadequate equipment. My head started spinning and my stomach churned. All he really had to do was take one breath and the expansion of his chest could have triggered its release.

My God.

If ever there was a doubt I would relentlessly pursue the people in charge of Owen's stunt, it was erased right then and there. I immediately decided to retain the Robbs as my counsel and instructed them to draw up whatever papers they needed to launch the lawsuit. The Robbs agreed to work on a contingency basis while financing the lawsuit, as it would've been difficult for me to afford it.

I flew home that afternoon and spent the weekend communicating with the Robbs and my Calgary lawyers. They laid out all my options for a suit on behalf of me and the children. They also explained all the parties I needed to include in the suit and why.

I instructed them to get the best experts possible, regardless of cost, and to spare no expense in helping me fulfill my promise to Owen. I would do my part to ensure justice was served at any cost. As I stated at his funeral, there would be a day of reckoning.

After plenty of discussion, my lawyers told me the only decision left revolved around whether or not to include Owen's parents in the suit. My lawyers suggested I should.

My gut reaction, however, was to exclude them. I had a feeling that their involvement would open the door for the Hart children to interfere. The lawyers respectfully concurred.

After a sleepless night, I was bothered by concerns I wasn't doing the right thing. Owen was always very protective of his parents and if they were entitled to something I decided they should get it. That's what he would want.

I informed the lawyers of my change of heart and we met with Stu and Helen to explain I would include them as collateral plaintiffs if they so desired. I told them they would have little say in the suit but would also be free of any requirements or stress. There was absolutely no benefit for me to include them, but I knew it was the right thing to do.

Three days later, on June 15, 1999, I walked into a crowded hotel conference room in Kansas City to tell the world I was ready to take on Vince McMahon and a number of other defendants in a fight much more real than anything the WWF had ever staged in their ring.

With Stu, Helen, Bret and my lawyers by my side I looked into a sea of cameras and blinding lights to announce I had filed a 118-page wrongful death lawsuit at the Jackson County courthouse. It listed forty-six counts of negligence against McMahon and twelve others, including the WWF's parent company Titan Sports, the riggers who set up the stunt, the manufacturers of the harness and clip, as well as the City of Kansas City, which owned and operated the arena.

Labeling their conduct, "wanton, willful, callous, reckless and depraved," I spoke of the conscious disregard for Owen's safety that had caused his tragic fall. I lashed out at McMahon specifically for continuing on with the show. I spoke of how the decision was disrespectful but perfectly demonstrated the mindset of McMahon and the WWF.

As for damages, we simply asked for a Kansas City jury to determine what was "fair and reasonable." Given that Gary Robb had already set a U.S. legal record with a $350 million jury verdict in a case involving a helicopter crash (it was later reduced significantly), the media speculated we could be awarded as much as $500 million.

However, my only goal was to have my day in court. I wanted the world to see how negligent and irresponsible those involved with the stunt had been.

With tears in my eyes and a lump in my throat, I spoke of my children growing up without their dad, about my loneliness and how I hoped Owen hadn't died in vain.

"In the efforts to increase ticket sales and market share the WWF has deliberately chosen to promote profit at the expense of the most basic safety of its performers," I said.

"Our legal and factual allegation is that Owen Hart died because this makeshift contraption was totally inadequate for this intended purpose," added Gary Robb, revealing to the press for the first time the quick release clip was intended to rig sailboats.

I pointed out wrestlers had no union of any sort to protect their jobs if they decided to question a promoter's demand. I hoped my suit would help ensure nothing like this would ever happen again. (I didn't realize until I read it in the papers the next day that in my anger and determination I had pounded my fist on the table several times as I spoke.)

Helen spoke briefly of how much she missed her baby of the bunch. Bret lent his support by talking about how Owen was the only good thing about the WWF.

"Neither myself nor any of my brothers or sisters are parties to this legal action—that's the way it should be," said Bret. "This case is about Martha and it's about Owen's children."

Throughout the half-hour press conference a black and white photo of Owen sat in front of me as a reminder this was all about the senseless death of a great father, husband, son and brother.

On his behalf I had just declared war against the WWF and twelve other defendants, who were armed with some of the most powerful lawyers in America. And it felt good.

We flew home immediately following the press conference. That night would be the first I'd spend in my new house.

While I was in Kansas City, Virginia had completed the move. In addition to putting everything away, she also saw to thoughtful details like hanging up pictures and making the beds. For months and months I called her to ask where certain things were and she knew exactly where to direct me. As part of her incredibly sweet gesture, she packed all of Owen's clothes and belongings and stored them in the basement, where they remain relatively untouched to this day. It was a very emotional task for her, as she too loved Owen dearly.

Lying alone in the bedroom Owen and I designed, the sadness of sleeping by myself in our dream house was temporarily fought off by a deep sense of pride and duty. I had launched a lawsuit and had top-notch lawyers who believed in me and believed in my case.

I woke up the next morning, got the kids ready and drove them to school, then went into a cafe to grab a coffee. While standing in line I was shocked to see myself on the front page of the *National Post*. I couldn't believe it was me, I wasn't expecting it. Here I was, just a mother trying to raise my family and live my life, and all this crazy stuff was happening around me. It was like some strange dream.

As I'd soon realize, it was only the beginning of a very nasty, very public war between Vince and me that would soon include a major battle with the first family of wrestling, the Harts themselves.

Several days before we announced the lawsuit, Vince had infuriated me once again. He wrote a letter to the editor, published in the *Calgary Sun*, saying he had gone to great lengths to pay for Owen's funeral. How this could possibly be true was unknown to me since I had specifically instructed the funeral home to ensure that I paid for everything that had to do with Owen and his funeral. Demonstrating his pettiness, Vince virtually item-ized all the things he paid for, including sunglasses, arm bands, lawn cleanup at the Harts and a Canadian flag.

At a cost of $40,000 it sure would have been easy for me to let the WWF pay—especially considering I suddenly had every reason to be worried about my financial situation. I was so uncertain about my future, I even went as far as to call my bank and instruct my advisors to reposition all our aggressive investments into more conservative ventures. However, I wanted it known that I had paid the bill, not him.

The police investigation into Owen's fall determined the quick-release clip attached to the back of his harness had triggered prematurely. Nothing had malfunctioned. It was classified an accident.

However, two weeks after the fall the Kansas City Police elected to open a criminal investigation that revolved around the equipment, the way it was used and whether Owen was properly trained to use it.

"In looking at the rigging, I have a concern whether this was the safest way to do this stunt," Major Gregory Mills told the *Kansas City Star*.

"We went into this thinking it was an unfortunate accident," Mills told the *Calgary Sun*. "We thought we'd get to that conclusion right away, but now I'm not comfortable stopping at this point."

Mills said if indeed their findings warranted an arrest, the charges laid would likely be involuntary manslaughter, which holds a maximum prison sentence of seven years.

I was thrilled at the news. Having seen how ridiculous the nautical clip was, I was encouraged to hear those responsible could face jail time.

That summer my lawyers were busy gathering evidence, talking to stunt and rigging experts and building our case while we waited and waited for a trial judge to be assigned. The phone was constantly ringing with questions or information and the fax machine was constantly transmitting. There was a lot to be done.

I had returned to my route with Canada Post in an attempt to take my mind off the lawsuit, my loneliness and all the stress in my life. I also returned to the pool to teach water fitness. I felt I needed every dime I could to stop the rapid depletion of savings.

Not willing to let the kids suffer in any way, I was determined to work as hard as I could to preserve the lifestyle they were accustomed to. There were piano lessons, art classes, tutoring, ballet, figure skating and private school to pay for, and I would somehow find a way to do it.

So many people in my life, including my co-workers, were doing what they could to help me through this time. I had trouble concentrating, was overly sensitive and moody. I would constantly mis-sort the mail; my fitness classes at the pool had grown stale and boring. Everyone was more than kind to me, and all of them would tell me not to worry about anything. They excused my preoccupation for the time being as they just wanted me to get better.

A lady I worked with named Virginia gave me a book entitled *Healing after Loss*. It was filled with short inspirational, uplifting passages and was the only book I could focus on long enough to read. She wrote inside the cover, "Martha you will sing again!" I prayed it would be true because it sure didn't seem that way.

The stress of it all slowly started to affect my mind and body. One day while working at the post office I had totally convinced myself none of it had happened. Owen didn't die, I wasn't suing Vince, I didn't live alone, I wasn't a single mother—it was all just a bad dream. I had been working at the post office just days before Owen's incident, and in my moment of delirium I turned back time to the Friday before he died. I started to worry I was going crazy and realized I needed to get a grip on myself.

After all, that's what it was all was about: control. Controlling my emotions, my responses and my reactions. Self-control on every level was the key because if I couldn't hold it together how could my kids?

The irony of it all was that everyone thought I was doing just fine. I appeared stoic and hardy, but that was just what I was projecting, not what I was really feeling. Rarely did I cry or show emotion in front of anyone, but when I was alone with my thoughts the tears often flowed.

I thought if others saw what a mess I was I would lose their respect and never regain it. It just wasn't like me to invite others into my personal zone anyway. I liked to solve my problems in my own way—with much introspection.

One of the most important people helping me through it all was my mother. She could always be counted on to help take care of the kids. She also kept a close eye on me.

I recall an incident early in the summer. I saw Owen's handwriting on the kitchen message board and froze in my tracks. It was a surreal reality check and suddenly it was all too much. I started shaking and became short of breath.

My mother looked over, saw something was wrong and rushed to my side. "Martha, you only have to make it through today," she said, bracing my arms and looking into my eyes as they filled with tears.

"I know I can make it through the day without Owen," I said. "But how do I make it through the rest of my life?"

Hugging me in the way only a mother could, she reminded me of the key to it all: "One day at a time." It sounds like such simple, basic advice, but they were words I needed to hear over and over.

The problem with depression was that today was like yesterday and tomorrow would only be a repeat of today. There was no end in sight, and at that time I failed to see any improvements on a daily basis.

Still, I hadn't lost hope, which was encouraging, and was determined to continue pursuing my psychology degree at the University of Calgary in the fall. I had already been attending classes for three years and my mind was set on graduating in 2003. My dear friends Dr. Paul Wellings and his wife Magdi forever encouraged me to continue on at school. I figured with the degree I could get a good job in human resources at Canada Post, feel more secure and be better off financially.

Problem was, upon my return to school I just couldn't concentrate. Still in a constant state of grieving, my mind was also swimming with concerns over the lawsuit, the kids, financial insecurity and my identity. I couldn't retain any information, often prompting me to hurl my books in frustration. I contemplated dropping out.

However, I was buoyed by a surprisingly good test result on my first exam, which gave me hope that I could endure. I was a fairly disciplined person already but I had to further discipline and train myself to close my mind to other things while allowing myself to focus on one task at a time.

Still, I had to keep myself occupied constantly. Throughout the summer I was only sleeping a few hours each night. Refusing to take medication of any sort to combat insomnia, stress or grief, I would often lie awake, staring at the ceiling while awful images entered my mind.

I was predominantly haunted by Owen's fall. In my mind I kept seeing the clip snap open and Owen falling helplessly into the abyss. I wondered, as I did when I had actually been on the catwalk, what went through his mind as he fell those eight long stories.

Over and over again my thoughts would torture me. On a nightly basis I would squeeze my eyes shut and rattle my head back and forth on my pillow as if I could shake out the pictures playing in my head.

And so, after putting the children to bed, I would escape my house for a workout, a run or a movie, or I'd meet a girlfriend at a smoky little coffee shop.

Some nights I wouldn't get home until 2 or 3 A.M. It was then I'd instantly fall into a deep sleep, only to wake up a few hours later to get the kids ready and rush off to work or school. With all the nervous energy I had, staying busy was my coping mechanism. Yet there was still a pall cast over my life.

In addition to my waking thoughts, what also haunted me were the awful dreams I had of Owen. I had dreams in which I knew Owen's fall was going to happen but I couldn't warn him; dreams about his fall and dreams that I was falling; dreams he survived the fall but he was permanently injured; dreams where he came back from the dead and was trying to exist among the living. In my dreams I would tell him that he couldn't keep coming back because he was confusing everyone. In one dream I even told him I was going to have to bury him deeper. I had dreams where he was trying to grab me and he was telling me to come with him. He would say "Martha, come with me, we can work it out."

Occasionally the dreams had nice elements to them, where I got to talk to him and tell him all the things that were happening with the kids and with me. But they were nevertheless heartbreaking because I knew he was gone.

The saddest dream I had came to me during a particularly stressful time in the lawsuit. In the dream, Owen asked me why I was so sad. He started to cry, yet I knew he wasn't sad. I could feel he was completely happy—he was crying for me. I woke up in the dead of night, deeply disturbed and sobbing uncontrollably. Strangely, I haven't dreamed of him since.

Through the first six months living without Owen it was his sheer physical absence that hurt the most: not having him around or hearing his voice, sleeping alone night after night, no more phone calls. After that it was his helpfulness and guidance I really missed. All the details of daily life were wearing on me.

I soon started having serious problems with Oje. He began misbehaving at school. He seemed fine at home, perhaps because he didn't want to upset me, but his behavior was beginning to affect his performance at school. His teachers contacted me, concerned that this once happy, playful, popular child was becoming somewhat anti-social. Oje had always been a polite, well-mannered boy, so his teachers were increasingly alarmed at his sudden indifference.

Immediately, the school and I took major steps to help Oje deal with his pain and grief. We set up an intense system of extra work and daily monitoring, and we removed privileges, allowing Oje to be rewarded for any positive changes. As hard as it was, I refused to let him use his father's death as a crutch in any way. It was a very scary period for me but over time he once again became the happy young man who will forever make me smile.

Athena had her own share of troubles. She started experiencing night-mares and night terrors and would wake up almost every night screaming uncontrollably. I didn't know what to do with her because half the time she wasn't even awake. Athena also kept talking about her dad, asking when he would be coming back or when he would be waking up.

"Why was he in that funny bed?" she would ask, referring to the coffin.

One of the most important parts of my day throughout the summer included my daily visits to Owen's gravesite. It was there I'd sit in my car or lie by his grave talking to him in my head. The serenity calmed me.

Eventually I bought a park bench I could sit on, and it was there I forged a beautiful relationship with a lovely old man named Doug Blake. Doug, who was in his eighties, had recently lost his wife. She was buried next to Owen. I often picked up coffee and muffins for our regular "meet-ings," during which we'd talk of our dearly departed spouses and cry on one another's shoulder.

Midway through the summer Gary Robb flew to Calgary to update Stu, Helen and me on the progress of the lawsuit. It was then he fully explained the importance of putting a damage figure on the table to trigger pre-trial interest on any award. More importantly, he explained the defense lawyers would rely heavily on delay tactics, and such a number would serve to deter such maneuvers. As trial lawyers who fully intended to see this through in a court of law, he explained it was still prudent to trigger that interest.

However, I refused. This wasn't about money, it was about justice. Besides, how could I ever possibly attach a dollar figure to Owen's life?

I told him I didn't care about the money. When I lost Owen I lost everything, and I felt those responsible should be brought to justice through trial, not through some settlement.

We knew the WWF's lawyers would try testing my resolve by delaying as many things as possible so it came as no surprise the first judge assigned was struck by the defendants, as was their right. The second judge selected had actually attended the WWF show Owen died at and had to resign.

The wait continued.

Throughout all this, the person I leaned on the most was Bret—and he just so happened to be leaning quite heavily on me too. From day one he was my biggest supporter, standing by my side at all times and helping any way he could.

At the time of Owen's death, Bret's marriage to Julie had dissolved. Despite being divorced he was entertaining ideas of reconciling. He was a caring dad and missed being close to his four kids. He had been given time off by the WCW to cope with Owen's loss and was very confused on several fronts.

Neither one of us knew where our lives were going at that point, and we spent countless hours, days and weeks together talking to one another about some of the problems we had in common.

Being with him was comforting, as he was the only person that didn't treat me with kid gloves. For a long time after Owen died I knew exactly what everyone was thinking when they spoke to me. I could feel their sorrow for me.

Bret, on the other hand, treated me normally. He had his own problems, and through talking about them he took my mind off my issues. Our friendship grew.

Throughout the summer though, he was a man in the middle of an ugly war brewing at the Hart house. Days after Owen's death, he began feeling the wrath of sisters Ellie and Diana, who resented the fact he was supporting me in my fight against the WWF. While both sisters were in the midst of horrific marital problems, they were nonetheless furious with Bret's stance because it threatened to bite the WWF hand they hoped would feed them. Diana's husband Davey Boy was an aging, unemployed wrestler, and Ellie's spouse, Jim Neidhart, only had a low-level wrestling gig far from the WWF's spotlight. Neither had many options outside the WWF and both sisters were completely dependent on their husbands' earnings.

With hopes of helping their husbands' careers, both sisters made it clear from the outset they would do whatever they could to disrupt my lawsuit—even though it included their parents and would affect their niece, Athena, and nephew, Oje. Ellie later admitted as much.

They left nasty, hurtful messages on Bret's answering machine with regularity, telling him he was a self-centered egomaniac who was supporting me simply because of his vendetta with Vince. I had learned over the years how awful both of them could be, but I couldn't understand how they could be so terrible to one brother after another brother had just died.

It was clear they couldn't see past their own miserable lives to realize the suit wasn't about them. It was about Owen. It was about justice. It was about right from wrong.

Bruce also had harsh words for Bret, as Bruce was still clinging to the hopeless belief the WWF would hire him on in some capacity. He and Ross were in the midst of trying to resurrect *Stampede Wrestling* in Calgary following a seven-year hiatus and were working to use some of the WWF's talent for upcoming shows.

Because so many in his family were such backstabbers, poor Bret didn't know who he could count on. Siblings like Ross, Georgia and Smith were suspiciously silent while they maintained close ties to Ellie, Diana and Bruce.

I appreciated Keith, Alison and Wayne who elected to stay out of the politics of it all, as I knew they were in a tough spot having to choose sides. The Harts were being torn apart on an issue that should have united them.

Earlier in the summer, Smith made his own selfish stand by approaching my lawyers with an insulting, yet laughable, claim that he had lost an asset in Owen. It was so pathetic I hardly had time to get angry about it.

Regardless of their thoughts, all I asked was that they didn't work against me in any way. They all had a right to employment and Lord knows I'd never begrudge someone for trying to make a living. But they could have worked for Vince without having to comment on the issue. Instead, several opted to sell me out.

Hurt immensely by the destruction of what was left of his family, Bret stuck with me through it all. It pulled Bret and I closer together and I was grateful he was able to give me a voice at the house, albeit one that often got drowned out by shouts. Stu and Helen respected and listened to Bret.

Angry, confused and broken-hearted, Bret and I were thrust together in a way neither one of us could have imagined. Different in so many ways, we never would have gravitated to one another otherwise. We were both suffering from grief. We both missed Owen and were each other's link to him. I was his best friend at that time and he was mine.

And while our united stand was crucial to our recovery and sanity, we became almost too dependent on one another. That quickly changed as we both turned our focus on regaining control of our own lives independently.

Still, his support with the lawsuit was unwavering and for that I was, and am, thankful.

On July 27, Vince McMahon did his first television interview since Owen's death two months earlier. Appearing on TSN's *Off the Record*, Vince finally addressed the widespread criticism following his decision to continue the show Owen died at.

"Quite frankly, for better or for worse—and people are going to think a lot less of me for saying this—at the time we didn't think of not continuing," said McMahon. "There was no disrespect intended, although there may have been from your standpoint."

Vince went on to say he chose not to announce Owen's death to the live audience for concern over how fans would have felt or what they would have done. He said he didn't blame the Canadian public for seeing him as the bad guy in all of this and that he didn't want to get back into the debate over funeral expenses. "I'm at a disadvantage," he said. "Naturally the sympathy is justifiably with Martha."

Vince then took dead aim at Bret. He spoke about a meeting he'd had with Bret at Owen's funeral. "I couldn't believe what I was hearing," said Vince. "I'd ruined his marriage, I'd ruined his career. All he wanted to talk about was himself, nothing to do with his brother. It was like looking in the eyes of a skeleton in some respects. It seemed like he wasn't human."

Then came the ultimate insult to me.

"I would suggest one of the reasons there is a such a bad P.R.-type situation here really doesn't rest so much with Martha as it does with Bret," said Vince. "In a vulnerable situation as Martha was, I credit Bret for being in her ear, and I just don't know that some of the actions taken by Martha and the family don't solely rest on Bret's shoulders."

It was a ridiculous accusation, as I didn't need anybody in my ear. I knew exactly what I was doing. My husband had been killed and those responsible needed to be held accountable. No one in the world needed to tell me that.

Several days later, Jackson County prosecutor Bob Baird announced criminal charges would not be laid against the WWF, the riggers or anyone involved in the botched stunt.

I was disappointed, but the crown prosecutor explained to me that while he certainly could build a criminal case for gross negligence, his chances of successful prosecution were not high enough for the state to incur the cost of the case.

He reassured me his decision would have no bearing on my civil suit. Criminal charges revolved around intent to harm, while the civil suit was based on negligence and damages.

I thought right away about the O.J. Simpson case and how Ronald Goldman's father worked so hard to finally obtain civil justice despite the fact the suspected killer escaped prosecution. He won, and I was determined to win too.

Then came news Davey Boy was indeed being rewarded for Diana's tireless efforts to defend the WWF. After being flown first-class to New York City by McMahon, Davey and Diana were taken by limo to the Waldorf-Astoria where he was signed to a five-year, multi-million dollar deal.

I couldn't believe it.

Prior to hearing the news, Bret took a pretty good jab at Davey in his weekly column in the *Calgary Sun*. "Saw a strange sight the other day," wrote Bret. "Dogs rolling in manure and loving every minute of it. For some reason it made me think of how the British Bulldog will do anything to work for the WWF."

In a subsequent column Bret took another jab. "There were these four little pigs in the pig races. The guy there told me they'd sell out their mothers and brothers and sisters to the slaughterhouse just for those mini donuts. Kind of reminds me of, er, I won't go there this week."

Upon announcing his return, Davey said he couldn't figure out why Bret attacked him, informing columnist Rick Bell, "He even called my wife [Diana] on the phone and said, 'If I see you on the street, I'll run you over, you——.'"

Things were getting so nasty, and we didn't even have a judge selected or a court date set.

In addition to all of this, I was convinced the WWF was watching me. One day I was followed for quite some time. After I pulled into my driveway, I jumped out of my car and went to confront the men. They sped away.

My lawyers had warned me that someone might be hired to follow me to see if I had started dating anyone. My lawyers stressed the importance of not seeing anyone, to the point that they made me sign a document stating I'd remain single. It was easy to sign, as I had absolutely no desire to pursue any relationships. In fact, I was shocked and repulsed by a number of advances, since I'd never experienced them while with Owen.

Although unnerving, being followed didn't surprise me much. The WWF's lawyers made it quite clear they would do whatever they could to improve their case. They requested all of Owen's medical records to see if he had any ailments that might have contributed to his fall. They also wanted my records, presumably to see if I was in good enough health to withstand a lengthy legal battle. They wanted tax receipts for the last ten years and bank account statements.

They tried everything they could. I couldn't fault them for it, though, because they were just trying to fight for their client.

Try as they might, my friends and my family could not comfort me completely because they couldn't truly understand what I was going through. My best friend Lisa Hartzell, who is a flight attendant, would try cheering me up by taking me on great little trips from London to Paris, Houston to L.A., or even just to Toronto for a day. My sister Virginia would try anything from gifts to dinners, and my mom would clean my house from top to bottom while helping with the kids. However, such kind gestures only served to divert my mind for small periods of time.

I felt guilty I wasn't getting better fast enough, so in the late fall I decided I would participate in a grief group at the Rockyview Hospital, which I still attend.

I was willing to do the hard work or whatever it took to get through it all. It was helpful to be with people in a similar situation. I did feel I was at a bit of a disadvantage, though. Compared to others, I felt delayed in my grief—the lingering lawsuit would not allow me any closure, which was frustrating. Oddly enough, the group sessions left me as empty as they did fulfilled, something I still can't explain.

Despite everything, the grief and stress were getting to me. I was agitated and restless all the time. It was like my mind was on fast-forward and my body needed to catch up. I had been a runner for years but now I felt the need to run nonstop. I would run morning and night, and sometimes several times in between. Depending on my day, it afforded me the flexibility to either do some hard thinking or clear my mind.

I was obsessed with running. My mind was constantly in a state of exhaustion and I needed my body to be the same. I think it also helped me release a lot of my anger and frustration, two emotions I rarely showed.

However, even running started taking its toll on me. The arches in my feet were falling, my toenails were turning black and my calf muscles were so knotted up I could hardly walk. Yet, despite ligament problems in my left knee, I still ran. Maybe I just wanted to run away.

I also developed eating problems for the first time in my life. I had long maintained a healthy, well-balanced diet but suddenly I would go on binges where I couldn't stop eating.

I chalked it up to being lonely and trying to fill the emptiness somehow. I monitored the problem closely, and by using good nutrition as my guide I was able to ride it out without any weight gain.

Other times I'd go a week without eating much at all, which affected my circulation. My hands would become bluish due to the lack of protein in my system.

One of the worst side effects grief had on me was my trembling hands. It got to the point they would shake even when I felt I wasn't under stress. It was embarrassing. It always made me look nervous, as if my nerves were just frazzled and I couldn't hide it. I wasn't frightened by it, just annoyed.

However, nothing annoyed me more than the battle now raging around me every day.

While the family was busy taking pot shots at one another, the WWF fired its first legal salvo at me in the fall of 1999 by way of a countersuit. Their claim was that I had breached Owen's contract, which stated any legal action taken against the WWF must be litigated in its home state of Connecticut (where punitive damages weren't awarded, as it turns out, thus generally making awards much lower).

While Owen, not I, had signed his contract, their argument centered on the notion I was bound to his contract because I had acted as administratrix of his estate, therefore taking on his responsibilities. Did that also mean I'd have to get in the ring to fulfill the remaining years of his deal, too?

Our contention was the contract was terminated when Owen died. Further, the contract did not cover the event of negligence outside of the ring by the defendants that precipitated Owen's death. As Pam pointed out to the media, the accident happened in Missouri, we filed the suit in Missouri and it should therefore be heard in Missouri.

While it seemed a ridiculous motion, it threatened to wipe me out financially. I knew they'd come back swinging and sure enough their gloves were now off. They were suing me for $75,000 as well as all their legal fees, which would ultimately be in the millions of dollars. My guess was that $75,000 represented the expense of flying WWF talent to the funeral.

My lawyers had been nervous about telling me all this. When I asked if there was any merit to the motion, they said that while they were confident it would be unsuccessful there were no guarantees in law.

It forced me to protect myself by hiring one of the best law firms in Connecticut—Zeldes, Needle and Cooper—at considerable expense. The motion likely wouldn't be heard by a judge until the summer of 2000 but it hung over me like a dark cloud.

Now the attacks were coming from absolutely every angle imaginable. Owen had been taken from me in such violent fashion, and now everything he and I worked for could also be taken away.

The family in-fighting had now become relentless. The kids put increasing pressure on Stu and Helen to agree to compensation out of court.

Despite the fact we had not received a settlement offer of any kind, Linda McMahon told CNBC "[the WWF] would love to be able to settle and work through this ordeal with Mrs. Hart … in a way that will take care of her and her children for the rest of their lives."

One WWF spokesman, Jim Byrne, went one further, suggesting my lawyers had "put their own interests ahead of the family." It was ridiculous posturing.

Their comments came days after World Wrestling Federation Entertainment Inc. had raised $170 million US on its first day of public trading on the Nasdaq. Shares in the company had risen 53 per cent that day, giving the company a market value of $2.3 billion, of which Linda and her family had a stake worth $1.9 billion. Of course it would be easy for them to buy me off.

I wanted something more however—accountability. We had heard all their "whiskey talk" about taking care of me, but the point I couldn't stress enough was they hadn't taken care of Owen. And for that I intended on following this through.

I opted not to respond to their comments, however, leaving my lawyer Ed Pipella to shoot down their claims.

"They're trying to make things more difficult," Ed told the *Calgary Herald*, pointing out the WWF had filed a counter-suit against me. "That's hardly the way (Linda McMahon) suggests that Martha will be looked after."

There were days I never thought I'd get out of this war. I figured this could all go on for years, and I knew that's what they wanted. They had tried intimidation and media tactics—who knows what else they'd try to deter me in my quest. On many days it just seemed so incredibly hopeless, but I felt such a sense of duty to Owen to fight on.

In early November a touching documentary about Owen was released by filmmakers from High Road Productions. After producer Paul Jay failed to come through on a promised public premiere, I scrambled to invite family and close friends to gather at a quiet local nightspot for a private screening and celebration of Owen's life. It would later air on local TV as well as A&E.

I was happy with the hour-long tribute. I wanted people to see Owen for who he was as a person, not as a wrestler.

I was especially touched by a comment from Mick Foley (a.k.a. Mankind). It did well to sum up Owen's life.

"Owen definitely had his priorities," said Foley. "Some people say they live for wrestling. I think they have it backwards. Owen had his priorities in the right order because he lived for his family and just wrestled to live."

Through all the darkness, confusion and conflict at that time, at the very least we had solidarity among Owen's parents, my lawyers and me.

Or so I hoped. Whatever solidarity we had didn't last.

My greatest fears were realized in November 1999, when Helen phoned my lawyer, Pam, to request all of our legal documents. Although she was certainly entitled to see everything we were doing, the red flags went up immediately. My lawyers suspected right away she was talking to outside counsel with an eye on settling.

Stu was eighty-five at the time and rapidly losing his faculties. Helen was seventy-seven and in poor health. It was obvious neither one of them would have made such a request had it not been for Ellie, Diana and Bruce. To my knowledge they were nagging their parents on an almost daily basis to settle with Vince out of court.

In fact, as we later learned in a sworn deposition by Helen, Ellie was actively working on behalf of the defense. I suspected and feared that McMahon and the WWF were encouraging Ellie and Diana to have Stu and Helen settle or fire our counsel. Months later we'd find that to be the case.

"I believe that Ellie is suffering from serious domestic, personal and financial problems, which are adversely affecting her judgment and that she is intent on settling an old score with her brother [our son] Bret," said Helen in an affidavit months after the fact.

"She has said that she will do anything necessary to assist [WWF lead counsel] Jerry McDevitt and Vince McMahon in this lawsuit against Martha, even if it means hurting us. My husband and I do not believe it is right that Mr. McDevitt and Mr. McMahon would try to communicate to us about the lawsuit through our daughter, Ellie. We wish these efforts would stop."

In a desperate effort to help her wrestler husband, Jim, keep his job with the WWF, Ellie was being "manipulated" by McDevitt (the WWF's lead counsel) and McMahon into pressuring the parents to "let Vince take care of us."

I understood that if one party, namely Stu or Helen, settled, this would prejudice the other parties' claims, including mine and the children's. In effect, Ellie's interference threatened to erase my lawsuit.

Although Oje, Athena and I stood to gain the lion's share of any settlement they might strike, this wasn't about money. I wanted our day in court. Justice needed to be served.

Upon hearing of Helen's request, I exploded in the lawyer's office. I knew from day one it was going to be a mistake to bring Owen's parents on board. I just knew it would be nothing but trouble.

Ellie was complaining to Pam about the money. Her selfish concerns revolved around the possibility that Stu and Helen could die before the case was settled. She knew if that were to happen, the Hart kids would get none of the money the parents were sure to gain from the lawsuit.

Bret tried to quell the situation by offering to give his parents whatever money they needed to make ends meet until the suit was resolved. But once the trust was broken, I knew we would have a hard time keeping Owen's parents onside. I had invited these people on with all the right intentions and they threatened to screw it all up based on their children's greed.

The battle lines within the Hart family had been drawn. On one side stood Bret and I working hard to ensure justice was served on Owen's behalf. On the other stood Ellie, Diana and, to a lesser degree, Bruce. Somewhere in the middle stood Georgia and Ross, who claimed to be neutral while maintaining close ties with the troublemakers. I couldn't trust them because they wouldn't take a firm stand either way.

Georgia had been a friend of mine for years, which made her stance all the more disappointing. I think her reluctance to support me revolved around the possibility her son Ted would lose any chance he had at wrestling in the WWF. He had been signed by them while still in his teens.

In her deposition, Georgia said she had no concerns with Ted being employed by them. Being a mother myself, I was alarmed by such a stand. I wouldn't want my son working for a company that obviously had little regard for the safety of their employees.

Keith was silent. He always tried to be the peacekeeper. However, a year later he got fired up and blasted Ellie and Diana for their conduct. Keith had been close to Owen, and he cried for his little brother every time he saw me that summer. He was also old enough to remember Owen as a child and would get teary-eyed whenever he saw Oje, who bears a striking resemblance to his dad. Smith was Smith, keeping to himself, while Wayne and Alison remained silent but supportive.

Other than Bret, no one had the guts to tell Ellie, Diana and Bruce they were being very selfish in their approach. Despite the horrible things his siblings were saying and doing to him, Bret continued going to the Hart house to reassure his parents they needed to stay the course and let our lawyers handle everything.

Poor Stu and Helen, whose health was suffering from the stress of it all, were caught in the middle of a firestorm. The stress had little to do with our case—my lawyers and I had that under control. It had everything to do with the nagging kids.

Stu and Helen's hearts had been broken by Owen's death and now they were understandably torn. Who should they listen to?

Even though my kids and I were the biggest victims, Stu and Helen heard the plight of their desperate, money-strapped children on a daily basis. I knew Oje, Athena and I mattered little to Stu and Helen compared to their kids, so I counted heavily on Bret's calming presence to ensure they remained onside.

Realizing any chance of obtaining justice could be ruined by all the meddling going on, I asked my lawyers if anything could be done to ensure whatever money the parents might be entitled to would still be awarded to their estate in the event of their deaths.

In an effort to keep everyone as united as possible, my lawyers composed an allocation agreement document to be signed by all ten of the Hart siblings. It was designed to preserve the share Owen's parents would be entitled to in the suit even if they died before the case was resolved.

To my utter shock, Bruce, Ellie and Diana refused to sign it.

This led me to believe they saw greater benefits for themselves from the WWF if they did their part to hamper our efforts to continue towards a trial.

Everyone else was on board. Bret signed it, but announced he wanted no money out of the deal. He simply wanted to show his support.

The WWF's lawyers were still working hard to get the case heard outside of Jackson County. They suggested the Kansas City police were not being impartial.

Through the WWF's maneuvering, the Supreme Court of Missouri eventually went outside the district, appointing Judge Douglas Long. In early 2000—seven months after we launched the civil suit—we were set to meet with him.

He set the trial date for February 5, 2001, which opened the doors for us to start deposing a list of close to 200 witnesses, experts, family members and anybody else who could shed light on how negligent the WWF and others involved had been. My lawyers were looking for facts to support a claim to justify punitive damages and I wanted the facts to disclose what really happened.

Although I had certainly made progress in terms of healing, every day still felt empty. Although I was happy we finally had a court date, it was also somewhat depressing as I knew my whole life would be put on hold for another year.

Helen was the first person to be deposed by both sets of lawyers because we were worried about her health. It was during the second of her two depositions that I first laid eyes on the fleet of more than a dozen lawyers working for the defense. At first sight the WWF's lead counsel, Jerry McDevitt, didn't strike me as the type of polished lawyer I expected to battle in such a high-profile, high-stakes case.

He was a tall, thin man in his fifties who wore glasses, and I assumed his unhealthy, hard-living look stemmed, in part, from his frequent cigarette breaks. His suits were slightly outdated, his tousled gray hair rested on his collar and he had an untrimmed mustache. He didn't fit the profile of the typical lawyer.

Despite my first impressions, however, he proved to be a bright, highly skilled and dangerous attorney. It was he who delivered concrete evidence during Helen's second deposition that made me realize just how dirty this fight would be and how far some of the siblings would go to chop us at the knees.

Shortly into the gathering, McDevitt made a deliberate move to drop several sheets of paper on the table in front of us. He might as well have dropped a bomb.

My lawyers and I were shocked to see he was in possession of our allocation agreement as well as other confidential documents concerning my retainer agreement with counsel. We had no idea how long the defense had had them nor what other documents they might be privy to.

The only thing we knew was that the one document had obviously been taken from Stu and Helen by Ellie and sent to McDevitt. The allocation agreement was sent to him by Diana's fax machine.

"I did not originally know how WWF counsel got copies of confidential documents which I kept in my home concerning the case—I thought I kept them in a secure place," said Helen in an affidavit later that year. "I now know, and Ellie has admitted, that she took these confidential papers and copied them without my or my husband's knowledge or consent and passed these papers on to the WWF lawyers. I do not condone this conduct. We are taking steps to put further papers under lock and key but I do not know what other confidential papers Ellie may have copied and supplied to WWF lawyers."

My lawyers immediately cried foul, charging it was unethical to possess such documents without informing us immediately. McDevitt and his team responded by accusing my lawyers of similarly underhanded tactics concerning the allocation agreement. They contended such a document was designed to buy favorable testimony from the siblings in exchange for the possibility of monetary gains.

I was shocked at the implication. It was clear to me none of the Hart siblings had any pertinent information to offer the case. They weren't there the night Owen died, so why would I try to buy "favorable" testimony from them?

The boardroom scene soon deteriorated into a shouting match and we wound up walking out of the deposition that day.

Never-ending objections forced lawyers to call Judge Long for rulings so often he wound up assigning another judge to be present at all our depositions, just to make sure they were completed. So nasty were some of the exchanges between counsel, we needed constant supervision.

Soon after the defense questioned the allocation agreement we rescinded it to show just how good our faith was and that our intentions regarding the allocation agreement were pure. Everyone who signed the original agreement gladly signed on to rescind it.

Nonetheless, the allegations made by the WWF had significant consequences. The WWF wanted to cross-examine my lawyers about the allocation agreement and to cross-examine the Hart children. The purpose was to try to demonstrate improper conduct by my lawyers and infer there was tainted evidence from the Hart children. While we didn't believe any of the allegations would be sustained, they had to be vigorously defended.

It was clear at this point the WWF was relying heavily on trying to muddy the waters and grind me down by delaying and rescheduling as many things as possible. I tried not to let it get me down. I had to remember what this case was really all about: a 229-pound man being dangled eights stories above the ground with a nautical clip designed to release on six pounds of pressure.

Soon after the depositions restarted I regained plenty of confidence. We unveiled hordes of evidence to support our gross negligence claim.

THE INVESTIGATION

"One of the greatest delusions in the world is the hope that the evils of this world can be cured by legislation."
—THOMAS REED

Having rigged various stunts for the WWF for close to three years, Joe Branam knew Vince McMahon was more than willing to put his wrestlers at risk.

As president of his own theatrical rigging and supply company for more than twenty-one years, Branam was as qualified as anyone in the world to determine what was and wasn't safe in terms of rigging flying stunts. He had done work for Disney and MGM Grand in Vegas and had rigged for everyone from the Rolling Stones, Elton John and Ricky Martin to Robin Williams, 'N Sync and Boyz II Men.

As part of his relationship with the WWF, Branam had "flown" The Undertaker, Shawn Michaels and even McMahon himself in the past, using locking carabiners, as was the industry's safety standard. However, on at least three separate occasions, the WWF's Steve Taylor had told Branam that McMahon wanted quick release snap shackles for the stunt. In fact, Branam recalls they seemed "almost obsessed" with the idea. They argued it would look better for the camera.

Branam repeatedly shot down the idea, telling them in no uncertain terms that he would never use such devices for humans. They simply weren't designed for such a purpose. It was far too risky. His only use for snap shackles in the stunt game revolved around dropping curtains or other props, not people.

In fact, the sole purpose of using the device would be to save less than two seconds on such a stunt. That's exactly what the WWF was looking for—quick release for the cameras. They didn't want anyone fumbling around in the ring, trying to unhook themselves while precious time ticked away on their broadcast.

In November 1998, Branam's right-hand man, Randy Beckman, had rigged up Owen for a "fly in" in St. Louis, Missouri. It was there Owen was lowered into the ring area by way of a locking carabiner, flapping his arms, only to be left hanging and beat up by several wrestlers before being lifted back to the rafters. The setup provided safety backup—redundancy as it's known in the stunt world—and did not require Owen to disconnect from the rigging at any time.

In St. Louis that day Beckman was shocked to have to seek out Owen in the dressing room hours before the event and inform him of a stunt Owen claimed to know nothing about. It was a scenario virtually unheard of in the stunt industry.

Beckman characterized Owen as cooperative and pleasant. Owen was willing to do a rehearsal in spite of tremendous fear. He white knuckled his way along the catwalk, gasping for air as he tried calming himself. Beckman told Owen he didn't have to do the stunt if he was scared or uncomfortable, but Owen felt that by not doing it, he risked losing his job.

Later that night, when Owen was being lowered during the show, Beckman recalls Owen saying in all seriousness, "Don't drop me, I'm scared."

WWF stage manager Tim Rogers witnessed that afternoon scene of extreme discomfort, which Beckman later relayed to Steve Taylor, VP of Event Operations.

In May 1999, the WWF contacted Branam's company and asked for a quote on another stunt involving Owen in Orlando, Florida. The bid of $5,000, the same price charged for the identical stunt in St. Louis, was rejected with claims from Taylor that "it wasn't in the budget."

Knowing McMahon's desire to use the snap shackle, combined with Owen's tremendous fear, Branam grew instantly concerned. He knew the industry was littered with marginal riggers in Orlando and was concerned the WWF would hire anyone who agreed to do it as long as it saved the company a few bucks.

He instructed Beckman to call the WWF again, offering to reduce the cost by $2,000 as well as promising to take care of all shipping costs. Beckman told Taylor of Branam's concerns and that he was willing to discount the price to ensure the stunt was done without compromising Owen's safety.

Taylor later called back and left a phone message saying the Orlando job had been canceled. He said Owen's stunt had been written out of the script but that he'd call "next time."

The next thing Beckman and Branam heard was that Owen had died.

"There was no doubt in my mind that the reason the WWF didn't use our company and chose an unknown rigger was to save money and to get someone who would use the snap shackle like the WWF wanted," said Beckman in a sworn affidavit.

"It was my experience in working with the WWF that they just wanted to go right in and do their stunts in a rushed manner. The WWF was also unprepared and very degrading to their performers." On his headset in St. Louis he recalled hearing production people mocking Owen, saying, "Look at this guy, he looks like an idiot."

Neither Branam nor Beckman had ever heard of the man hired out of Orlando to rig the stunt, Bobby Talbert. None of the other expert riggers contacted by my lawyers had heard of him either.

Talbert was an independent rigger who had been in and out of the business for about seven years. He had spent part of the previous two years as a subcontractor who, on a few occasions, had assisted another rigger set up a similar drop-in stunt for Sting of the WCW. During that time Talbert had worked intermitantly as a special rigger for Universal Studios in Orlando, Florida. The night of May 23, 1999, was Talbert's first job with the WWF. We never had a chance to depose Talbert, but according to WCW stunt coordinator Ellis Edwards, Talbert had very little to do with Sting's drop-ins. Edwards was insulted by insinuations Talbert was "his" rigger, saying Talbert only worked as an assistant for him on three occasions. By no means was he in charge of Sting's stunt, which Edwards spent months preparing the wrestler for. Edwards insisted he always used two snap shackle clips for redundancy and that it was crucial to give the talent time to prepare for a stunt—not just one afternoon.

Edwards said if the stunt had been rigged the way he did it, a performer could not inadvertantly be released by squirming or moving their arms around. However, he said that the way Talbert set it up, Owen should have been told not to move at all and that a simple cape adjustment could have triggered the clip.

In discussions with homicide detective William Martin about how competitive the rigging business had become, Talbert said after the accident that his hiring for Owen's stunt was a real break. "Yeah, we just got, I don't know if you want to call it lucky now, but …"

Talbert told police he had been contacted by Taylor about a month before the fatal stunt. Taylor told him the WWF had other people rig "drop-ins" in the past but that they were "not good for the camera shots because they performed the stunts too slow."

Taylor called again before the Kansas City show and originally asked Talbert to do a "slide for life" stunt. It would have entailed hooking a wrestler to an anchored guide wire on which he'd slide into the ring from above. However, Talbert told Taylor he wouldn't have enough time to set it up on such short notice.

So, mere days before the event the WWF called again, wondering if Talbert could do a drop-in using the snap shackle for three shows. The stunt would involve Owen and midget Max Mini at the same time, using two snap shackles and a tether connecting the two men. Talbert made a verbal agreement to do the job and flew to Kansas City to set up the stunt using whatever equipment he found appropriate.

"[Taylor] said they had somebody do it before but it was way too slow for the camera," said Talbert, who met with Taylor in Orlando for the first time a month before Owen's fatal stunt.

Talbert claimed all the equipment used was new and that it had been tested by using a 250-pound sand bag before Owen hesitantly did a trial run. His assistant, Matt Allmen, who was asked to join Talbert just three days before the stunt, was also allegedly lowered without incident. To this day it has yet to be proven the quick release snap shackle had actually been used for the trial runs.

Owen was told by Taylor to do a rehearsal that afternoon, but when Owen deliberately showed up late, they opted to scrap plans to include Max Mini that night. Talbert next met Owen again on the catwalk that night during the show.

It was important to me to learn Talbert attached the snap shackle to a metal ring on the back of Owen's jacket as opposed to the front where Owen would instinctively have been able to hold onto the cable until he was in view of the crowd. It also made me realize Owen might never have seen the clip. If he had, I figure he would have questioned its sturdiness and reliability. He was always so careful and inquisitive, not to mention scared of these particular descents. After all, part of the stunt involved flapping his arms like a chicken, which certainly would have put all sorts of stresses on the clip itself.

Talbert told police he then took the release cord connected to the snap shackle behind Owen's neck and brought it across Owen's right shoulder to tape it to the front of his vest using gaff tape, allowing a small amount of slack. This cord was Owen's lifeline and Talbert claims he told Owen that afternoon, "As long as you don't put your hands on this, nothing's going to happen."

Obviously Owen wasn't supposed to pull on the cord until he had descended into the ring. As experts would later testify something as simple as a deep breath from Owen's massive chest could easily have put enough tension on the taped cord to trigger his release. What's more, Talbert and the local teamsters rigger Jim Vinzant, who helped prepare Owen for his descent, both confirmed Owen was having difficulty adjusting his cape, which continually hampered the use of his arms.

Vinzant, who had to help lift up Owen's cape to allow him to step over the catwalk railing, said it was clear Owen was inexperienced with the stunt. He added that he would not have had Owen perform the stunt with the harness system that was used because it provided minimal safety.

Police suspected perhaps it was the constant efforts to readjust his cape and the strings attaching it that led to his triggering of the clip. There was conflicting testimony concerning whether anybody was actually looking at Owen when the clip opened. Talbert told police he was looking away, but Ellis Edwards said that he spoke to Talbert afterwards and was told by Talbert he was looking right at Owen. We never had a chance to clear up this contradiction. Regardless, it all could have been avoided if the WWF hadn't asked that the snap shackle be used in the first place.

The police confirmed their suspicions after Detective Martin flew to Hollywood to meet with Tom DeWier of the International Stunt Association. DeWier had been in the stunt business for eighteen years and had even been nominated for an Academy Award for technical achievement for the design of equipment used in rigging stunts.

Upon inspecting photos of the equipment used, he concluded it was set up in a "sloppy" fashion but was "adequate," outside of the clip.

He said the harness/vest used was designed for stunts where people are dragged, not suspended. His concern revolved around its design, which transfers a person's entire body weight into their chest and torso area when they're suspended. He said it has proven to be so uncomfortable that he had seen it affect people's breathing to the point of their blacking out.

More importantly, he said he would never have suspended a human using a snap shackle, or pelican release as he called it, higher than ten to twelve feet off the ground without backup. Anything higher and he would insist on a locking carabiner.

He stated when he deals with actors he does not allow them to have any control over the stunt, as their focus is generally on their performance.

In DeWier's opinion, Talbert didn't focus on the two weakest links of the stunt—the release and the nervous wrestler. He also would have ensured there was more slack given to the release cord to reduce the chance of an accidental trigger.

DeWier also accompanied Detective Martin to an associate's garage where similar equipment was tested to re-create how the stunt was performed. After several hours of testing, it was determined the cape Owen wore may indeed have played a significant role in what went wrong. It was discovered tension on the cape, which was secured around Owen's neck and draped over his vest, would have caused his breathing to be restricted once he began free hanging.

If the collar of the cape was manipulated in a manner to release tension it could easily have put tension on the release cord, which needed only one sixteenth of an inch to open the clip—roughly equivalent to the thickness of the lead in a pencil.

During testing the snap shackle was accidentally tripped on several occasions by way of body and arm movement aimed at adjusting the makeshift cape.

Several experts pointed out a locking carabiner was the only equipment safe for human use. A spokesman from Lewmar told police the snap shackle was designed for leisure sail boats, specifically for the quick release of the spinnaker sail. Lewmar's technical manager, Mark Gibson, told Pam and Gary the same thing when they flew to England to depose him. When asked if it was suitable to use the snap shackle to dangle a human seventy-eight feet above the ground he was short.

"It would not be the correct thing to do, and it would be a highly unsafe practice because the product is designed to open under load," said Gibson.

He said no one had ever called his company to ask if it was suitable for human use. However, after learning bungee-cord operations were using it in some fashion he said steps were taken to reiterate to distributors that the equipment was for marine use only.

"From the knowledge I have, I would not think it is the proper use of that shackle at all. Definitely not," he said when asked of its use in Owen's stunt. "It is not designed to hold people."

He said if anyone would have asked about the possibility of using it to rig humans, he said, "I would have insisted it was not used at all."

Lewmar's Matthew Townsend had a long history in the marine industry and was the product manager for the hatch and hardware division.

"We would never have believed it credible that anyone from the stunt industry would use a product like that," said Townsend. He added the company never considered stamping it with a warning because it was sold by specialists to specialists in the boating industry.

Lewmar's finance director, Mark Swales, said using the snap shackle in any stunt capacity amounted to "lunacy." Lewmar was one of the leading suppliers of their kind in the marine industry, and he explained the clip was often used in the Super Bowl of yacht racing, the America's Cup, on the spinnaker of the boat. It would be used at the front of the yacht to take down the mast quickly to get the boat under wind and change direction.

"The triggerlatch shackle is not designed to lower people from seventy-eight feet, fifty feet or twenty feet," said Swales. "Totally improper."

I remember thinking that I would drop the lawsuit if Vince hooked himself up to that ridiculous contraption once he knew how improper it was.

Garry Foy was one of the industry's top experts. He lived in California and had rigged "flying" effects for seventeen years, including stunts for the Academy Awards. Foy reviewed the police file and photographs of the equipment for Owen's stunt. He then flew from Nevada to Kansas City to review the equipment and costuming used in the stunt and said in a sworn affidavit the WWF was grossly negligent in the design and performance of the stunt. He said it most certainly did not meet industry standards in several significant respects, which amounted to recklessness.

"The snap shackle was a totally inappropriate device for use in this stunt as it is intended by its very nature to fail, i.e., release," said Foy.

"No one in their right mind would suspend a human being from the top of an arena with this type of equipment, knowing that it is designed to release quickly and open."

He went further by saying the pull-ring setup taped across Owen's chest "would in and itself have pulled up on the release pin and caused the snap shackle to release," thanks to the cape tied around Owen's neck and draped over the rigging lines.

"Simply the weight of his body when suspended and/or his chest movement when breathing or adjusting his costume would inevitably cause the release to be triggered," said Foy. "There is only about eight-and-a-half pounds [actually, it's six pounds] of pull and a tiny travel of approximately one sixteenth of an inch required to release this quick release."

Foy said he had never heard of Talbert and said it was obvious from his work in this case he was unqualified for the job.

Calling it "a conscious disregard for the safety and well-being of their performers," Foy said the stunt should have used at least two separate wires for redundancy. As well, a carabiner should have been the obvious choice.

"By using inappropriate equipment and personnel, the WWF... created a high degree of probability that Mr. Hart would not survive the performance of this stunt," said Foy.

World Wrestling Federation lawyer Edward Kaufman bolstered our case when he admitted in his deposition that Vince McMahon had hired a safety and stunt coordinator named Michael Bledsoe in the wake of Owen's death. It was an obvious admission their safety standards needed to be augmented.

"The fact that the WWF instituted a stunt/safety officer position after Mr. Hart's death is further proof and acknowledgement of their negligence in not doing so earlier, and also demonstrates the feasibility of their having this position in place previously," said high-ranking industry expert Manny Chavez, a safety consultant for all film and television productions at Walt Disney, Touchstone and Hollywood Pictures.

"The snap shackle used for the stunt was ... being used outside the scope of its intended use. A locking carabiner is safer and does not have the potential of an accidental release. It also has the ability to release quickly when the lock is removed."

Another expert rigger shocked by the negligence involved was Brian Smyj, who went as far as to fly in to Kansas City to inspect Kemper Arena as well as the rigging and costume use for Owen's stunt.

Besides his long list of movie credits, Smyj also happened to own the world record for the longest and fastest rappel, which took place at the World Trade Center. It went from the 108th floor to basement level four as part of police rescue training for the New York and New Jersey Port Authority.

Smyj was shocked that a company as wealthy and successful as the WWF would stoop to hiring a "hacker" for such a dangerous endeavor.

"In the stunt industry, people employed at the Universal Stunt Show are known to be 'the bottom of the barrel' people in the industry," said Smyj in reference to Talbert. "They make about $30 per show. In my opinion, it was outrageously negligent for the WWF to employ a person with this inadequate background and no feature film or TV experience to have been responsible for Mr. Hart's rigging. There is no question that they could have afforded to hire qualified and experienced people in the stunt industry, and in fact did, prior to this stunt. They were grossly negligent in not having procedures and personnel in place to adequately check Mr. Talbert's credentials."

Appalled the WWF would use a quick release snap shackle in the manner it did, Smyj also pointed out, contrary to Talbert's claims, much of the rigging equipment had clearly been used for industrial purposes, rendering it inappropriate for human use.

"It is my opinion that the WWF management, including Vince McMahon, knew or should have known that there was a high probability that their action in using inadequate equipment and an unqualified stunt rigger would lead to a high probability that Mr. Hart would be injured," said Smyj.

"It is apparent from Mr. Joe Branam's statement that they were specifically advised by Mr. Branam of this potential danger [yet] found someone who would use the snap shackle they desired anyway. This is outrageous and egregious conduct, which demonstrates a complete indifference to, and conscious disregard for, the safety of the performer, Owen Hart."

Such testimony from experts in the field came as a great relief. We were finally getting to the bottom of what the whole case was about.

When I learned Talbert was from Orlando I immediately thought back to a conversation I had a week before Owen's death with a representative from the WWF office. She had called asking to speak to Owen when I was almost out the door to pick him up at the airport.

She explained the company needed Owen's measurements for a vest they had to make for him. I inquired about the purpose of the vest and she proceeded to tell me about this stunt they were planning at the Kemper Arena. She said that Owen was to be suspended above the arena and then lowered into the ring on cue. I commented on the danger of it.

"We have top experts that are flying in from L.A.," she reassured me. "They do this stuff all the time. They are the best in the business."

Owen was just returning from a typical ten-day tour, so it seemed a little strange to me they wouldn't have fit him for the vest while he was on the road. When I questioned her on this point she simply said, "We just decided today that he would be doing this. Please give him the message. We need these measurements A.S.A.P. if we are going to be ready for this Sunday's pay-per-view."

As I dashed out to the airport I remember thinking to myself that everything the WWF does seems to be done in such a hurried frenzy. It seemed to me not much thought or consideration was put into many of their actions. This little escapade was no exception.

"Since when did Owen become a stunt man?" I remember thinking to myself.

As part of the discovery process, we had access to the video captured by a WWF ringside cameraman mere seconds after Owen hit the ring. The eight-minute video included footage of police and paramedics running into the ring and working on Owen before he was transported out.

It was very distressing to watch. The hardest thing was he looked normal, as if he should have just been able to get up. Although it was clear he was unconscious, his skin looked okay on the video. As ridiculous as it sounds, I just felt like saying, "Wake up." All I was looking at were limited views of his head and body. He didn't look broken or bloody. It seemed as though they worked on him a long time to try to stabilize him but I guessed that was normal.

Those who wandered in and out of the picture ringside told the story with their facial expressions. They knew it didn't look good.

(Although I hated to do it, we decided to show the video to Owen's parents later in the lawsuit to remind them of exactly what had happened to their son. We figured at that point Stu and Helen had been brainwashed by the children into forgetting what this lawsuit was all about—Owen.)

Reading over the autopsy report was similarly unpleasant. The medical examiner, Dr. Thomas Young, pointed out there were no skull fractures or injuries to the brain, neck or spinal column. The only external injury of note he found during the autopsy was a four-inch laceration that cut through to the bone and disfigured his left elbow. That explained the blood sample taken from the ring that pooled next to a nearby stain of fake blood tested by the police.

Young said Owen's aorta was essentially ripped from his heart upon impact and that he died from the shock of internal blood loss as it filled the left side of his chest. Official cause of death was blunt chest trauma.

"It would have taken a few minutes for him to lose consciousness," said Young in an affidavit. "Up until that time, the findings are consistent with his experiencing pain and suffering. There is no evidence that he suffered any injury that would have caused him to lose consciousness immediately."

Such testimony, while disturbing, added to our claim Owen had endured pain and suffering.

"Usually with disruption or injury to the aorta frequently there is a lot of pain," confirmed Young, who added Owen likely lived several minutes after hitting the canvas. "Not only on the aorta but the other injuries as well. The injury to the arm, the chest wall, the bruising and the injury to the aorta, all of these things would have caused pain."

Another disturbing part of the investigation process involved the report of a video sold on e-bay dubbed the Owen Hart Death Video. The police looked into an e-bay claim a man sitting in the eighth row at Kemper Arena that night had the only footage of Owen's actual fall. It was on sale for $16 but turned out to be a hoax.

There are plenty of sick people out there.

Another crucial part of establishing our losses was proving what sort of quality person Owen was as a father, husband, brother and friend to all. Helen obviously spoke glowingly of her boy, saying we, as a couple, never missed anyone's birthday or forgot to buy someone a Christmas gift.

When asked for a special example of an incident demonstrating his thoughtfulness, Helen smiled. "Oh there were so many," she said. She began talking of how Owen had set up a romantic weekend at the finest hotel in Calgary for her and Stu's fiftieth anniversary.

"Room service, a romantic suite, a jacuzzi … everything was paid for by him, and he came up to see that things were just right. The candles were lit, there were flowers and fruit … it was a memorable occasion for us."

When asked about me, Helen said, "Martha and the children were his primary consideration." Helen also spoke of how Owen had provided financial assistance to at least half of his siblings including Alison, Bruce, Smith, Georgia and her husband, B.J.

Helen's talk of his caring and cautious nature also helped us establish that Owen had put all his trust in the riggers.

Ellie was the only person we deposed in Calgary. She did a wonderful job proving she had no credibility—she was all over the place, rambling on and making irrational comments. She didn't come across well, which was exactly what I expected.

She admitted then she had taken our legal documents from her parents and faxed them to WWF lawyers, but insisted she had done nothing wrong. "I did fax some stuff to Jerry McDevitt but it wasn't confidential," she said. "It was sitting there loud and clear on [Helen's] pillow."

She had harsh words for Bret, called her sister Alison a "kook" and called a handful of people liars, including Alison's two young children; her father's doctor; my attorneys; Gary and Anita Robb; as well as Ed Pipella and Pam. The irony of her testimony was that all she claimed to want was the truth about what happened to Owen the night he died. Yet when questioned whether she had ever asked anyone what really happened she couldn't say that she had. She hadn't, which said a lot about her motives.

One of the only things she said that made any sense was her description of Owen. "Owen was a happy person, a fulfilled person. He loved his wife and children. He was there for my parents every step of the way," said Ellie.

She recalled her final conversation with Owen involved an argument over her abusive husband, Jim. "Sometimes his bluntness with me bothered me, like when he told me my husband was an idiot and to get past him. Thing is, he was right about it."

She pointed out, "[Owen] was there if I ever needed him."

Too bad she didn't afford him the same loyalty, I thought.

Keith and Wayne were both called for depositions by the defense in regards to the allocation agreement. However, they both refuted any notions I was trying to buy testimony by clarifying they signed it simply to support me.

The defense lawyers also tried to reduce the amount of lost wages we would lay claim to by trying to establish information from Ellie that Owen was going to retire in two years. Keith shot this attempt down saying retirement plans were Owen's private business and were never discussed between the two.

As part of the police investigation, attempts were made through the WCW to interview Sting concerning his stunt, which was said by Talbert to be identical in nature to Owen's—a claim that WCW stunt coordinator Ellis Edwards disputes. Sting refused, saying he did not want to get involved. However, it was revealed Sting had practiced the stunt for several months, starting out with small drops and gradually increasing them.

Many of the wrestlers quite likely didn't even have to be told by WWF or WCW officials to keep their mouths shut about what everyone knew would be a legally contentious issue. For obvious reasons, a number of them declined to speak on the record with my lawyer, Pam. However, out of respect to Owen many agreed to share whatever information they could as long as their names weren't brought to light.

Unfortunately, The Undertaker (Mark Calloway) wasn't one of them. We had heard he was present for Owen's rehearsal and overheard some things said by Owen regarding his concern over the stunt. However, my repeated phone calls to Calloway's house went unreturned. Was he hiding something? Almost everybody else we approached who worked with Vince talked to us or at least returned the call, so why wouldn't he?

One of the wrestling wives who had known Vince McMahon for many years gave us some convincing testimony on the inherent pressure to do whatever he asked or risk being unemployed.

To her, the WWF had a prison mentality. "They own you," she said.

According to her, Owen didn't really have any choice whether he did or didn't do the stunt. "The WWF uses a lot of manipulation. 'If you don't want to do this we've got Joe Blow sitting over here and he'll be glad to do it,'" she said. "The constant intimidation and threats to your job—they exist daily."

Several people confirmed Owen forgot to pull the release cord when he landed in the ring during rehearsal, proving he was unfamiliar with the equipment.

As far as Owen's value to and future with the company, one WWF official said he was revered. "He is somebody who, in my eyes, the company would suffer greatly if they did not have him on the roster. He was … one of the top guys because he was entertaining. He was one of the best wrestlers we had on the roster and he was somebody that everybody loved. Owen would have had a job for as long as he wanted with this company."

Several wrestlers testified Owen had voiced concern and displeasure to them surrounding this fatal stunt and/or his previous stunt. Several wrestlers in the dressing room before the show said he didn't want to do it, and one reported Owen had thrown his vest across the room in frustration. Another said Owen told him his cape was getting in the way.

One wrestler said he saw Owen pacing on the night in question and asked if he was nervous. Owen said he was and reiterated he did not like doing the stunt. Two wrestlers echoed the industry credo: "In this business you don't ever tell anybody you don't want to do something."

A former roommate of Owen's said Owen admitted he was "scared to death" after one of his earlier aerial stunts. He said that Owen said he couldn't believe they had him "go up there like we're a bunch of trapeze artists. There is no net, there is nothing."

Several wrestlers and one of the production people said it was obvious after just a few minutes that Owen was dead and the bulk of performers disagreed with the decision to continue the show.

A wrestler who had been subjected to an 80-foot stunt without safety backups said there was a complete disregard for the safety of the talent, while a rigger confirmed that McMahon took unnecessary risks and had a reputation for cutting corners to save costs.

Throughout the course of ten months I had made at least a half-dozen trips to Kansas City as part of excruciating three- and four-day deposition hearings. It was there I sat in the Robbs' boardroom, staring out the window at the American flag waving in front of the Kansas City courthouse. I contemplated endlessly, "If there really is any justice, where is it?"

Out the front windows of the Robbs' office I could see Kemper Arena in the distance, which served as yet another reminder of my nightmare and determination for some retribution for the terrible wrongs committed.

In the spring of 2000 we started letting people out of the lawsuit when we determined they bore no responsibility for what happened to Owen.

Gary and Pam had flown to England to depose Lewmar representatives about their nautical clip before I decided to drop them from the suit. The WWF's defense lawyers were furious, in part, we figured, because Lewmar had $50 million in insurance money.

At the time we weren't thinking about settlements of any kind. Besides, I knew they weren't guilty—the clip was not intended in any way to be used for the stunt. It just did what it was designed to do—release quickly on load.

We also dropped our suit against AMSPEC, the company that manufactured the harness Owen wore. The manufacturers of the rope and cable were also excused.

That summer a Connecticut court heard the WWF's motion to move the court case to Connecticut. It had been one of many looming concerns.

The preliminary hearing sought to find out if I was indeed bound to Owen's contract because I administrated his estate. If so, it would have opened the door for a second hearing, which threatened to force us to dismantle our Missouri case and refile it in Connecticut.

We awaited the judge's ruling on the matter. It was just one more reason why I was feeling more and more pressure to end it all.

As the one-year anniversary of Owen's death approached, Bruce and Ross thought it would be touching to do an Owen Hart tribute show at a *Stampede Wrestling* card. They asked Stu to attend. He thankfully declined because the show was to involve talent from the WWF. "It would be in poor taste for me to be celebrating," Stu told the *Calgary Sun*.

It wound up being canceled.

The WWF itself also decided to come to Calgary within weeks of the anniversary, which I saw as a major slap in the face. I made my displeasure clear in the local papers, especially when I knew the WWF wanted Stu to sit ringside for the show.

Diana and the others were going to take him down to the Saddledome show at Vince's request, to essentially use him as a puppet. I was furious. What would that look like?

We decided we couldn't have Stu appear there, so Pam arranged with Keith to sequester Stu. Helen was in the hospital while Keith took Stu out of town. Diana and the others showed up at the Hart house looking for Stu and were very angry we "kidnapped" him. As crazy as it all sounded, we knew it was the only way to ensure Stu missed the show.

CNN wanted to do something on the first-year anniversary but the Robbs understandably quashed it for fear it could damage our case.

The local papers were also interested in interviews and the *Sun* offered to let me write a tribute column, which I poured my heart into. Although I was extremely proud of it, my lawyers went berserk the next day when they opened the paper. Their major concern was that I had referred to the snap shackle as "practically the equivalent of a paper clip."

I had to sign an agreement with my lawyers saying it was my own opinion and that they didn't tell me to write anything about the clip. They were worried it would run in the *Kansas City Star*, which they said could've tainted the jury pool and given more credence to the WWF's transfer request.

All I was trying to do was honor my husband with a touching tribute and it was blowing up in my face. Horrified by their reaction, I told my lawyers I didn't care if I had done damage because the column was between me and Owen. I felt compelled to say what I had said.

On top of all this, my lawyers were starting to get angry as they still wanted me to put a number on the table. The lawsuit was getting messier than they imagined it would.

I, too, was obviously frustrated because little on the merits of the case was being covered. There was so much unimportant garbage. I wanted to get to the meat of the issue.

It was obvious the defense lawyers were delaying because they had nothing to lose by doing so. They had a poor case. So, according to my lawyers, the only way to stop such delays was to table an offer. That way, if they didn't accept, the interest would start running. As it was explained to me, we had already lost $1.5 million to $2 million in pre-trial interest. I felt like the WWF lawyers were laughing at me, as that money alone could have essentially paid their legal fees.

I finally decided on May 24th—366 days after Owen died—to put a number on the table. After months of arguing with my lawyers and demanding they never again ask for a number, I finally went to them with my decision. My lawyers were shocked.

The decision was so agonizing. Attaching any sort of number to Owen's life made me physically ill, leaving me bed-ridden for almost a week. I had never had to make such a critical decision in my life before and immediately afterwards I beat myself up twenty-four hours a day thinking about it. What kind of person was I to do that?

I had to remind myself the only reason I could live with the decision was that it was a strategy to stop the WWF from delaying the case.

The number we picked was $32 million US.

It was determined with the help of a statistics professor from Washington State University, who calculated a number of factors, including lost income and pain and suffering. In a nutshell we calculated his loss of income at $16 million and elected to double that due to his worth to his family.

When the documents had been prepared, I was still numb from the decision. I broke down crying in the law office several times as I could barely sign the paper. Just thinking about that horrible moment still upsets me.

The lawyers told me several times I was doing the right thing but if I wasn't comfortable with it they'd shred the paper. Realizing I was too distraught to drive, Pam took me to a coffee shop where we talked for over an hour while I sobbed.

We submitted the number the next day, making it clear it wasn't our intention to settle—this was being done solely to trigger pre-trial interest. The figure was low enough we felt certain we could do better at trial—and that was still our intention. (By this time we even had a scale model of Kemper Arena constructed for the court case.)

They had sixty days to accept or the meter started running.

A few days later we met in front of Judge Long.

He questioned the phraseology of the allocation agreement and ruled the defense lawyers could cross-examine my lawyers and the family on the issue. This served to lengthen the deposition list and made it impossible for us to proceed with our Feb. 5, 2001, trial. As a result we lost the trial date, despite two later, favorable rulings from the court of appeals.

When I lost my trial date, I almost lost my mind. We had worked so hard to get that date and now it was gone—dust in the wind.

The appeals court agreed with me and my lawyers that Judge Long should not allow questioning regarding the allocation agreement. The Missouri Court of Appeals ruled that these documents should be returned to us and not be referred to during the rest of the case.

But no arrangement could be made for a new trial date. We would have to wait for the final court of appeals decision in October 2001, by the Missouri Supreme Court of Appeals, before we could even arrange for a new trial date hearing with Judge Long. In spite of this development, we were still preparing for trial. We kept moving forward with our depositions.

Exactly sixty days after tabling our $32 million offer, I was overwhelmed by fears it could finally all be over. On that day the window would officially close on our offer. After that day the interest started accruing, which was our sole intent.

I had never dreamed they'd agree to pay such a figure. However, my sudden fear was that because the WWF was a billion-dollar company they could most certainly decide to end this shareholder's nightmare by accepting. Then where would my justice be?

I became frantic and immediately called Pam. Strange as it sounds, I had never thought of such a scenario, as I was always bent on going to trial. I felt so empty when I realized in the end the case would only be about money. "That's all it could ever be about," she said. Then there was silence.

I had never thought of that before.

As I stood in the middle of my kitchen stunned, I hung my head wondering how I could let Owen's life be reduced to a check. To me, the money was dirty.

However, instead of spiraling into yet another tunnel of depression it hit me like a flash of light: I would create my own justice by building an incredible institution in his name.

The Owen Hart Foundation—that would make it clean.

It would reflect the way he conducted his life, being kind, generous and caring towards others. It would be designed to help those who worked hard but still needed a hand.

I realized no one was ever going to be convicted or go to jail and there wouldn't be any changes to wrestling. That's not where he'd want to make a difference anyway. He'd be proud if he could be a part of something good that would reflect his personality.

Besides, I started thinking that once the trial ended in a year—or two years or three years—what if the judge didn't believe we were 100 percent right? There was always that risk, especially considering McMahon employed some of the sharpest lawyers in the land.

And then what would I have to show for all this? Heck, we didn't even have a trial date anymore because of all the delays. At that point I had some of the family fighting against me and the WWF suing me and suggesting I was trying to buy witnesses; only 80 of 200 depositions had been completed, there was no trial date in sight and I was spending all my time in boardrooms.

That wasn't living. Instead, I could make it all disappear and start working on something Owen would be proud of.

For so long I wondered how it would all end, and now that I knew what we'd do with the money after the trial, I felt as though a tremendous burden had been lifted. Although my goal still was to go to trial, I resolved the end result would be the foundation. While the money would never be enough justice for me, I would create another level of it with the foundation. The funny thing was I didn't know a thing about building a foundation.

I couldn't wait to learn.

Two weeks later, they countered with a settlement offer of $17 million US.

THE SETTLEMENT

"Always forgive your enemies; nothing annoys them so much."
—OSCAR WILDE

Settlement was a new concept to me.

The prospect of ending the lawsuit right then and there was overwhelmingly tempting. Seventeen million dollars was obviously a lot of money—it would have been the highest wrongful death settlement in Missouri history. But the defense didn't want any punitives attached. Generally, punitives were only something awarded in special circumstances, and there is never a guarantee that they can be attained.

I had been so uptight and dedicated to the suit I couldn't even live my life. More importantly I could see my kids suffering—they forever had my divided attention. Even if I was doing something with them, my mind was always worried we were going to lose everything—the house, the lifestyle, the school and the activities. It was a prospect Owen would have been sick about. Yet, that threat still loomed by virtue of the WWF's countersuit.

And suddenly I could make it all go away with a simple nod.

However, my lawyers and I didn't think it was a very good business tactic to accept the first offer, so we rejected it cold. I worried because I knew some of the Harts would be stirred into a frenzy when they heard of the money I had turned down. They were.

To my advantage, daily interest was now being accrued on any settlement monies sure to be realized, which did well to keep the lines of communication open between the two sides.

Still, no concrete progress was being made, so we agreed to a mediation hearing. It was an important day for me as I wanted the opportunity to sit across the table from Vince and tell him of the terrible loss I'd had to live with for some time now.

Vince was also the product of a single mother, so I figured he could relate to what my kids were going through. However, I didn't know if he could truly appreciate what the job of raising kids alone was like. He had no idea how my life had changed and how exhausted I was by trying to carry out all my responsibilities.

I wanted him to know my pride for my children was self-contained as I had no one to share it with. He needed to hear that my children still cried for their dad and missed him, and that I too cried on an almost daily basis. He needed to be reminded I was still haunted by Owen's fall, the negligence involved and the fact he died alone. He was robbed of what promised to be fifty of the best years of his life.

I wanted Vince to know this was not a business deal—this was about Owen's life. Indeed, I did get my chance to make Vince squirm that day by looking him in the eye and telling him of my pain.

Otherwise, the exercise failed miserably. The mediator was not mediating. He seemed more interested in chatting up Vince McMahon. He thought $17 million was fine, as it was $3 million over the previous largest settlement ever awarded in Missouri for a wrongful death settlement, a $14- million settlement also obtained by Robb & Robb.

We ended up walking out.

However, as we did so, I found out Helen was hoping to make her way over to the other side of the room to talk to Vince. Of all the shockingly inappropriate acts carried out by some of the Harts throughout the entire ordeal, poor Helen almost capped them all. However, it wasn't a self-motivated move. When questioned about her mission, she revealed she had been asked by Bruce to approach Vince for a job.

What made it so sad was that months earlier Diana used her mother in a similarly disgusting fashion, asking Helen to pass along a package to

Jerry McDevitt for Vince. I intercepted the package, labeled "From Diana Hart," which Helen admitted contained a resume and profile of Diana's new, wannabe-wrestler boyfriend.

Embarrassed for Helen, I had grabbed it away from her. Still, I ended up mailing it to Vince anyway out of pity. I should have thrown it out but I felt so badly that Helen had been put in that position.

Bret later told me that when Bruce heard Helen wasn't able to submit his verbal job application he was furious at her.

Two weeks later Pam took it upon herself to study relevant Missouri case law. Together, the two of us sat in her Calgary boardroom mapping out the particulars of all the recent cases relevant to personal injury so we knew where we stood with regards to the appropriate dollar figure.

I didn't care about the money. I just wanted to make sure I didn't get taken advantage of. There was no way I was going to let the WWF get off easy in the eyes of the law.

Days later the defense bumped their offer significantly and we took it. The settlement included the WWF, Vince and Linda McMahon, Bobby Talbert, Matt Allman, the City of Kansas City and the two city riggers who stood on the catwalk that night. With all that was facing me, it was the most rational decision I could make.

My seventeen months of hell were finally over, and an incredible sense of relief swept over me. The lawyers drew up the papers and one week later I returned to Kansas City for what I hoped would be the last time in my life.

Still needing a rubber stamp from our judge, we sat in the courtroom for more than two hours with my patient kids dressed in their sharp, white school uniforms. Throughout it all I stared endlessly at the seal of justice that hung on the wall opposite the witness stand where I was questioned for most of the proceedings.

Even though I didn't get the jury trial I had planned on, the final hearing was a reassuring substitute. At the end of the day it would be entered into the records that I had indeed endured a lengthy legal process that wound up recognizing wrongs had been committed. It was hard that morning to officially relinquish any rights to pursue the matter any further, but at the same time it was also very liberating.

When our final courtroom appearance was adjourned, I took Oje and Athena by their tiny hands and we went together to Kemper Arena. Walking in with an eight and five-year-old who were still buzzing from the limo ride, I looked up at the rafters from which Owen fell. I put my arms around the two most precious things I have left in this world and fought back tears.

I wanted them to see where Owen died because as time went on I didn't want them to look back and have any unanswered questions. I wanted them to have closure.

I pointed up to the catwalk and explained how Owen fell.

Athena said, "That must have really hurt daddy."

Oje said nothing. He wanted to leave.

We had come a long way as a trio since the night I had sat them down on the edge of the bed to tell them daddy wasn't coming home. And in the future we'd now be better prepared to weather the harsh realities and challenges life would bring. As I squeezed them ever closer I felt a tremendous sense of accomplishment and relief.

"You did so well," Oje told me, referring to my courtroom testimony. Just like his father, he always knew the right things to say.

We had endured the most horrific of circumstances I could ever have dreamed of and turned it into something good. What's more, I felt we were going to use those experiences to help ensure friends and neighbors in our city could have better lives through Owen's legacy foundation. The stress in my life was suddenly gone, as was the pressure and burden of having to ensure that the man I loved more than anyone did not die in vain.

Still, I knew there would be an emptiness—a void I might never fill. Part of that emptiness stemmed from the loss of my extended family, the Harts. As I moved forward, I knew most of the Harts would never again be part of my life. That was my choice.

We carried the same last name but that was as far as it would go. I would never consider myself, or my children, a part of that family anymore.

I vowed to respect Owen's parents, and I would stay in touch with a select few of his siblings. However, my teenage suspicions dating back seventeen years had been proven conclusively over the last seventeen months—Owen was a white sheep in a black family.

There was too much betrayal, too many lies, too much hatred. That's not what Owen was about, nor was it something I wanted my children to have anything to do with.

I decided months earlier I would set aside $2 million of my settlement share to start the foundation. Owen would be proud to know that even in death he would be helping people who are trying to help themselves. In that regard, we had truly come out winners.

I know in my heart I did everything I could for Owen. I imagined he'd say, "Quit crying for me because I'm okay. It's you that has to wake up every day and face challenges."

And I would. My thrust from the beginning was that the WWF had to recognize what they had done to me and my children. At long last, they finally had.

I decided then and there I would not carry any bitterness. I couldn't. I couldn't carry any extra baggage anyway.

Later that day, while a flood of raw emotions swept over me, I felt compelled to write a handwritten letter to Vince McMahon. In order to go on in a healthy direction and to really start living again, I needed to let everything go. Yes, I was angry with Vince, but I certainly didn't hate him and I wanted him to know that.

The one-page letter had an element of forgiveness woven through it, although I didn't come right out and say it. The real message in the letter was that I wanted him to think about how he lived his life, and that what really mattered was whether you were a good person or not.

I told him how hard it was to live without Owen but that I still believed in living a good life. I told him I believed everyone had the capacity to be a good person including him.

I knew as his life passed him by I would creep into his thoughts from time to time, and when I did, I wanted him to know that above all I did not hate him. I didn't hate anyone for that matter. Hate weighs you down, and my load in life was hard enough to pull already.

Vince had always struck me as the kind of man who was basically untouchable. With his empire now worth several billions of dollars, he could forever surround himself with a horde of "yes" men.

Unfortunately for all of us, age and death are the great equalizers, and I feel if you don't know where you go when you die you will never know how to live. I thought I would remind him of this fact, hoping he might think a little harder about how he lives his life. My opinion was that he is an extremely lonely man who puts so much time into his work because it diverts him from his own personal issues. My hope was that he would start making decisions in a more cautious manner, especially where other people's lives are involved.

I never heard back from Vince, although a week later he sent a check for more than $50,000 to be donated to the Alberta Children's Hospital in Owen's name. The money represented proceeds from the sale of an unendorsed Owen tribute magazine the WWF had sold.

He couriered a copy of his donation letter to my house, which stated what a great husband and man Owen was. I took it as a sign he'd received my letter and appreciated its content.

Writing the letter to Vince was an important part of my ability to move on. It gave me great peace. Another significant part of my healing process began in the courtroom minutes before our ugly legal battle was to officially come to an end.

Jerry McDevitt made the first move by asking me if he could approach my children to say hello. He was so moved by the sight of them, he dug into his legal bag and pulled out the only thing he had to offer: the coveted mints he always turned to after his cigarette breaks. I found it to be a simple, yet moving gesture.

After the hearing, he shook my hand and wished me well. I knew he meant it. His fellow counselors also approached my lawyers and me with handshakes symbolizing at that point we were no longer rivals, we were just people. And now, the fighting was over.

My goal through it all was to bring awareness to the wrongs that had been committed, and by the end of the long, drawn-out legal battle I felt I had succeeded. I wanted those responsible for Owen's death to feel my pain, to realize all the damage that had been done. By the end of the process I had placed the majority of responsibility on Vince's shoulders, as he took great pride in being the man who made all the decisions for the WWF.

At the end of the day I did feel that Vince was deeply sorry for what happened. However, I think it was the long legal process that hammered home my message: that I believed it was his company's lack of consideration that led to Owen's death.

In my eyes, they needed to be shown there are consequences attached to every decision and that people need to be held responsible for their behavior. It's important that individuals conduct their lives with integrity and honesty. Some people do tend to forget that.

I hoped the message would get through. I think it did.

Courtroom journalists and legal journals reported the settlement to be $18 million US. As part of the arrangement I agreed not to comment on any figures. However, they knew I would not agree to be silenced in any other way. I wanted the world to hear what they did to me and, more importantly, what they did to Owen.

The settlement date coincided with the bungled U.S. presidential election. What could have been a front-page story became an afterthought placed towards the back of the newspaper, near the obituaries where this all began.

I had quite a few requests from television stations in New York and various other major U.S. cities to do interviews following the settlement. *People* magazine had also lined something up. However, many of them backed out when the election turned into a long, drawn-out fiasco.

In Canada the settlement still garnered major headlines. The next day, I was up at 5 A.M. doing live television and radio interviews and opening my door to a steady stream of journalists who I sat down with one-on-one to end a year-and-a-half of relative silence. Rather than set up a generic press conference I wanted to give personal accounts of the hell I'd gone through.

I had bitten my tongue so many times on the advice of my legal counsel and now I felt it was my turn to set the record straight. I told the press I was relieved the legal battle was over and that I could now begin work on the foundation in Owen's name.

I spoke of the dissention in the family and revealed how several Hart kids tried derailing my suit while others stood by and let it happen. I made it clear to journalists from across the country and the world I wanted nothing to do with most of the Harts ever again.

In the days and weeks ahead one of the biggest issues I still needed to resolve revolved around the betrayal I felt at the hands of some of Owen's brothers and sisters. I really needed to let go of all the pain, heartache and feelings of disappointment certain siblings caused me.

Several of them, namely, Ellie, Diana and Bruce, made the mistake of thinking the legal battle was all about them. It wasn't. I made it clear so many times that it wasn't even about Oje, Athena or me. It was about Owen.

No one is capable of supporting someone else if their only interest is self-serving, and I guess the lesson I learned is that you really shouldn't expect anything from anyone. If there are no expectations then there can't be disappointment.

I know that all of Owen's brothers and sisters must have loved him in some capacity and were sorry about what happened to him. However, several of them couldn't see past their own interests to appreciate and acknowledge the wrongs that had actually been committed.

Their judgment was clouded and they acted like starved animals. Money was their food and they chased it shamelessly.

As a result, their lack of support and the emotional trauma they put me through will stand as a wedge between us forever. Although I forgive them for all their wrongdoing and wish them well, I feel many of them no longer deserve to know me or my children.

When the settlement checks from the WWF arrived several months later, it spurred an unexpected wave of emotion. Called by my Calgary lawyers to pick them up, Keith was instructed to bring his parents to ensure Ellie or any of the others who worked against our lawsuit didn't get a chance to get their hands on the money.

The sight of the amount on the checks was sickening to both Keith and me. We both started to cry as we couldn't help but think the whole nightmare had amounted to two pieces of paper.

Thank God for the foundation. I had all sorts of incredible ideas for the type of things I wanted to do with it but I didn't know how to make my dreams a reality.

I approached longtime friend Colleen Gray. She helped lead me to the Calgary Foundation, which would ultimately administer the Owen Hart Foundation. Together Colleen and I spent the next several months in various meetings to set up the parameters and incorporate the foundation's programs.

Our mission was to help those with limited resources but unlimited potential. We wanted to help hard-working people build or rebuild their lives, not with band-aid solutions but with an eye on solving problems long-term. The foundation consists of three components. The first is a scholarship fund that gives out high-impact scholarships annually to students at Calgary's Forest Lawn High School—so far, 21 scholarships have been given out. As someone who always had part-time jobs throughout high school I knew the value of targeting a school like Forest Lawn where 75 percent of its student body also worked.

The second component is a housing program. Upon completion of a two-year educational program that prepares candidates for home ownership, we aid select applicants by assisting in a mortgage downpayment— so far, we've provided 17 homes this way. I had grown up in a working-class neighborhood and saw first-hand how hard it was for families to save for a house purchase. I wanted to aid in that process because I knew of the pride involved in home ownership.

The final component recognizes and contributes to other worthwhile causes like Calgary's Youville Women's residence, Easter Seals and the Children's Hospital, for all of which the foundation helps raise funds and awareness. The Partnership Fund has also helped the Kids' Help Phone as well as the Peace Heroes Program in local high schools to teach kids to increase self-esteem and respect for themselves and others. This program complements the scholarship program.

One of the programs I was most proud to be associated with was the Owen Hart Memorial Fund set up at the Children's Hospital. Using more than $200,000 donated in lieu of flowers by Owen's grieving fans, we helped set up a basic needs fund that assists low-income families traveling to the hospital with their sick kids. It assists with hotel expenses, food, transportation, parking and other costs incurred by such visitors.

As part of my charity work, I personally funded a project at the Rockyview Hospital to provide the addition of a grief counseling office. I had benefited greatly from the programs I attended there and it was my way of saying thanks.

In December 2000, it was with great pride I announced the Owen Hart Foundation was born. Almost a year later I stood at a press conference at which I presented two hard-working single mothers with keys to brand new homes the foundation helped pay for. The smiles on those women's faces mirrored the tremendous happiness and sense of accomplishment I felt. I had followed through on my word and made sure I would help promote change through Owen's name.

Not only would his legacy help me move forward and add new meaning to my life, it would forever serve as a reminder that the man who touched so many lives during his life could still do so long after his death.

EPILOGUE:
Life Goes On

"We are not permitted to choose the frame of our destiny. But what we put into it is ours."
—DAG HAMMARSKJÖLD

From time to time, the phone will ring with a request to speak to Owen. It's been more than three years since he died, but no matter how many times it happens, it always seems to catch me off guard.

I have yet to come up with a comfortable way to address such inquiries although I generally try everything I can to avoid saying, "Owen has passed away." Such words have never come easy, and I doubt they ever will.

Whether it's a misguided phone call, a piece of mail bearing his name, a wrestling logo or a song, my days are filled with endless reminders of the life I used to lead—the life I used to love.

Not a day goes by Owen doesn't cross my mind. The aroma of fresh flowers still takes me back to the days my home smelled like a flower shop as hundreds of well-wishers inundated me with bouquets and cards of condolences. Family pictures of Owen that used to sit on the mantel have since been moved to less prominent areas where the kids and I can still honor him without dwelling on our loss.

Throughout the legal process I wore my wedding ring because I was representing my husband, as was my duty. However, after I signed the settlement and felt I had done all I could for him, I took it off and set it aside in a special place along with Owen's ring. It was part of my credo that I would no longer live in the past and that I was going to continue building a new life. Unfortunately, while I focused heavily on doing what I said I would do, I was unaware I'd soon be embroiled in yet another public battle with the Harts.

Early in the year 2001 the WWF announced it was returning to Calgary almost two years to the day Owen died. They had done the same thing a year earlier and once again I found it upsetting as I knew the timing was not at all coincidental. I had come to grips with the fact I'd forever see and hear of the WWF's exploits, as it was still one of the highest profile entertainment companies in the world.

At Christmas it had been hard for me to buy presents for my children, as the toy stores are littered with a wide variety of licensed wrestling merchandise. The sight of their logo always seemed to trigger an emotional response; it felt as if daggers tore through my heart every time I laid eyes on it.

By Oje's birthday in March I had resolved a lot of those issues. I realized Vince McMahon and his motley crew were not going to go away anytime soon. I'd started to make peace with them.

But what bothered me most about the WWF coming to town was that Stu was rumored to be a ringside participant of some sort as part of the show. I had forgiven the WWF in many ways, but I wasn't excusing them of their responsibility in Owen's death. I stated publicly I felt any Hart member who would attend the show for whatever reason was being disrespectful to Owen's memory. My pleas to the family were in vain.

I had lunch with Bret that day and he was sure it was all some sort of misunderstanding and that his father would not attend. That morning he had gone to the Hart house to reiterate how inappropriate it would be for them to support the WWF. It was a pay-per-view show broadcast worldwide and I figured Vince's plan was to show Stu ringside as some sort of vindication in Owen's death.

Bret insisted his father not go. Sadly, Bret's demands had little effect as Diana, Bruce, Smith and Ellie brought Stu along for a front row display. They were all in their glory for what I felt was the biggest mockery of Owen's death I could ever have imagined. I felt it was as if Vince was laughing at them all, saying "Your son and brother died in my ring and still you all run after me, my money and my fame."

I was not surprised to see the siblings on the show lapping up the attention. Smith went as far as to rub it in Bret's face, holding up a sign saying, "Hi Bret."

After all the WWF had put me through, seeing Stu cater to the WWF's whims deeply disturbed me. To see Owen's own father sitting there just for the sake of trying to get one of his other children or in-laws a job was pathetic. I called Helen up during the show to ask her what was going on. "How could you do this? How could you allow this to happen? What kind of family is this anyway?" I screamed.

I was outraged and fed up with the lack of moral character I witnessed over and over again with this family. I had had it. Up until that point I had been kind to Owen's parents, dropping off Christmas presents, inviting them to dinners, calling to chat. But that would all end now. This was the final straw.

I said to Helen, "I am ashamed of all of you and you should all be ashamed of yourselves. Go to hell!"

Then I hung up. I didn't plan on speaking to her ever again.

That summer I did well to put it all behind me as I was more concerned with reconnecting with my children. For obvious reasons we hadn't had a good summer in three years. I took them on a number of trips, including an African safari in the Serengeti, which did well to further cleanse my mind and reintroduce the beauty of life.

My serenity was short-lived. Upon my return I was told Diana was about to come out with an explosive tell-all book about her life in the famous Hart family.

It so full of hatred, bitterness and lies I had little choice but to protect myself and Owen's memory by issuing a libel notice threatening to launch a lawsuit. It was hate literature, plain and simple, used to lash out at several siblings and me. I wanted the book pulled.

It was so full of anger and factual errors, Calgary icon Ed Whalen considered jumping on board the lawsuit with me for what he called "a fairytale" book. Bret deemed it "pornographic."

Toronto Star book reviewer Michael Holmes called it "terribly underwritten, ridiculously simplistic, pointlessly episodic, repetitive and error-riddled, even with the assistance of co-writer Kirstie McLellan. It's one of the most manipulative, megamaniacal, deliberately unselfconscious books I've ever read … Reading it makes you feel dirty." Other than that he didn't really say what he thought of it.

Once again I was facing litigation and it was a major stress for me. I had to rummage through her filth to compile a laundry list of damaging comments aimed at destroying my reputation and that of my family's. She even attacked my poor mother and sister Virginia. Suddenly I was put in the position of having to spend my time gathering evidence to disprove her claims. When the publishers were presented with my documents pointing out her inaccuracies and malice, her publisher did not hesitate to remove the book from bookstores soon thereafter. The publisher issued an apology, paid my legal expenses and made a donation to Owen's foundation.

The timing of Diana's book couldn't have been worse as its release came at the same time her mother Helen lay in a Calgary hospital, battling for her life following a serious of seizures.

I visited Helen in the hospital. She was hooked up to life support and slipped in and out of a coma. Waking slightly upon my arrival, she smiled and then grimaced as if she was going to cry. I told her not to cry even though tears were streaming down my own face.

I told her I was happy she woke up so I could get the chance to talk to her. I held her hand and told her I loved her, Owen loved her and that God loved her too. It was the first time I had spoken to her since my distraught call five months earlier. She tried to respond, and I could tell she was saying, "I love you too," but because of all the tubes placed in her mouth she couldn't make a sound.

I brought her a little green leather-bound bible and put it in her hand. I knew if I was on my deathbed I'd want to have my bible with me, and I thought she would appreciate the gesture. In it I wrote, "Helen don't be afraid, go to the light and let it warm you. You will be remembered, you will be missed. I love you, Martha."

She died six days later, on November 4, 2001.

I wanted to go to her funeral but I knew there would probably be some tension. I hadn't seen some of the family members since Owen's funeral two-and-a-half years earlier and I wasn't looking forward to it—especially with all the newly generated hostility stemming from Diana's book.

Mind you, I wasn't the only one who had issues with the book. Many of the family members were upset with the content as well. Bret stated publicly his mother would have been appalled with Diana's book and that he was glad Helen passed away before she had a chance to read it.

Yet, the day after Helen died, Diana appeared on a local morning show promoting the book, and days later she was on Dave Rutherford's talk show on QR77 radio for a half-hour interview. Bret called in to the show and ended up having an on-air fight with Diana. The family's dysfunction was being broadcast across Calgary. At one point he told her to shut up.

Helen's funeral was held on Friday, November 9, 2001. Bret, Keith and Ross invited me to ride in the family limos but I chose to go accompanied by my mother, sister, Pam Fischer and a friend. It was a decision that didn't sit well with some.

It was a strange feeling because I felt like I wasn't really in the family and yet I wasn't really out either. Upon our arrival, I was apprehensive about entering the funeral home. Once inside, my group and I were escorted to the family area. I waited in the wings as I did not want my presence to act as any type of distraction. Nor did I want any confrontations.

From where I was standing I could see many of the family members I had issues with—Diana, Ellie, Davey Boy. I couldn't help thinking how awkward it was going to be for me to be sitting with all the family, especially the ones who had worked against me. Knowing how unstable some of them were, I was more than a little concerned there might be an outbreak like something seen on *Jerry Springer*. As it turned out there wasn't.

The most touching portion of Helen's service came near its conclusion when Stu got up to speak. Bret had to help him shuffle his crippled, eighty-six-year-old body up to the podium to address the crowd in honor of his life partner.

Although he tended to ramble incoherently late in life, his speech on this day was short and powerful. "I will never get over losing Helen … I don't have enough time," he said. It was so sad and so true.

When the service was over the family members gathered in the garage, filing into their limos for the procession. I didn't know how I would be received but I wanted to go and hug Stu. I was worried I might never see him again.

On the way there Bruce approached me and gave me big, long hug. I hugged him back twice because I knew he was very upset and I felt Helen's funeral wasn't a place to bring up past hurts, it was a place to help mend them. I also embraced Georgia as I knew how much her mother meant to her. I finally tracked Stu down and gave him the type of hug we had exchanged so many times in the past.

For me, the saddest part about losing Helen was that it represented yet another little piece of Owen I had lost.

Seeing Stu in such a fragile state both mentally and physically made it easy for me to forgive him for making his appearance at the WWF event against my wishes. I knew he loved Owen dearly and must have been too weak to fend off the pressure placed on him by his children to attend the show.

I married into this family and with Owen gone—and now Helen—I knew I had made the right decision to distance myself. I didn't belong there any more.

Helen's funeral confirmed I had done well to take steps toward a new life. It also marked the last time I would see many members of the family, including Bret. After the lawsuit was completed, he and I continued to drift further and further apart as our lives took very different paths. I will always be grateful to him for helping me through the darkest days of my life.

A concussion forced Bret to retire as a wrestler in 2000 but he maintained wrestling ties abroad as a spokesman for a short time. He still has a high profile in Calgary through the local junior hockey team that bears his name (The Hitmen) as well as a weekly newspaper column in the *Calgary Sun*. He too has distanced himself from most of the family and hasn't remarried. In June 2002, at age 44, Bret was involved in a bicycle crash that caused a stroke that paralyzed the left side of his body. In his time of crisis I supported him. Thankfully, his condition continues to improve through rigorous rehab. Since recovering from his stroke, Bret, who once told me his soul would shatter if he ever befriended Vince McMahon again, did just that.

Alison and I are still close. She's a sweet, hardworking librarian who has done a great job raising her two daughters alone. She is one person in the Hart family I will always support any way I can.

Ross still teaches school and dabbles in the family wrestling camp. My dealings with him are limited, as they are with Wayne.

Bruce is a part-time teacher still involved in the family wrestling school. I still empathize with him and his plight—his estranged wife Andrea left in a very public fashion for her brother-in-law, Davey Boy. I thought of Bruce endlessly during a court case in which Davey Boy was charged with uttering death threats to Diana. After several charges were dropped, photos ran in the local papers of Davey Boy walking out of the courthouse hand in hand with Andrea.

On May 19, 2002, Davey Boy died of a heart attack at age 39 while vacationing with Andrea. News reports indicated that the autopsy revealed his most likely cause of death was the abuse of steroids. I sent my condolences to his children but did not attend his funeral. Andrea and Bruce have since reconciled and are now living together again.

I still talk with Keith, who continues to work as a teacher during the day and a fire-fighter at night. He's fought so hard to overcome the heart-break of his divorce and continues to be a wonderful dad for his three teenage boys. In November 2002 Keith married a second time to his long-time girlfriend Joan; I couldn't have been happier for him.

I've had nothing to do with Ellie or Diana, and never will.

Georgia is the only one of Owen's siblings whose marriage is still intact. She's a sweet woman with a good heart. I'm sure she never meant any harm, but her lack of support for me when I needed it most will always stand in the way of rekindling our once-strong friendship.

October 16, 2003, was a sad day for everyone in the Hart family as Stu Hart passed away peacefully at the Rockyview Hospital. He was 88. He had been plagued by poor health the last few years of his life, suffering from congestive heart failure and diabetes, amongst other ailments. Stu simply had no fight left in him. Over the past few years my contact with Stu was confined to seeing him at the odd function. When I did see him I was always more than respectful to a great man who raised 12 kids the best he could. He truly was an exceptional man, and I still feel bad some of the family members that he taught to protect one another have allowed things to deteriorate as they have. The lengthy funeral attracted the likes of Premier Ralph Klein, Vince McMahon, a handful of wrestlers and hundreds of Calgarians who heard touching tributes from several people including Bruce, Bret and Ross. Having taken the children to see their grandfather days before he passed away, I elected to take them to the funeral where I saw many of the family members I hadn't seen since Helen died almost two years earlier. My feeling is I have likely seen many of them for the very last time.

Despite the unfortunate fallout that led me to distance myself even further from the Hart family, I wish them all well.

The WWF is still as powerful as ever, recently buying out the WCW to become the world's undisputed heavyweight champion of pro wrestling. Vince McMahon has a wrestling monopoly and because of it I'd imagine wrestlers are now exploited more than ever.

Young children are still being targeted as an audience, and the WWF continues to profit off the sleaze Owen detested. I don't let my kids watch it, nor do they seem the slightest bit interested.

McMahon made headlines in 2001 when he took a $35-million loss on the failed XFL football league, yet it barely put a dent in his billion-dollar portfolio. In May 2002, McMahon's empire took another hit when the WWF lost a lawsuit to the World Wildlife Fund over use of the initials. McMahon immediately started billing the company as WWE (World

Wrestling Entertainment). Ratings began to slip heavily in 2002 and have not recovered.

The company's presence no longer haunts me, although it was disturbing to see an ad for one of their pay per views read, "Let the bodies hit the floor."

One of the byproducts of my charity work has been the opportunity to do some public speaking, as I try hard to bring awareness to my cause and other worthwhile charities. Before Owen died I had never spoken to a group larger than my family. Now I'm relating my story to groups as large as 10,000 people.

The message I try to convey revolves around my philosophy that life is about faith and commitment. Whether it's commitment to love, your kids, your work or whatever is important in your life, it's the commitment that keeps you dedicated and loyal during the most difficult of times.

Faith is about believing and trusting things happen for a reason. As long as you keep your faith and make honest decisions, I believe life unfolds in a manner that will ensure your just rewards are realized.

Throughout my life and throughout my tremendous loss, I focused heavily on these two important disciplines to see me through.

Every May I host a fundraiser for the foundation—it's always the hardest month of the year for me. Not only is it the month Owen was born and the month he died, it also plays host to Mother's Day, which further reminds me I'm alone.

The sole beneficiary of the May fundraiser for the first three years was the Youville Women's Residence for abused women. I had been involved with the women prior to Owen's death through my water fitness classes, which they attended as part of their therapy. I always felt so sad for the girls and wanted to do something more to help them. I still work at the pool, maintain my job at the post office and have now graduated from university with a degree in Psychology and am now pursuing a second degree in Sociology. My plan is to enter into the master's program.

Being a widow, you face a lot of changes in your friendships. Most of the people in my life before Owen died still play prominent roles, although several couples we called friends now struggle to incorporate me, as a single woman, into their social calendar.

As a single mother I've worked hard to ensure neither of my children is pitied or looked-down on in any way. My kids enjoy a full slate of activities and I endeavor to drive them to everything myself.

Oje's flair with a paintbrush mirrors his father's artistic flair in the ring, and he's become a good little defenseman on the ice. Athena recently skated out before one of Oje's hockey games carrying a Canadian flag as her father often did in the ring—it was a proud moment for me.

Our Friday night pizza and swimming ritual carries on, as do our regular trips to the zoo. Both used to supply painful reminders of what we had lost. The memories they now trigger serve as delightful nostalgia.

Holidays are still tough on all of us, especially Father's Day. It's the one day each year I take the children to Owen's grave. We have a picnic on the bench I donated and we discuss happy times spent with Dad. I stress to the children that they do have a father, he's just not here. The kids seem to truly enjoy this day and always hug and kiss his tombstone before we leave.

The transition from wife to single mother has been a struggle for all of us, although I've worked extremely hard on so many fronts to ensure Oje and Athena are loved and cared for as much as any child with two committed parents. To help us compensate for our loss, many people have rallied around us, helping any way they can. This has served the children well and is greatly appreciated by me.

Unfortunately, some others perceived us as a weaker family unit early on, something I fought very hard to disprove. Just because we weren't a nuclear family anymore didn't mean the children were any less supervised or disciplined. They're good students, great little people and a wonderful source of pride and amusement.

My mother moved into a condo close to my home so she could be on call to help with the kids at all times. She is a godsend. At age seventy-nine she delights in taking the kids bowling, swimming or anywhere else they desire, including the local amusement park where she, too, rides the roller coaster.

My sister Virginia has also played a crucial role in easing my parenting duties. She's a constant source of support, doing whatever she can to help. I don't know what I would do without either of them.

Still, my life was, and still is, a lonely stroll. Some of the most frustrating times come when I could simply use another strong set of helping hands like when one of the kids is sick. It's then I curse the fact I don't have the help only a loving spouse can provide.

The funny thing is that Owen wasn't there a lot of the time, and I would more often than not have to conduct all the family business on my own anyway. But the fact that he was really gone for good somehow accentuated the drudgery of these everyday tasks and responsibilities.

I see so much of Owen in Oje. Watching him play chess reminds me of how Owen was when planning his pranks—always thinking three steps ahead. While he's as laid back as his father was, there's nothing Oje enjoys more than making someone laugh. That was Owen's gift, too.

After stumbling across one of his rubber mice, which he strategically placed in my bed, I told Oje, "Your dad would've had a great time with you—you are a goofball just like him."

Oje took it as the greatest compliment. "Am I really as funny as dad was?" he often asks.

For all of Oje's silliness, he has a very mature side for a ten-year-old. As I was tucking him into bed one night last spring, he stared up at me with his father's big blue eyes and broke my heart.

"Mom, I'm the only kid of five hundred people at my school that doesn't have a dad," he said. "Why didn't he just quit?"

I was shocked by the question as Oje generally avoids talk of Owen. In fact, when questioned about his father by other children, his standard response is a polite, "I don't want to talk about that now."

"Why did it have to be *my* dad? He meant so much to me," said Oje, who still has figurines of his dad throughout his room.

It's times like those I too wonder why it happened to us. It's something I try not to question, though, for fear I will never know.

I had no answer for Oje, telling him I didn't know. Unsure what to say next, I explained the good work of the foundation would not have happened otherwise. I told him to remember the feelings he had for his dad because they were important. I added that he was lucky he had a dad for a short while who really loved him rather than a dad his whole life who didn't care about him.

I knew that from experience. My dad got the chance to be a dad but never took it, whereas Owen was such a great dad and never really got the opportunity.

Athena still likes to talk about Owen and remembers a surprising number of things about him considering she was only three-and-a-half when he died. She still starts a lot of questions beginning with the phrase, "Remember when dad …"

I'm just so glad Owen was such a great father for her and I take plenty of solace in the fact that his limited time on earth did well to create many pleasant memories for all of us.

I find comfort in knowing my last words to him were "I love you."

To this day, the 1965 Mustang Owen drove on our dates is untouched in the garage. There are also boxes and boxes filled with thousands of letters from fans all over the world who were devastated when he died. The room that would have housed our third child remains empty, the bags from Owen's final trip remain unpacked and his wardrobe is neatly packed away in the basement.

For some reason I can't even think of getting rid of them. I thought maybe when Oje grew up he might want to see his father's clothes or drive the car his dad took such great pride in.

We love him, we miss him. That will never change.

Still, this is not the life I chose and worked for, and, on some days I still feel cheated and robbed. Sometimes I'll be driving and I'll just break down. It's those moments alone that continue to get the best of me.

Right now, I'm not where I want to be but I'm comforted by the thought that I'm in the process of getting there.

Among the many gifts Owen gave me in life, one of the most precious were his words to me that final night together on the sofa—to move on if anything should happen to him. I believe in the philosophy that lives unshared are wasted lives. The power to love and be loved is truly the greatest gift. Still, I'm a long way from doing so.

I always knew Owen and I were a special couple but I realize that even more now. I can admit there were times during our pre-wedding fiasco, his long road trips and throughout the lawsuit I wondered if it would've been easier or better if I never met him at all. But then I would have missed out on all the wonderful things he brought to my life.

Owen's death shattered my heart into a near irreparable state, but what I didn't expect was that in its place a bigger one would grow—a heart of humility and compassion, which guides me to help those I can and to inspire others to be helpful and generous.

Yet, it seems that no matter how busy I keep myself and regardless of the direction my life takes I can't help but miss Owen so much.

All the hurt and scars I carry, created by my own pain, have allowed me to understand pain of all kinds, loneliness on every level and compassion at any cost. It is helping others to have a better life that makes my life better. It provides the depth I need while distancing me from my own worries and heartaches.

And yet something lingers.

Just as I needed to focus on taking it one day at a time throughout my road to recovery, I now think a lot more about living for the moment.

For me and Owen it was always about looking forward. I don't do that as much any more. Nor do I live in the past. Now I savor precious little moments with the kids, at work, in school. Whatever triumphant little moments we're afforded in life are often short-lived and under-appreciated as we stare ahead at the bigger picture. No more. I just wish I had done that before—lived more for the day.

I miss the love notes, I miss the late night phone calls, I miss the kisses and I miss his smile. He made me a happier person. He made me a better person. And he did it without changing who I was. He truly was a gift.

I'd do anything for him to come back just one day to see how hard I worked for his justice, how far the good work of the foundation has reached and how beautiful our children are. I'd even enjoy letting him play another prank on me. Still, the fact remains Owen died of a broken heart—the same thing I live with every day.

INDEX